MARCO ⊕ POLO

D0995007

GRAN CANARIA

www.marco-polo.com

Do You Feel Like ...

... adventurous hikes, beautiful views, colonial flair, subtropical gardens, sleepy mountain villages or pre-historic caves? A few ideas on Gran Canaria just the way you want them.

GREAT HIKES

- **Caldera de Bandama**
  Walk around the crater on a trail with beautiful views. You can also walk down into the crater.
  page 146

- **Pico de las Nieves**
  Follow a spectacular trail from Cruz Grande to the highest peak on the island.
  page 203

- **Roque Nublo** ▶
  The most popular hiking route on the island goes to the »cloud rock«.
  page 217

DISTANT VIEWS

- **Mirador de Unamuno**
  »Stone thunderstorm« is what the Basque philosopher Miguel de Unamuno called Gran Canaria's mountain ranges.
  page 139

- **Mirador Balcón**
  Along the GC 200 high above the western coast there are various observation points where it's worth stopping to look.
  page 160

◀ **Santa Ana Cathedral**
  Take a lift to the observation platform on the southern tower of the cathedral of Las Palmas.
  page 179

Do You Feel Like ... • CONTENTS

5

CAVES FOR LIVING AND OTHER THINGS

- **Barranco de Guayadeque**
  There is a cave village in the gorge and a cave chapel. There are even several restaurants in caves for visitors.
  page 133
- **Cenobio de Valerón**
  The cave labyrinth carved into the tuff stone is one of the most impressive cultural remnants of the aboriginal inhabitants.
  page 147
- **Quatro Puertas**
  Near the old royal city of Telde four caves are hidden in a mountain – with traces that point to an old cultic site.
  page 241

EXOTIC FLORA

- **Jardín de la Marquesa**
  The subtropical garden belonging to an old noble family is located in the middle of a banana plantation.
  page 145
- **Parque Botánico Maspalomas**
  An as yet young botanical garden with decorative plants from all over the world.
  page 187
- **Jardín Canario** ▶
  Awesome Canarian flora and dragon trees near the capital city.
  page 233

COZY PLACES

- **Embalse de Soria**
  A picturesque hamlet above a reservoir bordered by palm trees.
  page 137
- **Tejeda**
  Expansive almond orchards around a mountain village are especially enchanting when they blossom in February.
  page 235
- **Teror**
  This rural town is known for its pilgrimage church. A colourful market is held on Sundays around the church.
  page 241

COLONIAL ARCHITECTURE

- **Old city of Agüimes**
  Around the Moorish-style domed church narrow lanes invite exploring.
  page 131
- ◀ **Casa de Colón**
  Columbus' house in Las Palmas has decorative Renaissance portals, magnificent wooden ceilings and a secluded inner courtyards.
  page 179
- **Plaza San Juan in Telde**
  The old city square surprises with an intact 16th century ensemble and a basilica dedicated to John the Baptist.
  page 239

BACKGROUND

ENJOY GRAN CANARIA

Carneval celebrations in Las Palmas are colourful

TOURS

SIGHTS FROM
A TO Z

The cathedral in Arucas was only
built in the 20th century

Gran Canarians know how to celebrate, like here at the festival of the virgin of the cave in Artenara

PRACTICAL INFORMATION

PRICE CLASSES
Restaurants
(main course)
€€€€ = over €20
€€€ = €10 – €20
€€ = €8 – €15
€ = up to €8
Hotels (double room)
€€€€ = over €200
€€€ = €100 – €200
€€ = €60 – €100
€ = up to €80

Make a splash into the harbour
basin of Puerto de Mogán

BACKGROUND

Gran Canaria is a top spot for sun lovers with attractive beaches of fine-grained sand – here a view of Playa de las Canteras at Las Palmas. Yet the island's interior offers surprisingly untouched natural settings.

Facts

Nature

Gran Canaria, which gave the entire Canary archipelago its name, is almost in the middle of the island group. It is the third-largest of the Canary Islands after Tenerife and Fuerteventura and is extremely popular among visitors from western and northern Europe.

The Canary Islands (**Islas Canarias**) are a group of seven larger and six smaller islands in the Atlantic, about 100 – 300km (60 – 180mi) from the north-west coast of Africa (Morocco/Western Sahara) and about 1,300km/800mi from Cádiz on the Spanish mainland. The entire archipelago extends 500km/300mi from east to west and 200km/120mi from north to south. Geographically the islands are part of Africa, but politically and socially they are definitely European.

Canary Islands

Until the end of the 20th century there were varied theories on **the origin of the Canary Islands**. Some thought they were part of the sunken continent Atlantis, others believed that the Canary Islands were once part of Africa. The present theory is that the Canaries are elevations of the 4,000m/13,000ft-deep floor of the Atlantic, which is between 150 and 180 million years old here. Tectonic forces from the collision of the European and Atlantic plates caused the eastward-drifting ocean floor to be broken up and compressed, so that parts of it were pushed upwards like wedges. Magma oozed out along the cracks from the Middle Tertiary Period (c30 – 40 million years ago; ▶ MARCO POLO Insight, p. 220).

In 1999 an expedition with the research ship Meteor eliminated any remaining doubts about the volcanic origins of the islands. Scientists on board took countless rock samples from the ocean floor at depths up to 2,500m/8,200ft over a period of weeks. The results showed that all the rocks were of volcanic origin. The Canary Islands did indeed

> **?** MARCO ⏣ POLO INSIGHT
>
> *Origin of the island name*
>
> Pliny (AD 23 – 79) gave the name of today's Gran Canaria as »Canaria«. He claimed that it derived from the large dogs (Latin »canis«, meaning »dog«) that were thought to live there. While there were already dogs on the Canaries at that time, they were not unusually large. Another explanation refers to the canora bird (from Latin »canere«, »to sing«). The name possibly also comes from Cabo Caunaria (presumably today's Cap Bojador) on the coast of Africa.

The landscape near Artenara is beautiful – and not only when the almond trees are in blossom in January and February

Canary Islands

emerge out of the ocean in numerous eruptions and stages of development. The land mass above the surface of the water is only the top of these eruptions. Tenerife and La Gomera probably appeared out of the sea 8 – 12 million years ago, Fuerteventura 16 – 20 million years ago and Gran Canaria 13 – 14 million years ago, while the age of La Palma and El Hierro is only 2 – 3 million years.

Evidence of volcanoes There have always been volcanic eruptions on the Canaries. The most recent took place in 1949 and 1971 on La Palma, and in 2011 off the coast of El Hiero. The underwater eruption near the Canary island, which is located about 240km/140mi west of Gran Canaria, was preceded in July 2011 by a mild earthquake and the town La Restinga had to be evacuated for a short time. Then in October steaming pyroclasts were thrown into the air about 1.5km/1mi from the southern point of El Hiero, while a huge area of sulphur formed on the water's surface. The new underwater volcano was named El Discreto.
In 1730 –1736 and 1824 large parts of Lanzarote were completely destroyed by eruptions. Gran Canaria and Fuerteventura have not experienced any eruptions in modern times (the last one on Gran Canaria is thought to have been about 3,000 years ago), but these two islands also have volcanic characteristics. Fuerteventura and Lanzarote are marked by moderately high volcanic peaks. Gran Canaria is dominated by former volcanic pipes at the centre of the island;

moreover, several calderas indicate a volcanic history. The geological term **caldera** refers to a former volcanic crater that was expanded to a cauldron shape by cave-ins and later erosion or by explosions. One possible origin is that during an eruption so much magma was thrown to the surface that a huge hollow formed below. Eventually the surface collapsed and only the edge of the crater remained standing.

Caldera de Bandama in the north-east of the island is a well-known example of a cauldron-shaped crater on Gran Canaria. **Caldera Pinos de Gáldar**, in the north between Artenara and Valleseco, is believed to be the most recent example of volcanic activity on Gran Canaria. It originated when the peak of the volcano was blown away during an explosion.

The most common volcanic rock is the bluish-black **basalt**, which can be found in the cliffs between Agaete and Mogán. **Trachyte** is light in colour and has a rough surface, while greyish-green **phonolite** is often used as gravel or for building. **Tuff** is easy to work and thus also often used in building. The ancient Canarians enlarged existing caves in the tuff layers of the barrancos and added new ones. Dark, glassy **obsidian** was named after its discoverer, the Roman Obsidius. The most astonishing characteristic of the light-coloured **pumice** is that it floats. It is actually a rock foam made of gaseous, thickening lava. It holds water well and is thus used on the Canaries for dry farming.

Landscape

Gran Canaria, with a diameter of about 50km/30mi and a circumference of about 240km/140mi, is almost completely circular. After Tenerife and Fuerteventura it is the third-largest island of the Canaries. The centre of Gran Canaria consists of a mountain range. The highest peak is **Pozo de las Nieves** (1,949m/6,394ft), which is surrounded by several peaks that are almost the same height and therefore less dominant than Teide on Tenerife. Bizarre rocks like the **Roque Nublo** (1,813m/5,948ft) are characteristic of Gran Canaria. These are the remains of extensive rock coverings. While the surrounding rock was eroded away, the harder parts, which were originally volcanic pipes, remained.

The central mountain range, also called the **Cumbre**, divides the island into two completely different types of landscapes. The northern slopes are covered with lush vegetation while the south is more like a desert, except for some fertile valleys. Deep valleys (**barrancos**) radiate from the Cumbre to the coasts. The largest canyons are in the west and south of Gran Canaria; the barrancos of Agaete, Aldea, Mogán and Fataga are especially impressive. The mountains fall steeply in cliffs to the coast in the west; in the north they gradually turn into hills bordered by cliffs and a surf coast.

The only sand or pebble **beaches** are at the mouths of barrancos. In the east and south coastal plains with some large beaches border the

Facts and Figures

Canary Islands (span. Islas Canarias)
Major islands: Gran Canaria, Lanzarote, Fuerteventura,
Tenerife, La Palma, La Gomera and El Hierro

Area:
1,560sq km/ 591sq mi
(all Canary islands: 7,541sq km/2,912sq mi)
Gran Canaria is the third-largest island in the archipelago.

Population: **850,000**
(all Canary islands: 2.1 million)
Las Palmas de Gran Canaria is the
largest city on the Canaries:
population **383,000**

Population density:
**545 people per sq km/
1,417 per sq mi**
(by comparison: Tenerife
446 people per sq km/
1,160 people per sq mi)

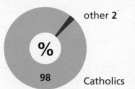

Spa

1300km/807mi

Canaries

Africa

300km/
186mi

Gran Canaria

©BAEDEKER

▶ **Tourism**

About 19% come from **Great Britain**.
But most of the visitors come from Spain.

30%

of all tourists who visit Spain
visit the Canaries (by comparison:
35% the Balearics).

Guests and beds:

2.9 Mio. foreign guests (2013)

about 160,000 guest beds

▶ **Religion**

other 2

%

98

Catholics

▶ **Government**

Gran Canaria is **part of the Autonom
Region of the Canary Islands**
(Comunidad Autónoma de Canarias
Highest **political authority:**
»Cabildo Insular« (island council).

▶ **Tourist centres**

MASPALOMAS
PLAYA DEL INGLÉS
PUERTO RICO
PUERTO DE MOGÁN

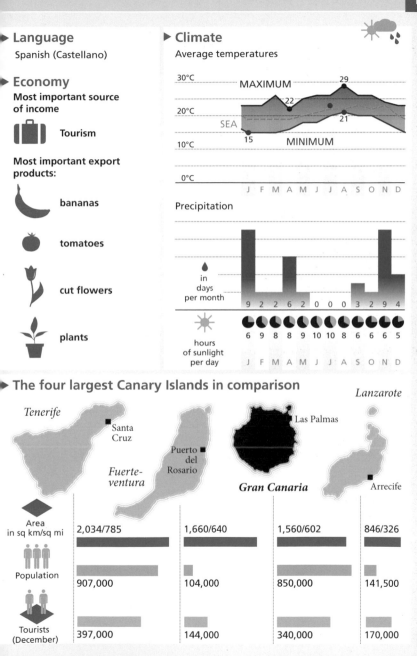

Sunset at Roque Nublo with a view of Mount Teide on Tenerife

mountains. The most beautiful and longest beaches are near Maspalomas/Playa del Inglés. The extensive beaches and dunes were once attributed to frequent sandstorms from Africa, but since the sand is mainly made of carbonates, it can only have originated in the coastal shelf. As the land became elevated, sand terraces of various heights were formed.

There are no perennial rivers on Gran Canaria, but some springs, including those near Firgas and Los Berrazales in Barranco de Agaete, are very productive.

PLANTS AND ANIMALS

Unique flora   Canary Islands flora is unique for two reasons. On the one hand, plants from almost every zone of vegetation on earth exist in a relatively limited area; on the other hand, there is an unusually **large percentage of endemic plants**, i.e. plants that exist only here. Canarian flora includes almost 3,000 different species, many of which were introduced as agricultural and decorative plants. It is estimated that about 1,300 species of plants on the island already existed in prehistoric times. Of these 30% are endemic. Due to this biological diversity UNESCO declared about 100,000ha/250,000ac to be a biosphere reserve. Many fossils of fruits and leaves that have been found in the Mediterranean region, in the Alps and in southern Russia

MARCO ⊕ POLO INSIGHT   **?**

New discoveries

Even today new species and plants are being discovered on the Canary Islands. Among the most exciting recent finds are Dracaena tamaranae, a species of dragon tree that was discovered in 1996. It grows in areas that are rocky and not easily accessible in the dry southern part of the island. It differs from other dragon trees in size, the position of the leaves and the form of the roots. Presently about 50 trees are known of in their natural environment.

prove that plants that only grow on the Canary Islands today were once common over larger areas. Climatic changes at the end of the present Tertiary period (beginning of the ice age, drying out of the Sahara) forced plants out of their earlier territories, but they were able to survive on the isolated Canary Islands. Moreover, extreme differences in elevation on the western Canaries and on Gran Canaria made it possible for the plants to survive by migrating to different altitudes.

The varying elevation and trade winds caused the different zones of vegetation on the Canaries.

Vegetation zones

The lowest level is dry as a desert. Along with succulents like Canary Island spurge, the Canarian date palm grows here. In the south this zone has an elevation of up to 1,000m/3,300ft, while in the north it is restricted to the coast. Here the natural vegetation between 200m/650ft and 600m/2,000ft includes varieties of juniper and dragon trees; laurel trees appear above 600m/2,000ft. The deciduous zone, which is always green, borders the fayal-brezal formation (faya = bog myrtle; brezo = tree heath) at an altitude of 1,100m/3,600ft. Tree heath grows up to 15m/50ft high, but can also develop into a shrub or dwarf shrub. Together with the laurel zone, the fayal-brezal heathland is also called »Monte Verde«. In the northern half of the western Canaries the pine forest zone begins at 1,500m/5,000ft; in the southern half Canary pine already grows at 1,000m/3,300ft.

The unique and most characteristic plant of the Canaries is the dragon tree (Dracaena draco). It is a member of the **Ruscaceae family**, and with its tall trunk and branched crown is a close relative of the

Dragon tree

Island of Contrasts

Gran Canaria's south offers nothing but sunshine and endless beaches. But the scenery in the often cloudy north is completely different: lush greenery everywhere. The interior is spectacular with its strangely shaped mountains and pretty villages.

❶ Pinar de Tamadaba

The light pine forest covers the 1,444m/4,738ft high Tamadaba. The pine trees are vital to the island's water supply since they cause the water in the passat clouds to condense.

❷ Embalse Caidero de la Niña

This reservoir was built in the mid-20th century in the interior to relieve Gran Canaria's constant water shortage. Today the emphasis is on desalination plants.

❸ Caldera de Bandama

The crater cauldron is visible evidence of the island's volcanic past. It was made about 5,000 years ago in a violent explosion.

❹ Roque Nublo

»Cloud mountain« is a striking rock column and the remains of a former volcano pipe.

❺ Pozo de las Nieves

Pozo or Pico de las Nieves with 1,949m/6,394ft is the highest mountain on the island. Despite the name (snow fountain) there is hardly ever any snow here.

❻ Barranco de Fataga

From the centre of the island deep gorges like Barranco de Fataga lead out to the coast. The floors of the narrow valleys are used for agriculture.

❼ Dunas de Maspalomas

Nowhere else on the Canary Islands are the sand dunes as extensive as here. It was created several thousand years ago during the last glacial period. At that time sea level was up to 90m/300ft lower than it is now.

Just like the western Canaries Gran Canaria's north is lush and green

yucca. Dragon trees grow relatively quickly. A few old specimens are even up to 20m/65ft high. The ends of dragon tree branches form a bunch of dark green, long, sword-like leaves. Since the dragon tree only forms branches after about ten years, when it first blossoms, the young ones bear no resemblance to the old trees. As they have no annual rings, the age can only be determined by the number of branches, but the branches grow at irregular intervals. Dragon trees had a special meaning for the early Canarians, who used the »dragon's blood«, the sap that oozed from the trunk and turned red on exposure to air, as an ointment.

Canary date palm
The Canary date palm (Phoenix canariensis) has spread from the islands into the entire Mediterranean region. It is closely related to the North African and Arab date palm, but its trunk is shorter and its crown fuller and more decorative with larger fans. However, its fruits are woody and not edible. Beautiful examples of Phoenix canariensis can be seen in southern Gran Canaria, especially in Barranco de Fataga.

Canary pine
The long, flexible needles of the Canary pine (Pinus canariensis) always grow in groups of three. The hard reddish wood was and still is used for panelled ceilings and balconies. The pines (in Spanish »tea«) grow at an elevation of 1,000 – 2,000m/3,300 – 6,600ft and are able to condense water out of the passing clouds. It drips from their needles like rain. This filtered water not only irrigates the trees but is also an important part of the island's **water supply**.

Canary laurel
Even though the forests of the Canaries have been decimated over the course of centuries, some laurel forest remains on Gran Canaria. The most accessible area is in the north of the island at Moya (**Los Tilos**). Canary laurel (Laurus canariensis), like the Canary pine, also contributes to the island's water supply. It is usually around 8 – 10m/27 – 33ft high, but can reach 20m/66ft; its dark green leaves, which can be used as bay leaf, are pointed and elliptical. Los Tilos forest has about 15 different varieties of laurel, but all look very similar: It takes some effort to distinguish them by their leaves and bark.

Crassula
Crassulacaea are **succulent plants** that can grow in arid places. They store water for dry periods; rosette leaves reduce evaporation. On the Canary Islands there are more than 80 varieties of Crassulacaea, which remain green and can get to be very old.

Canary spurge
Canary spurge prefers dry mountain slopes and rocks. It is called »**cardón**« on the Canaries. At first glance this native of the Canaries looks like a cactus, but it differs from cacti in the poisonous milky sap in its branches, roots and fruit and in its inconspicuous leaves.

Canary spurge grows slowly. The giant ones that can be seen in the southern part of the island may be hundreds of years old.

Another typical succulent is the prickly pear (Opuntia ficus indica). **Prickly pear**
It was introduced to the Canaries in the 16th century and often covers the slopes of the island up to the middle elevations. Its edible fruit is sold on the island. Picking them is not recommended because of their very fine thorns. Cochineals (scale insects) are grown on prickly pears and processed for their red dye. This industry is now significant only on Lanzarote.

Along with the prickly pear and a few varieties of agave, the Spanish **Decorative**
conquerors brought several varieties of luxuriously blooming plants **plants**
to the islands. Oleander, hibiscus and of course bougainvillea abound
in the winter months **poinsettias** blossom red
in many places on Gran Canaria.
These dense bushes can grow to be 3
– 4m/10 – 13ft high. The **bird of paradise** or **strelitzia** with its
unique flowers looks very exotic.

The **cultivation of various food plants** also changed the original island vegetation. The lower and middle elevations are now covered with banana plants, fruit trees, vegetables

> **?** *Named after a princess*
>
> **MARCO POLO INSIGHT**
>
> Strelitzia (Strelitzia reginae), now a separate genus, was considered to be part of the Musaceae family (banana) and owes its name to Charlotte Sophia of Mecklenburg-Strelitz (1744 – 1818), a German princess who married King George III of England

and vineyards. The cultivation of **citrus fruits** is well-developed.
Exotic fruits include mangos, papayas and guava; avocados ripen
wonderfully under the Canarian sun. In the mountains, mainly
around Tejeda and Valseguillo, there are also expansive almond orchards.

The banana is by far the **most important cultivated plant** (▶ MAR- **Banana**
CO POLO Insight, p. 38). The variety that has been cultivated on the
Canaries since the late 19th century, Musa cavendishii, is small and
resistant to weather; it was imported from Indochina. The trunk of
the banana plant consists of a number of long, stiff and juicy leaf
shafts. At the end of the shaft is a long, fibrous leaf. When the plant
is about one year old the flower forms, with the female part at the
bottom and the male part at the top. Depending on how much sunlight they get and the altitude, the bananas ripen in 4 – 6 months. A
bunch of bananas weighs on average 25 – 30kg/55 – 66lb, sometimes
even up to 60kg/130lb. The plants die after the bananas ripen, but in
the meantime they will have formed offspring. Of these the strongest
survives and matures and will itself flower after a year.

The island of »eternal spring« lives up to its reputation: blossoming plants at Roque Nublo in the central mountains

Fauna   The fauna of Gran Canaria is far less extensive than the flora, but again there is a relatively large number of endemic species. Of the 328 species that are protected in Spain, 63 live on the Canaries.

Mammals   Apart from rabbits, hedgehogs and bats there are no endemic large mammals.

Reptiles   It is reassuring to know that neither scorpions nor poisonous snakes inhabit the islands. **Lizards** can be seen everywhere, as well as the occasional slow worm, a legless lizard. The largest lizard is the 80cm/30in Lacerta stehlini, which is endemic to Gran Canaria.

There is great diversity in the birds on the island. Blackbirds, blue tits, a type of robin, chaffinches, woodpeckers, various kinds of pigeons, buzzards, kestrels as well as seagulls and ibis live here. Occasionally the song of the capirote, the Canary nightingale, can be heard. But anyone looking for the yellow **canary** songbird outdoors will be disappointed. There is only an inconspicuous variety, the Canary serin (►MARCO POLO Insight p. 26). | Birds

Gran Canaria is home to a very large number of endemic insects. Butterfly fans are in their element. The Canary admiral as well as the brimstone butterfly with orange front wings stand out. The largest variety is the monarch, which can have a wingspan of up to 10cm/4in. | Insects

The waters around the Canary Islands teem with fish. Salmon, tuna, squid, moray eel, bass, skate and sprat are among them. Mullet is caught around the islands and many menus include vieja, a variety of mullet that only lives in these waters. | Marine life

The rocky coastal areas are the territory of conger eels. Dangerous sharks have never been seen along the coast, but **swarms of dolphins and whales** accompany the ferries. Almost 20 different kinds of whales have been sighted off the coasts of the Canaries, including some endangered ones. Pilot whales can be seen relatively often; they are recognizable by their round heads. They can be 4 – 5m/13 – 16ft long and weigh up to 1.5t.

> **?** MARCO POLO INSIGHT
>
> *Danger for whales*
>
> Whale watching around the islands has increased dramatically in the last ten years. Many boats recklessly get too close to the whales, which can alarm them. The fast ferries that run between Gran Canaria and Tenerife also endanger the whales: Accidents happen regularly since the whales cannot manoeuvre fast enough to get out of the way.

NATURE PROTECTION AND ECOLOGY

The tourist boom and the construction that went along with it penetrated deeply the habitat of native flora. Many endemic species are threatened with extinction. In the **Jardín Canario** near Tafira efforts are being made to grow endangered species so that they can be transferred to their natural habitat. | Environmental factors

The deforestation that has taken place since the Spanish conquest and increased since the end of the 19th century has had devastating effects on the ecology. Large areas were deforested in order to increase agriculture. Thus on Gran Canaria less than 1% of the original renowned laurel forests remain. In past decades reforestation has been carried out on Gran Canaria, as the forest is essential for the island's water supply and prevents erosion. At first mainly eucalyptus trees

Canary Birds

Don't go looking for the yellow songbirds in their natural habitat. The ancestor of the domestic canary is the inconspicuous European serin (Serinus canaria).

It has grey-green feathers and doesn't sing nearly as nicely as its domestic cousin. The birds generally live in large flocks, mainly on Gran Canaria and the western Ca-

nary Islands. When Spanish invaders penetrated the interior of the Canary Islands in the 15th century, they found that the local people kept these birds in small cages. The Spanish conquerors, conscious of their value, took the birds back home as part of the spoils of war. The Portuguese had already brought canaries from Madeira and the Azores to Europe in the early 15th century. Spanish monks were the first to breed the birds. Astute businessmen sold only the males, thus securing the trade monopoly for themselves and keeping it for almost a century.

Symbol of Wealth

In those times only the nobility and wealthy commoners could afford to buy a canary. The little warblers soon became a **symbol of wealth** – in Italy, France and England as well as in Spain. The monks' lucrative monopoly ended in the mid-16th century, for reasons that are open to speculation. Some say that a trading ship en route to Livorno sank off the coast of Elba. The male canaries on board got away, and some mated on the mainland with the southern European serin (Serinus serinus), close relatives of theirs. Their young »were caught and bred«. But it is more likely that among the many males that were sold, an occasional female slipped through, as only an experienced breeder can tell the sex of a canary with certainty.

Coal Mines and a Football Club

In the 17th century the canary soon became the common man's pet in many parts of Europe. At that time many people in the Tyrol region of the Alps were miners; by raising and selling canaries they were able to supplement their income. Canaries not only helped support the family, but were taken into the mines to serve as a **living alarm system**. If a canary died suddenly in its cage, it usually meant that the poisonous, but colourless and odourless gas carbon monoxide was present. The miners then had little time to leave their tunnels and seek safety. The birds saved lives, a service they performed in coal pits and other mines around the world well into the 20th century. In England the city of Norwich became the centre for breeding canaries, as the birds were brought by Flemish immigrants fleeing from Spanish rule. They became a symbol of the city and gave Norwich City Football Club its nickname.

Popular Pet

Domestic canaries have become popular pets. There are now millions of them all over the world – on the Canary Islands as well, the home of their ancestors and their cousins who still live in the wild.

The pretty, colourful varieties are not to be found wild on Gran Canaria, but rather only a modest, colourless variety

were planted. In recent decades pines were used, albeit a fast-growing North American variety (*Pinus insignis*) instead of the local Pinus canariensis. Catastrophic forest fires in 2007 were a significant setback for the reforestation efforts.

Ecological problems of tourism

Air pollution on the Canaries is pleasantly moderate due to the warm climate, the almost constant wind and the lack of heating. Ecological problems derive mainly from the increase in tourism, which caused countless hotel complexes to be built in the 1970s and whole sections of the island to be covered in concrete. This uninhibited **building mania** can be seen in southern Gran Canaria, in Playa del Inglés, Maspalomas, Puerto Rico and other developed areas. While fewer building permits are now given for tourist facilities – in the past years the emphasis has been on quality tourism and improving infrastructure – there remain many projects that have been approved but not yet begun. Untouched sections of coastline will continue to be sacrificed for tourism. Until now ecologists have been able to hinder, for example, the addition of another 20,000 tourist beds at Playa de Veneguera in the near future.

Along with building over the land, mass tourism also makes problems in the disposal of refuse, water supply and treatment of waste water.

Lack of water

Fresh water is not plentiful on the Canaries. The population has grown in recent years and consumes more water. The thousands of tourists do not want to do without their daily shower: They use more than twice as much water per day as the local people. But agriculture is the largest consumer of water, most of which flows into banana plantations.

In the past reservoirs such as Presa de Soria holding up to 40 million cubic metres/10.5 billion gallons ensured the water supply to tourist centres in the south, but at present they are often empty. Thus the groundwater has increasingly been tapped. On Gran Canaria water is pumped from wells that usually have a diameter of 3m/10ft and are 150–200m/500–660ft deep, some even up to 300m/1,000ft. As a result, the water table has fallen in the past 25 years by 100m/330ft. More than half of approximately 2,000 wells and springs have dried up. Moreover, the further the water table sinks, the more seawater seeps in. This precarious situation has been alleviated somewhat in recent years through the building of **desalination plants**. The first was started in 1965 on Lanzarote. Today this island gets almost 100% of its water from the ocean. On Gran Canaria there are presently more than 100 small and large desalination plants; more than half of the island's water supply comes from the Atlantic. The desalination technology works well, but the problem is that the plants all run on fossil fuels, i.e. petroleum.

Maspalomas: holiday resorts as far as the eye can see

Nature protection was an unknown concept on the Canary Islands for a long time. However, things have changed since the 1990s. A visible sign is the lagoon at Maspalomas (Charca de Maspalomas). An almost finished hotel was torn down here and an area of 328ha/810 acres placed under protection. A law on the protection of nature covering compensation, government acquisition of nature zones and stricter measures against ecological crimes is now in effect.

Nature protection

In 1994 the Canary Islands parliament **established a national park** 20,000ha/49,400acres in size in the centre of the island around Roque Nublo. As building permits are no longer given for this area and agriculture is no longer allowed here, there is a lot of public opposition to this project, and little progress has been made on the park. But in 2005 UNESCO declared Gran Canaria to be a biosphere reserve, with about 43% of the island included and covering almost all of the western half of the island.

Climate

The Canary Islands have a warm temperate climate that justifies the phrase »eternal spring«.

Eternal spring | The climate is milder and more pleasant than one would expect in these latitudes. It is influenced mainly by **trade winds**, but also by the **high pressure areas off the Azores** and the cool **Canaries current**.

The biosphere reserve – a paradise for hikers

In general, the weather can change quickly on the Canaries. There are no long periods of bad weather. If the sun ever hides behind clouds, just drive a short distance further and it will be shining again.

The temperature varies remarkably little during the course of the year. The average winter temperature is around 19°C/66°F, while the summers rarely get above 24°C/75°F (▶ Practicalities, When to Go; climate table p. 17). In mountainous areas the temperatures are lower at higher elevations and tend to vary more during the course of the year. The influence of the Sahara on the climate is also noticeable at times: When the hot dry **calima** blows across from North Africa, mainly in July and August, the thermometer can suddenly rise about 10°C/18°F. Sometimes the fine sand and dust in the air reduces visibility to only about 100m/100yd. The heat wave generally only lasts for three to four days. Water temperatures in the winter are around 19°C/66°F, in the summer around 22°C/71°F.

Pleasant temperatures

Rainfall is generally limited to the winter months. It is caused by cyclones from northern latitudes. No rain has fallen on Fuerteventura and Lanzarote for years, and southern Gran Canaria no longer has much rain in the winter either. The northern coast gets about 500mm/20in of rain, the mid-range mountains about 600–800mm/25–30in annually, the higher elevations less. The **lowest altitude for snowfall** lies at about 1,200m/4,000ft, but generally snow lies only on the almost 2,000m/6,600ft-high Pozo or Pico de las Nieves for a short time in the winter.

Rainfall

Clouds form regularly over Gran Canaria and the western Canaries at the middle elevations in the early mornings, but disappear again towards evening. The clouds rarely bring rain, but they do cause precipitation in the form of fog and dew. The clouds occur almost all year and are caused by **trade winds** from the north-east that blow at up to force 4.

Trade winds

Unlike other climatic influences, the trade wind is consistent. It begins at the equator, where the sun warms the surface of the earth the most (inner tropic convergence, ITC). The warm air rises, then cools and moves at an altitude of 12–15km/7–9mi towards the poles. After cooling some more it sinks to the earth's surface at about 30° north and then flows back to the equator. However, the rotation of the earth diverts the wind streams from their course. In the northern hemisphere a north-east wind results; in the southern hemisphere its direction is south-east. Above 1,500m/5,000ft they are warm dry winds, and below that they are cooler and moister. As long as the upper and lower layers persist (**inversion**), hardly any clouds form, but if the flow runs into a mountain, the inversion is disrupted. The cooler, damper lower wind streams against the sunny warm mountain slopes, is warmed and begins to rise. Then it cools down again and the moisture condenses. **Clouds** form between 600m and 1,700m (2,000ft and 5,600ft), though not at night because of the cooler air. Since the winds blow from the north-east, clouds do not form in the south. Only warm, dry downdraughts occur there. The influence of the trade winds is reduced in the winter. The sun's rays strike the northern hemisphere at a much more acute angle (on 22 December the sun is directly above the Tropic of Capricorn), which causes the zone of trade winds to move southwards and the Canary Islands to be influenced by Atlantic low pressure systems at times.

Daylight hours Since the island is so close to the equator, the number of daylight hours does not vary as much between summer and winter on Gran Canaria as in northern Europe: The longest summer day has about 14 hours of daylight, the shortest winter day about 11 hours. **Twilight** is very short.

Population · Economy

Gran Canaria is by far the most populous of the Canary Islands. Most of the residents make their living from tourism.

POPULATION

Statistics The Autonomous Region of the Canary Islands has a population of about 2.1 million people; of these 850,000 live on Gran Canaria, which makes the island the most densely populated of the archipelago by far. There are about 545 people per sq km (1,417 per sq mi), while on Tenerife, the largest of the Canary Islands, the population density is only 446 per sq km (1,160 per sq mi; the corresponding figure for England is 395 per sq km or 1,027 per sq mi). The population of Gran Canaria increased dramatically in the 20th century, from only about 130,000 around 1900 to 330,000 by 1950 and 630,000 at the beginning of the 1980s. The largest urban area is Las Palmas de Gran Canaria; almost half of the island population lives in the capital city. Due to unemployment many Canarians had to emigrate in the past. South America was the destination of choice. Today, about 300,000 Canarians are said to be living in Caracas (Venezuela). In the meantime the South American countries accept only few immigrants, which is causing the population of Gran Canaria to grow again.

Gran Canarians love to celebrate enthusiastically – here at the Bajada de la Rama in Agaete

Anthropologists have proven that the Canarian people are different from mainland Spaniards. Many characteristics show that they are **descendants of the original inhabitants of the islands**.

Origins

The families have a **patriarchal structure**. The man is the head of the family; the woman takes care of the household and the children. As a result of the high rate of unemployment and low salaries, and due to the relatively high cost of living, the women are often forced to find some work to supplement the family income. Even though small families dominate in the cities, extended families often live together in rural areas. The number of children is declining, however.

Patriarchal structures

Welcome to Everyday Life!

Experience a different side of Gran Canaria and get in touch with Canarios. Here are some tips what to do away from the beach and the holiday resort.

PICNIC AT THE RESERVOIR

On sunny weekends the large picnic grounds on the shores of Presa Cuevas de las Niñas is a popular place where Canarios play and rest. There are a few barbecue grills and running water in the small pine grove; it's generally easy to make contact with other picnickers while barbecuing. The picnic grounds at the »Lake of the Girls' Caves« can be reached via a paved and signed road from Ayacata.

Presa Cuevas de las Niñas, on GC-605 between Ayacata and Mogán

AT THE ARUCAS RUM FACTORY

The distillery in Arucas is one of the few businesses on Gran Canaria that is open to visitors. A guided tour will show how rum is made. Experts are available to answer any question. The Spanish King and Plácido Domingo have been here too.

Destillería Arehucas, Arucas, Lugar de San Pedro 2, Tel. 928 62 49 00, Mo. – Fr. 10am – 1pm, in the winter until 2pm

LEARN SPANISH

Anyone interested in learning a bit of Spanish or refreshing what he or she already knows will be well taken care of at the Gran Canaria School of Languages. The classrooms are in the middle of the Santa Catalina quarter of Las Palmas only a few steps from Playa de las Canteras. There are group and individual courses to choose from and a cultural programme is also offered. They will also arrange accomodations close by if desired.

Gran Canaria School of Languages
Las Palmas, Calle Dr. Grau Bassas 27
Tel. 928 26 79 71
www.grancanariaschool.com

EXCURSIONS WITH THE SAVINGS BANK

If you speak Spanish, you can take part in the activities of the CICCA (Centro de Iniciativas de la Caja de Ahorras de Canarias). The Canarian Savings Bank offer includes, for example, birdwatching tours, guided hikes through the mountains or stargazing with an expert guide. The only cost is for transportation.

CICCA
Las Palmas, Calle Alameda de Colón 1
Tel. 928 36 86 87

PROMENADING ALONG THE CITY BEACH

Not only during the daytime but after dark as well Paseo de las Canteras is the main promenade of the residents of Las Palmas. Preferably on Saturday evening people will meet to eat or drink at one of the countless localities; children are taken along also until late at night.

Paseo de las Canteras, Las Palmas

ECONOMY

Tourism as »monocul- ture«

In past decades there has been a clear economic upswing on the Canary Islands. The average income on the islands is now higher than in many parts of Spain. But since the economy is completely dependent on tourism, the reduction in the number of visitors in the most recent years has caused serious economic problems. The service sector makes up about 80% of the regional economy, and about 70% of employed persons work in tourism. A slight economic recovery took place in 2011/2012, but it remains to be seen whether the increase in the number of tourists since then will continue.

Agricultural change

Over the centuries the agricultural export products have changed. The orchilla lichen, which flourished on Lanzarote and Fuerteventura, was valued in ancient times because it was used to make red or violet dye, giving the two eastern Canary Islands the name Purpuraria. After the Spanish conquest **sugar cane** was cultivated. However, this branch of the economy died out as early as the 16th century due to the competition from Central America. Then the main product was **wine**. In the 17th and 18th centuries, rich Canarian Malmsey wine was in great demand at European courts. But tastes changed; imported disease (mildew in 1852 and 1878) put an end to this branch of the economy. In the 19th century cochineal was raised. This cactus parasite, which is used to make a red dye, flourished on the fields of prickly pears, but lost its importance when aniline dyes were developed. At present **cochineal** is only used in lipsticks and to colour cordials, soft drinks and candy. The industry continues on a small scale on Lanzarote.

At that time the **banana** saved the economy (▶ MARCO POLO Insight, p. 38), when a small robust variety (Musa cavendishii) was imported from Indochina. Already in 1890 it was being cultivated on a large scale on Gran Canaria and the western Canaries. However, this branch of the economy too has faced problems for decades. Since the small but very tasty banana looks almost pitiful compared to the Central and South American competition, it is difficult to sell it in Europe. Moreover, production costs are much higher than in other countries. Even though production was subsidised for a long time by the Spanish government and the EU, it was no longer profitable for many farmers. Meanwhile the EU subsidies for banana farming have all but ceased. Banana cultivation is concentrated in the northern half of Gran Canaria. The delicious fruit flourishes at elevations up to 400m/1,300ft. Higher up the main crops are potatoes, grain, maize, sugar cane (especially around Arucas), cabbage, figs and other produce. In the south and south-west **tomatoes** are the most important products. Gran Canaria is the largest Canarian producer of tomatoes for the European market. The tomatoes produced from November to

Presa de la Cueva de las Niñas: one of the three large resevroirs southwest of Roque Nublo

May are exported. They are covered with plastic sheeting to protect them from the wind. A tomato plant needs three litres of water a day, which makes production expensive due to the high cost of water on Gran Canaria. The production costs for a kilo of tomatoes are more than twice that of Morocco, for example. The cultivation of cut flowers and flowering plants for export is increasing. **Winegrowing** on Gran Canaria is insignificant; there are only a few hundred hectares left around Tafira. The agricultural products most likely to bring a profit are the more exotic ones like mangos, papayas, avocados or cut flowers.

Livestock plays a secondary role. Beef and pork production only covers part of local needs. The area around Telde is the centre of cattle-raising on Gran Canaria, but the cattle are generally kept in pens since it is assumed that they could injure themselves on the uneven terrain.

Traditional Canarian fishing has been declining since 2000. At that time the negotiations on catch quotas and territories between the   Fishing

Short and Sweet

Banana plantations cover the western slopes – the rainfall is higher here – of the Canary Islands up to an elevation of 300m/1000ft. A dwarf variety, the Dwarf Cavendish Ladyfinger, which only reaches 2.5m/8ft in height, is planted here. While this variety might not look like Chiquita, etc., the bananas are unusually sweet and aromatic and are considered to be relatively resistant to the weather. Bananas began to be cultivated in a big way around 1890. But it only survived this long because of extensive subsidies and protective customs tariffs.

▶ **Banana plant**
Its size of 2 to 6 m (6.5 to 20 ft) means that it is often called a tree or a palm.

Fruit
A bunch of bananas weighs 25 – 50 kg (55 – 110 lbs) and carries 150 – 300 fruits, which are botanically part of the berry family.

Blossom
In the seventh month a banana plant forms a blossom that ususaly hangs downwards; this only happens once in the life of a plant.

Rhizome
Underground rootstock system

▶ **Banana production on the Canary Islands**
Every year more than 400 million kilogrammes of bananas are produced on the Canary Islands on about 9,000 hectares (22,000 acres) – mainly on Tenerife, La Palma and Gran Canaria. The fact that 10,000 people are employed in this sector shows the role it plays in the economy.

Distribution of banana production by island, 2012 in million kg

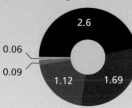

2.6
0.06
0.09
1.12
1.69

Tenerife
La Palma
Gran Canaria
La Gomera
El Hierro
Lanzarote,
Fuerteventura
(no cultivatio

▶ **Distribution**
Bananas grow mainly in tropical and subtropical regions where the temperatures are around 27°C/80°F, where the sun shines a lot and where there is high humidity. The banana belt is marked green on the map.

▶ **Production**
Bananas are cultivated in more than 150 countries. 106 million tons of bananas are produced every year. The major producers are:

Percentage (2012)

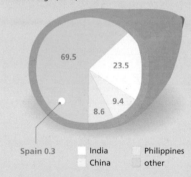

69.5

23.5

9.4

8.6

Spain 0.3

◼ India
◼ China
◼ Philippines
◼ other

Leaves
In many Asian countries the leaves are used as wrapping material or in place of plates.

Pseudostem
This is not a wooden trunk; it is actually a pseudostem; tightly packed sheaths make up the pseudostem

Sprouts
The banana plant forms offshoots to propagate. They reach their full height in nine months.

©BAEDEKER

Types of bananas
There are 400 to 900 varieties of bananas, of which about 100 are edible. Here are some of them:

Plantain (cooking banana)

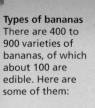

Dwarf Cavendish (dessert banana)

Dwarf Red (red fruit banana)

Gros Michel (dessert banana)

Ladyfinger/ Baby banana Canarian variety

A good catch – in Puerto de Mogán

European Union and Morocco failed. From 72,000t in 1999 the catch fell to 8,400t in 2003. At the same time **fish farming**, which is done in enclosures along the coast, increased several times over. Much of the fish consumed on the island has been imported for decades.

Industry
Industry produces about 17% of the gross regional product, but the high costs of importing raw materials and of energy continue to limit the development of this branch of the economy. A few smaller or mid-sized industries process foods, while others process wood and make paper and cardboard, building materials or fertiliser. Small businesses produce crafts such as embroidered articles.

Trade
The Canary Islands have been a **free trade zone** since 1852. This caused trade to boom. The lack of water, raw materials and energy, however, made economic development difficult. Thus the balance of trade has been negative for a long time. Imports are increasing, especially from the Spanish motherland. Important imports are crude oil, consumer products and food, as well as mechanical and electrical machines and vehicles. Exports are mainly agrarian.

Energy
The growing need for energy is met to a large extent by fossil fuels like **petroleum**. Alternative forms of energy are only used privately or on an experimental level. Solar energy is used on a small scale for desalinating seawater but some large businesses also have photovol-

taic systems. **Wind energy** is also used. The dry warm winds blow across the islands at an average speed of 40 km/h (24mph) especially in south-east Gran Canaria. By comparison: the average wind speed on the German coast of the North Sea is only 26 km/h (16mph). One of the most important wind power facilities is in Barranco de Tirajana on the southern coast of Gran Canaria. 67 wind generators here produce 20 megawatts of electricity.

The first tourists, mainly English and Scandinavians, came to Gran Canaria in the 1950s. They either went to Las Palmas or the Parador at Cruz de Tejeda. Around 1960 there were only 2,500 hotel beds on the island. In the late 1960s and early 1970s the building of the hotel city Maspalomas/Playa del Inglés drastically increased the number of visitors. The 1970s and 1980s saw a real boom in tourism. In the 1990s growth was interrupted more than once, but the trend continued upwards. In the record years of 1999 and 2000 about 10 million visitors came to the Canary Islands. After years of stagnation or declining numbers, there was a strong increase in 2011 – in that year 2.9 million foreign guests came to Gran Canaria.

Tourism

History

Guanches, Conquest and Autonomy

Research has found answers to the questions of when the Canary Islands were first settled, where the Guanches came from and what happened to them after the Spanish conquest of the islands.

MYTHOLOGY

Hardly any other group of islands on earth has been as shrouded in myth as the Canary Islands since the beginning of their history. Elysian Fields, Happy Isles, Islands of the Blessed, Gardens of the Hesperides and so on were the names used by ancient authors, such as Homer, Hesiod, Plato, Strabo, Virgil, Horace, Ptolemy and Plutarch, for islands at the western edge of the world which were supposed to be like paradise on earth. In the Middle Ages travellers, poets and scholars such as Isidore of Seville enthused about flowering islands in the distant west.

? MARCO POLO INSIGHT

»Guanche«

The name »Guanche« is often used for all the ancient peoples of the Canary Islands. However, this expression was originally applied only to the residents of Tenerife. The word »Guanche« comes from the ancient Canarian language and means »son of Tenerife«.

ANCIENT INHABITANTS

| From 500 BC | Settlement in several waves of immigration |
| **14th – 15th centuries** | Simple herding and farming culture |

Dated archaeological finds show that the Canaries were first settled after the birth of Christ. But more recent finds from 2009 near Tiagua on Lanzarote probably show that the Phoenicians had already landed on the Canaries around 1000 BC and had also built houses there. Excavations and research continue. But scientists now agree that the roots of the ancient Canarians go back to the Berber culture of **North Africa**. Examination of skeletons has shown that the ancient Canarians and North Africans are related. There are also similarities to the

Berbers settle on the islands

The most important early Canarian find: the Idol of Tara, which was found on Gran Canaria

MARCO ⊕ POLO TIP

! *On the trail of the Guanches* **Insider Tip**

No one interested in the Guanche culture should miss the Museo Canario in Las Palmas. The »cave palace« Cenobio de Valerón, the recently opened Parque Arqueológico de Arteara near Fataga and the excavations at La Guancha also give interesting insights into this ancient culture. A visit to the theme park Mundo Aborigen, a replica of an ancient Canarian village, is also fun.

Berber cultures; comparisons of language fragments as found in indigenous place names, in documents and inscriptions (petroglyphs) have also been fruitful. It is now assumed that the immigration from Africa to the Canaries took place in several waves, but it is still not clear why these people left their North African home. Possible causes are the growing desertification of the Sahara region and the oppression of the Roman occupation. There is also only speculation as to how the immigrants got to the islands. As no remains of boats have been found, it is assumed that reed boats were used which decayed later.

Guanche life and culture

When the Europeans conquered the Canaries in the 14th and 15th centuries they found a simple **herding and farming culture** which seemed to have no contact whatsoever to the rest of the world. The island was divided into two realms, each of which was ruled by a king, a **guanarteme**. The ruler of the western half of the island had his capital in Gáldar; the other ruled the eastern half of Gran Canaria from Telde. The royal succession was passed down the female line, but the culture was not a matriarchy. The ruler was not the woman but her husband, whom she chose and thus legitimised. The female succession is certain to have enhanced the position of women in the society. There is also evidence that women also played a role in religious rites. Little is known about the social structure. There were noblemen and farmers; nobility was not inherited, but awarded on the grounds of personal virtue.

The Guanches raised barley, wheat and pulses on small fields but had no ploughs. They kept goats as domestic livestock. The staple food was **gofio**, roasted barley which was milled and mixed with honey and water, kneaded and rolled into balls. Goat meat, milk and butter were also important parts of the diet. Seafood also played a role.

Most ancient Canarians lived in **caves**. These were especially suited to the climate. The cave interiors were made smooth; often wood ceilings were added. Sometimes artificial caves were made. This could lead to an elaborate system of caves, as seen in Cenobio de Valerón. There are also a few stone structures, especially tombs (e.g. the tumulus of Gáldar) and covered living pits as well as straw-covered clay huts. The **clothing** of the ancient Canarians must have seemed unusual to the Spanish invaders. The Guanches wore goatskins that were carefully sewn together with plant thorns. Fabric woven from palm

Mummies in Museo Canario in Las Palmas: after being embalmed the bodies were wrapped in grass mats or leather

and other fibres was also used for clothing. Their **tools and weapons** also appeared primitive to 15th-century Spaniards. The Guanches defended themselves only with wooden clubs and stones that they threw. In hand-to-hand combat they also used thin stone blades which were so sharp that they could be used as cutting tools. The ancient Canarians believed in an all-powerful supreme being, called »Acoran« (»the greatest, highest«) on Gran Canaria. Holy mountains, as the place where the divine and earthly worlds met, played a major role in religious rituals of the island people. Animal sacrifices and libations were made there.

It is remarkable that the world of the dead remained closely bound up with the world of the living. Settlement and funeral sites are not always easily distinguished. Natural and artificial caves served both as residential and as funeral sites. The dead from higher levels of so-

Mysterious mummies

ciety were mummified. The corpses were rubbed with goat butter and conserved with heat and smoke. The brain was never removed, and the internal organs only in some cases. These techniques of **mummification** were primitive compared to those of the ancient Egyptians. The mummies were not conserved for long, and the funeral grottoes were clearly used many times. The mummies found there, which can be seen in the Museo Canario in Las Palmas, were not very old.

Enigmatic rock inscriptions The little that has remained of the ancient Canarian language is mostly found in place names. **Similarities with the Berber languages** are evident. The islands did not have a unified language; rather different dialects were spoken on each one. Basic expressions like »gofio« and »tamarco« (fur cloak) existed on several islands.

When the Spanish conquered the Canaries the local people had no system of writing, but rock inscriptions have been found regularly even in recent times. The first were discovered in 1867 on La Palma (Cueva Belmaco); in 1870 an entire chapter of the history of the writing system was found on El Hierro (Los Letreros): A rock wall was inscribed with both symbols representing ideas and concepts, which the viewer has to interpret, and with signs that come close to modern alphabets. Transitions can be seen between the two writing systems. On Gran Canaria near **Barranco de Balos** (Lomo de los Letreros) spirals and concentric circles were found inscribed into rock (megalithic petroglyphs). Nothing comparable has been found on Tenerife and La Gomera. The inscriptions have not been deciphered, and it is doubtful that they ever will be, since souvenir hunters have removed large parts of the rocks. It is also not clear whether the inscriptions were made by the Canarians themselves or were left behind by visitors to the islands.

CONQUEST AND COLONIAL PERIOD

AD 23 – 79	The Canarians are mentioned in the Naturalis Historia of Pliny.
1312	Lancelotto Malocello lands on Lanzarote.
1478 – 83	Conquest of Gran Canaria
1479	The treaty of Alcáçovas gives the Canary Islands to Spain.
1492	Christopher Columbus lands on Gran Canaria during his first voyage of discovery.

First contact There has been much discussion on whether or not the **Phoenicians**, who were daring and skilful sailors, landed on the Canaries on their voyages of discovery along the West African coast in the first millennium BC. There is no proof. The first surviving report of a visit to the Canaries is by **Pliny the Elder** (AD 23 – 79). He described an expedition to the Canaries in his Naturalis Historia, which was made for the king of Mauretania, Juba II (d. AD 23). It is not known whether this expedition was a success, but at least the name »Canaria« appears for the first time in Pliny's text. The first clear evidence of a Roman landing on the Canaries comes in the form of 3rd or 4th-century pottery that was found on Lanzarote and La Graciosa. Up to the early 14th century it is likely that seafarers and adventurers occasionally reached the Canaries. These islands at the western edge of the then known world were mentioned many times in European, Byzantine and Arabic sources. However, due to their distance and the fact that there did not appear to be any material gain, the seafaring powers of Europe and the Near East showed no interest in dominating them.

Only in the 14th century did the Canaries get the attention of European seafaring powers. This began with reports of the travels of Lancelotto Malocello from Genoa: Malocello landed in 1312 on the island that was later named after him, Lanzarote, and liked it so much that he stayed there for several years. Many sailors, traders and pirates stopped at the Canary Islands after that. They hoped to get rich quickly by enslaving the indigenous people. Several documents of the second half of the 14th century refer to the wealth of the archipelago in human wares. As the sovereign of »all lands that have not yet been discovered«, in 1344 Pope Clement VI named Luís de la Cerda, a relative of the Spanish royal family, **King of the Canary Islands**, but this title did not include any claim to property. Luís de la Cerda's successor was Roberto de Bracamonte, who was also content with the title and took no steps to take possession of his domain. He left this to his cousin **Jean de Béthencourt** (1359 – 1425; ▶Famous People). Along with the Spanish nobleman **Gadifer de la Salle** (c1340 – 1422) the Norman Jean de Béthencourt was the first to try to conquer the Canary Islands for the Spanish crown. After the occupation of Lanzarote in 1402, Béthencourt was given the title »King of the Canary Islands«. In the following years he also gained the islands of Fuerteventura and El Hierro. But his attempts to conquer Gran Canaria and La Palma failed and he returned to the European mainland in 1406. He named his nephew Maciot de Béthencourt as viceroy of the islands. At the intervention of the Spanish king, Maciot de Béthencourt had to give back the title due to misrule, but profited from this situation several times: He sold the title to the royal ambassador Diego de Herrera, Prince Henry of Portugal and finally to the Spanish Count Hernán Peraza the Elder, one after the other. This left the possession of the Canaries completely unclear. Both the Spanish and the Portuguese sent ships in the following decades to conquer the islands. Only the **Treaty of Alcáçovas** in 1479 clarified the situation: The Canary Islands were awarded to Spain; Portugal got West Africa and any other offshore islands. When the Spanish landed on Gran

Conquest of the Canaries

To the New World on the Passat Winds

*On all of his voyages of discovery Christopher Columbus never sailed
directly west from Spain, but rather first to the Canary Islands.
He did this not only to stock up on food and water but
also to take advantage of the relatively stable
passat winds from the north-east.*

CUBA

PUERTO RICO

HISPANIOLA   WESTINDIAN ISLAN

TRINIDAD

Atlantic

Santa María

23m/75ft

▶ **Columbus' fleet**
Columbus undertook his
first voyage with three
ships: the two caravels
Pinta and *Niña* and
the flagship *Santa
María*, which ran
aground off the
coast of Haiti on
the way back.

▶ **Voyages of Columbus**

1 3. Aug. 1492 – 15. Mar. 1493
Columbus began his first voyage in Palos
de la Frontera. He (probably) first sailed
towards Gran Canaria in order to have
the rudder of the *Pinta* repaired. From
there he sailed on to La Gomera. On this
voyage Columbus discovered the
Bahamas, Cuba and Hispaniola and then
sailed back to Lisbon.

2 25. Sept. 1493 – 11. June 1496
On his second voyage - with 17 ship
and about 1,500 settlers - Columbus
stopped at La Gomera and El Hierro
On the way to Hispaniola he
discovered the Lesser Antilles.

Page 49

AZORES
Lisbon
Palos
Sanlúcar
Cadiz
MADEIRA
CANARY ISLANDS
CAPE VERDE ISLANDS

4
3

©BAEDEKER

Niña

21m/68ft   20m/65ft

▶ **Constantly blowing: the passat winds**

At the equator the sun, which stands almost directly overhead, warms the earth's surface. Warm air rises and cools off in the process, then flows towards the pole. At about 30 degrees latitude it sinks again and flows towards the equator close to the earth's surface. But the earth's rotation causes the winds in the northern hemisphere to flow from the north-east and in the southern hemisphere from the south-east, thus causing a north-east or south-east windstream. Columbus sailed westwards on these streams.

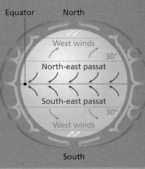

Equator   North
West winds
30°
North-east passat
South-east passat
30°
West winds
South

30. May, 1498 – 25. Nov. 1500

On his third voyage he stopped at Gomera again on his way to the New World. Columbus discovered Trinidad and Tobago and sighted the mouth of the Orinoco River.

4 9. May 1502 – 7. Nov. 1504

On his fourth voyage Columbus again anchored off La Gomera. His last voyage then brought him to the coast of Central America. He was the first European to land on the Central American mainland.

Tile picture at the church plaza in Ingenio – the life of the Canarians was probably not always this idyllic

Canaria in 1478 under the leadership of Juan Rejón, the island was ruled by two kings or »guanartemen«, as they were called. Tenesor Semidan, the ruler of the western part, governed from Gáldar; Dora-mas, the eastern ruler, was based in Telde. The Spanish founded Las Palmas in 1478 and conquered the rest of the island from here. Their capture of Tenesor Semidan was a decisive success. He was brought to Spain along with his entire entourage and baptised. Then he fought on the side of the Spanish conquerors, but only after many more bit-ter battles under the leadership of Pedro de Vera and Alonso Fernán-dez de Lugo were the Canarians conquered in 1483. In 1492 – 93 the Spanish conquered the island of La Palma. The Guanches on Tenerife held out and kept their independence the longest, but between 1494 and 1496 Alonso Fernández de Lugo also took this, the largest of the Canary Islands. A large part of the indigenous population was en-slaved and taken abroad. The surviving Guanches adapted to Spanish culture at an astonishing pace. Many intermarried with Spanish set-tlers, took on their language, religion, customs and traditions and adapted to the new economic situation. According to anthropological research most of the present Canarian population is descended from the ancient inhabitants.

After the Spanish conquest there were two different systems of ad- **Señorio**
ministration on the island: While Gran Canaria, La Palma and Ten- **status**
erife answered directly to the Spanish crown, Fuerteventura, La
Gomera, El Hierro and Lanzarote had the status of »señoríos« (**coun-
ties**) and were subject to the feudal rule of the noblemen who had
conquered the islands. The population had to pay taxes to the local
ruler and the Spanish empire. Only in 1812 did the Spanish parliament abolish the señorios.

On his first voyage of discovery in 1492, Christopher Columbus   **Interlude:**
(Spanish: Cristóbal Colón, 1451 – 1506) landed first at Gran Canaria   **Columbus**
and then La Gomera. On his later voyages (1493, 1498 and 1502) he
also stopped at these two islands.

The islands gained economic influence with the cultivation of sugar   **Pirate attacks**
cane and later wine. Its wealth made Gran Canaria the object of pi-
rate attacks in the 16th and 17th centuries. Time and again the English, Dutch and Portuguese tried to take Las Palmas, but never succeeded.

19TH/20TH CENTURIES

1820	Las Palmas becomes the capital of Gran Canaria.
1822	Santa Cruz becomes the capital of the Canary archipelago.
1852	The Canaries become a free trade zone.
1912	The islands gain local autonomy.
1927	The archipelago is divided into an eastern and a western province.
1936 – 39	Spanish Civil War
1982	The Canary Autonomous Region is formed.

In order to promote the economy of the Canaries, Queen Isabella II   **Free trade**
of Spain declared the islands to be a free trade zone in 1852. In 1912   **zone**
the »cabildos insulares« were established on the islands. The cabildos
of 1912 every island had its own **local government**. In 1927 the Canary Islands were divided into a western and an eastern province.
Since then Tenerife, La Gomera, La Palma and El Hierro have been
part of the province of Santa Cruz de Tenerife. The two Canary provinces in turn were combined in 1982 into the »Canarian Autonomous
Region«. Like the 16 other Spanish autonomous regions, the Canary
Islands gained a regional constitution under a **statute of autonomy**
as well as elected representative bodies. Since then the island parliament has met alternately in Santa Cruz de Tenerife and Las Palmas
de Gran Canaria.

MARCO ⊕ POLO INSIGHT

Galicia Greets France

On 15 July 1936 a twin-engine Dragon Rapide landed on Gando Airport by Las Palmas on Gran Canaria. On board were, along with the pilot C.W.H. Bebb, the retired Major Hugh Pollard, his daughter Diana and her friend Dorothy Watson – enroute on a secret mission.

Everything had run according to plan up to that point. Their cover as English tourists seemed to be intact. Pollard and the two girls went on to Santa Cruz de Tenerife. There they went to the »Clinica costa«, where they were to meet a certain Dr. Gabarda. Pollard said only one sentence: »Galicia saluda a Francia!« (Galicia greets France!). The doctor looked at the three visitors in astonishment. But the major only repeated the sentence. The doctor lost his temper: He wasn't interested in Galicia greeting France, he retorted. Pollard scraped together what little Spanish he knew, told the doctor that he had orders to tell him that Galicia greets France and that he and his companions would be in the Hotel Pino de Oro. That was the end of the conversation.

Secret Meeting Place

Bebb, the pilot, had stayed behind in the hotel in Las Palmas. He also had unusual encounters. One visitor who introduced himself as Captain Lucena badgered him with questions. For whom and why was he on Gran Canaria, who were his passengers and when was he leaving again? Bebb was suspicious. He had a secret mission. Could he trust the officer? Maybe he was on the other side! He did not want to take any risks, so he answered the questions ingenuously. The Spanish officer finally told him to go to a certain place at a certain time. In a villa in the mountains Bebb met a general named Orgaz and his interpreter, Don Bonny. But the minute interrogation of Bebb was just as fruitless as his first conversation with Captain Lucena in the hotel. The two Spaniards believed that they had the wrong man and sent him away with the warning to forget everything that he had heard.

The Unknown Passenger

On the morning of 18 July Bebb was woken up by three Spanish officers and brought to the military command. After waiting for hours, he was told at noon that it was time to go. Outside Bebb saw familiar faces – General Orgaz and Don Bonny. With an armed escort they went to Gando Airport, where Bebb's Dragon Rapide stood waiting in the middle of the runway. The airplane was ready to take off. Then the passengers appeared – three Spanish officers. One of them was in his mid-forties, a greying black-haired man, approached Bebb and introduced himself: »I am **General Franco**.« Bebb looked at him in astonishment. So this was the mysterious passenger that he was supposed to take to Spanish Morocco. Bebb did not know who he really was. General Franco entered the Dragon Rapide at 2.10pm. He exchanged his military uniform for a grey suit, shaved off his moustache and put on sunglasses. One of his co-conspirators gave him his diplomatic passport – in case there were complications during a stopover in French Morocco. On 19 July at 7am Bebb landed the plane in Tetuan, the capital of Spanish Morocco. Luis Botin slapped the English pilot on the shoulder and said: »One day you will understand what you have done for us.« Bebb laughed. He still considered it to be an adventure.

The Civil War

When Franco took command of the African forces, the Moroccan mercenaries and the foreign legion on 19 July in Tetuan, the rebellion against the government of the Popular Front, which took power in 1936, had already begun in Madrid. Franco's soldiers were taken to the Spanish mainland in Italian and German airplanes, where they soon conquered large areas with the help of Italian regular troops and the German »**Legion Condor**«.

In September 1936 a junta named the rebel Franco to »Generalissimo« and »Head of State«. After three years of battles with atrocities committed on both sides, Madrid fell in March 1939 to the hands of Franco's troops. The Spanish Civil War was over.

General Franco, who ruled Spain for almost 40 years

Spanish Civil War In July 1936 the Spanish military, including **General Francisco Franco** (1892 – 1975), who was at that time the military commander of the Canary Islands, revolted against the democratically elected republican government. The preparations for the coup that led to the Spanish Civil War (1936 – 39) were made on Tenerife. Franco assembled the island's garrison on 17 June 1936 near the town of Esperanza in order to gain their support.

Efforts at autonomy In the 1970s the autonomy of the Canaries from the Spanish motherland was a major topic in local politics. The separatists blamed the mainland Spanish (and foreigners) for their economic problems. Walls and rocks were covered with the demand of »Fuera Godos« (»Goths out«: Members of the Spanish nobility were originally called »Godos« because they claimed to be descended from Visigoth nobles; later all non-Canarians were called Godos).

The **separatism movement** climaxed in the years 1976 to 1978, when terrorists tried to enforce the slogan »Fuera Godos« with bombs. These attempts, which were supported by the Algerian government, did not cause any serious damage. The situation was defused when the Canaries got a degree of autonomy in 1982 as part of the decentralisation policies of the Spanish government. However, the topic of more independence – for example extensive autonomy within a Spanish state – comes up regularly in island politics.

Ties to the EU When Spain, which was transformed into a constitutional monarchy after the death of Franco in 1975, joined the European Union in 1986, there were initially no economic consequences for the Canary Islands: they had refused to join the EU in order to keep their status as a free trade zone and were the subject of a special agreement due to their location. In 1989 the Canarian parliament decided to join the EU anyway, above all to profit from EU subsidies and infrastructure aid, and to make it possible to export Canarian goods to Europe. The Canary Islands have been completely integrated into the EU since 1993.

RECENT DEVELOPMENTS

1990	Las Palmas gets a university.
2005	The island is made a biosphere reserve.
Since 2006	Unparalleled immigration from Africa

University town Decades of conflict in the cultural sector between the two Canary provinces Santa Cruz de Tenerife and Las Palmas de Gran Canaria were ended in 1990 when Las Palmas got its own university.

The election for the Canarian parliament in May 2011 was won by the conservative party Partido Popular (PP). They won 21 of the 60 seats. But this was not enough for a governing majority since the national-conservative Coalición Canaria (CC) joined the socialist party Partido Socialista Obrero Español (PSOE) in a governing coalition. The coalition is led by Minister President Paulino Rivero Baute (CC).

Political balance of power

In 2005 UNESCO declared 43% of the territory of Gran Canaria to be a biosphere reserve.

Biosphere reserve

The Canary Islands experienced an unparalleled invasion of illegal immigrants from Africa in 2006. Almost daily one or more boats landed along its coastlines with dozens of refugees. Many were then flown to the Spanish mainland, while others are taken back to their country of origin. Meanwhile the numbers have been reduced drastically mainly by the increased patrols off the Canarian coastline.

Illegal immigration

About one fourth of the forests on Gran Canaria were destroyed in summer 2007 in one of the most devastating forest fires in its history. A woodsman who was angry over losing his job had set the fire, and hot desert winds kept it blazing. Many residents lost all their possessions.

Forest fires

In early 2012 Spain found itself in a serious economic crisis. Unemployment climbed to 27% in 2013; on the Canaries it was even up to 30%. It was only the growing number of tourists that gave the islands reason for restrained optimism.

Economic crisis

Arts and Culture

Art History

The Guanches left an artistic legacy. In modern architecture traces of Gothic and Classicism can be seen. The balconies on typical Canarian houses are among the characteristic features.

ANCIENT CANARIAN ART

Some ceramic items from pre-Hispanic times have survived. They are free-form and were not made on a potter's wheel. Many have concave handles that also served as spouts. Most of them have smooth surfaces, but on some designs are etched into the surface. The forms varied from island to island. Thus ceramic objects from La Palma are characterised by impressed decoration, while those from Gran Canaria are especially artistic. Pintaderas, »stamps« with highly ornamented designs, are important as part of early Canarian ceramics. They were usually ceramic, more rarely made of wood, and were presumably used to »sign« objects. No two pintaderas are completely identical.

Idols were probably used in religious rites. Almost all that have been preserved are in fragmentary form. The Idol of Tara, possibly the oldest Canarian find, is the only one that has artistic value. It was discovered on Gran Canaria and can now be seen in the Museo Canario in Las Palmas. The statue with its grotesquely fat limbs appears female, even though it has no breasts (photo p. 42). Cave paintings were only found in Cueva Pintada in the north (Gáldar). The cave is decorated with coloured geometric patterns. All in all, there are few artistic items, and these are very plain.

ARCHITECTURAL HISTORY

After the Spanish conquest, European-style and above all Spanish-style churches and other buildings with modest pretensions were constructed. These might not be outstanding examples of architecture, but some of the buildings, which represent a wide variety of styles, are of interest. At first the **Gothic** style was used, for example the ribbed vaulting in the Catedral de Santa Ana in Las Palmas de Gran Canaria. Then Gothic and **Renaissance** elements were combined, as at Casa de Colón in Las Palmas. Gothic or Renaissance style combined with Moorish elements to form the **Mudejar** style. It was

Elaborate entrance to Casa de Colón in Las Palmas

developed in Spain by Mudejar architects, i.e. Moors who were »allowed to remain« in the country, but also by Christian builders who were influenced by the Moorish style. Its most important characteristics are horseshoe-shaped arches, stalactite vaulting and stucco ornaments. Mudejar style developed into the **Plateresque** style, beginning in the late 15th century in Spain. Façades were given intricate, detailed decorations. The Canary Islands developed a special variety of this style, often incorporating wooden ceilings made of Canary pine. They are richly decorated, in some cases in different colours. In the 17th century **Baroque** architecture appeared, but was used less than the Gothic or Renaissance style on Gran Canaria. However, many of the churches were given a Baroque remodelling.

Classicism left its mark from the 18th century, mainly in the façades. Austere composition and, compared to Baroque works, restrained use of statuary is expressed in the façade of the Catedral de Santa Ana in Las Palmas. The architecture of the 19th century is a mixture of various historical styles. A building boom has been in progress on Gran Canaria since the 1960s. Countless giant hotel complexes sprang up, especially in the south of the island. Tourist sites like Maspalomas/Playa del Inglés are planned communities. These aesthetically questionable solutions are points of controversy on the islands as well. Puerto de Mogán, where the two-storey white houses have colourfully decorated door and window frames as well as wrought-iron balconies, is generally considered to be an accomplished example of a holiday resort.

ARCHITECTURE

Urban and rural living
Here and there in the interior, one-storey farmhouses can be seen. They ususally have 30 – 40 sq m/300 – 450 sq ft of living space, but families spent much of their time in the partly covered and luxuriantly planted courtyards. The houses generally face south, so they need no shutters to keep out wind and rain. The single-storey urban dwellings are usually small and cramped; two-storey houses have outside steps made of wood or stone, a small balcony or – more rarely – a vestibule. With few exceptions even upper-class houses are relatively small; they hardly differ from more modest two-storey buildings. The shady inner courtyard with many plants forms the focal point of the house, with steps (generally on the left) going up to the living quarters on the top floor. Almost all houses are white-washed. This reflects sunlight, keeps the houses cool and repels insects, which avoid the white surfaces because they cannot hide on them.

Carved balconies
The most characteristic features of Canarian architecture are the elaborately carved balconies, windows and doors, all of which are

painted green, white or rust-brown; they have always been status symbols. The wooden balconies can be divided into two groups: those with shaped wooden balustrades, above which they are open to the roof; and those with a screen going up to the roof in the Arab style, which allows the occupants to look out without being seen. There are also various combinations of these forms.

Folklore

Fiestas play a central role in life on the Canaries. Sports like »lucha canaria« can only be found here.

The fiestas generally have religious origins and honour one of the islands' patron saints. As a rule they start with a procession followed by more secular entertainment. Music plays a large part in these festivities. The songs have passionate rhythms and melodies. Most of the time they are accompanied by a **timple**, a small stringed instrument.

Fiestas

There are grounds in every larger town where »**lucha canaria**« (Canarian wrestling) matches are held. Two wrestlers face off in a circular arena, 9 – 10m/30 – 33ft in diameter; each wrestler is part of a twelve-man team. A match consists of three rounds, each three minutes. The winner is the one who wrestles his opponent to the ground twice. »**Juego del palo**«, the Canarian stick fight, requires great skill. The two players confront each other with two sticks each and try to hit their opponent according to set rules. The body should be moved as little as possible (▶ MARCO POLO Insight, p. 106).

Traditional sports

Famous People

JEAN DE BÉTHENCOURT (1359 – 1425)

Jean de Béthencourt from Normandy was given the task of conquer-
ing the Canary Islands by Henry III of Castile. Béthencourt was accompanied by **Gadifer de la Salle**, with whom he had gone on a
»crusade« against Tunis in 1390. They gathered a fleet of ships for the
expedition and sailed from La Rochelle in 1402. When Béthencourt
finally sighted the first islands of the archipelago, he was so happy
that he named them Alegranza (joy) and La Graciosa (the graceful
one), even though they were barren, rocky places. The adventurers
dropped anchor at Lanzarote and took the island in a relatively short
time. Béthencourt returned to Spain the same year to get reinforce-
ments. At this time Henry III gave him the title »King of the Canary
Islands« – wrongly, in the opinion of Gadifer de la Salle, who took
part in no more conquests. Jean de Béthencourt subdued
Fuerteventura alone in 1405 and founded the capital Betancuria,
which was named after him. A short time later he also took El Hierro.
The French nobleman settled Norman and Spanish farmers on the
island; the local population was converted to Christianity. Then Béthencourt tried to conquer Gran Canaria and La Palma, but was
driven off by the local people. In 1406 Béthencourt named his nephew **Maciot de Béthencourt** viceroy of the islands. Béthencourt himself returned to France and died there in his castle in Granville in
1425.

French
conqueror

CHRISTOPH COLUMBUS (1451 – 1506)

Christopher Columbus (in Italian Cristoforo Colombo, in Spanish
Cristóbal Colón), who was born in Genoa, visited the Canary Islands
several times while on his voyages of discovery (▶MARCO POLO
Insight, p. 48) Columbus went to Lisbon in 1476 in order to pursue
his dream of discovering a westward passage to India. When no one
was willing to finance him he went on to Spain in 1485. In 1492 Ferdinand of Aragón and his wife Isabella of Castile signed an agreement that would make him viceroy of the discovered lands and give
him 10% of the profits from the trip. To this day it is not certain that
Columbus actually stopped at Gran Canaria on his first trip (1492 –
93). If he did so, he stayed not voluntarily but to repair the rudder of
the Pinta. During this short forced stop he is supposed to have stayed
in a house on the site of today's Casa de Colón in Las Palmas. Columbus left for La Gomera in late August 1492. His logbook shows that
he witnessed an eruption of the volcano Teide on Tenerife when sailing by. On La Gomera he took on water and food and met **Beatriz de**

Explorer

Bobadilla. While the residents like to tell about the love affair between the two, there is no historical evidence for it. On his second
(1493 – 96), third (1498 – 1500) and fourth (1502 – 04) crossings the
discoverer of America stopped at La Gomera and once on El Hierro
to take on supplies, but he never revisited Gran Canaria. Columbus
returned to Spain from his last trip a sick man and died in 1506 in
Valladolid.

NÉSTOR MARTÍN FERNÁNDEZ DE LA TORRE (1887 – 1938)

Painter The Néstor Museum in Las Palmas is devoted to the painter Néstor
Martín Fernández de la Torre, who was born on 7 February 1887 on
Gran Canaria. After studying at the school of art in Madrid, Néstor
de la Torre travelled throughout Europe. In London he studied the
work of the Pre-Raphaelites. His first successes as an artist came in
1908. In the next years Néstor de la Torre made numerous paintings
inspired by Symbolism that were displayed in international galleries.
He also painted murals like the one in the Teatro Pérez Galdós in Las
Palmas or in the casino in Santa Cruz de Tenerife. They often depict
idealised versions of the Canarian people. In 1934 Néstor de la Torre
started a campaign to revive Canarian folklore and architecture. It
was his idea to build Pueblo Canario, a Canarian village, but the idea
only materialised in 1939 in Las Palmas – a year after the artist died.
Water-colour pictures by Néstor de la Torre served as designs for the
buildings. In 1956 the Néstor Museum was opened in Pueblo Canario thanks to a donation by the artist's brothers.

JUSTUS FRANTZ (b.1944)

Pianist and The internationally known pianist and composer is among the most
conductor famous interpreters of Viennese music of the Classical and Romantic
periods. The musician's career began in 1967 when he won a musical
competition sponsored by German national television. His international fame as a pianist began in 1970: Frantz played under the direction of Herbert Karajan with the Berlin Philharmonic Orchestra. In
1975 he made his debut in the USA with the New York Philharmonic, conducted by Leonard Bernstein. From the late 1980s he began
visiting Gran Canaria, finally moving to Monte León, a hill behind
Maspalomas where many celebrities have villas. The »Casa de los
Músicos« soon became a refuge for celebrities. People like Steffi Graf
and former German Chancellor Helmut Schmidt have enjoyed the
peace and quiet of the finca that Justus Frantz gradually converted
into an organic farm with all sorts of domestic animals and a large

orchard. It has a vineyard and produces wine. In 1995 Frantz established the Philharmonia of the Nations, a unique orchestra with 196 musicians from 39 different countries and five continents. The orchestra performs all over the world under his baton, sometimes in unusual places such as the pope's summer residence, the ancient theatre of Ephesus or under the dome of the Reichstag in Berlin. Of course, the orchestra also plays on Gran Canaria, the conductor's chosen place of residence.

ALFREDO KRAUS (1927 – 1999)

The Spanish tenor Alfredo Kraus, son of an Austrian who emigrated to Gran Canaria after World War I, has the honour of having been born in the most famous house in Las Palmas, the **Casa de Colón**. He first studied engineering but soon turned to singing and completed his studies in Milan. In 1956 he debuted in Cairo as the Duke of Mantua; he broke through internationally in 1958 when he appeared on stage along with Maria Callas in his native country of Spain. He appeared in all of the world's greatest opera houses, including La Scala in Milan, the New York Metropolitan Opera and the Opéra Bastille in Paris. Kraus was considered to be one of the leading lyrical tenors, and was a specialist in Mozart. He was active until shortly before his death; in 1998 he gave his farewell performance in Berlin in the title role of Jules Massenet's Werther. While he was still

Opera singer

Alfredo Kraus was born in Casa de Colón

alive his hometown of Las Palmas inaugurated the Auditorio Alfredo Kraus, today one of the foremost cultural forums on the Canary Islands.

FERNANDO LEÓN Y CASTILLO (1842 – 1918)

Politician

Fernando León y Castillo from Telde was responsible to a large extent for Gran Canaria's economic upswing. He had gained fame as a politician on Gran Canaria in the 1870s; in 1881 he was appointed Spanish foreign minister in Madrid. Here he was able to work to Gran Canaria's advantage over and against the other Canarian islands by supporting the development of the harbour of Las Palmas. In a short time it became the major port of the islands.

JOSÉ LUJÁN PÉREZ (1756 – 1815)

Sculptor and architect

Statues of patron saints by José Luján Pérez can be found in the major churches of Gran Canaria and also on the entire Canary archipelago. He was born in the little town of Santa María de Guía in northern Gran Canaria. A bust and many wooden Baroque sculptures in the church honour the town's famous son. Luján Pérez worked on his home island not only as a sculptor, but also on the cathedral of Santa Ana as an architect.

BENITO PÉREZ GALDÓS (1843 – 1920)

Author

Benito Pérez Galdós is probably the most famous writer to come from the Canary Islands. The house where he was born on 10 May 1843 in Las Palmas and where he lived as a boy is now a museum. Pérez Galdós was the youngest of many children born to a moderately well-off army officer. After attending school in Las Palmas, he was sent to Madrid in 1863 to study law. He lived there until his death, except when he was making his numerous journeys around Europe. Pérez Galdós only returned to the Canary Islands once. They do not play a role in his works, the most important of which is Episodios Nacionales, the history of Spain in the 19th century told in the form of a 46-volume novel. It was Madrid that really fascinated Pérez Galdós. He wrote in his Memoirs of an Amnesiac: »I will skip my childhood since it is uninteresting or at least hardly any different from the experiences of my more or less industrious university years ...«. Pérez Galdós, who as an exponent of Spanish liberalism was controversial during his lifetime, is now considered to be the most important novelist in recent times in Spain.

JUAN REJÓN (d. 1481)

The conqueror of Gran Canaria came from Aragon and served in the
Castilian navy under the Catholic Monarchs Ferdinand and Isabella,
who appointed him to participate in the conquest of the Canary Islands. His expedition of three ships set out from Puerto de Santa
María near Cadiz in May 1478. On 24 June 1478 Rejón and his men
disembarked at Las Isletas. The first camp under palms was the origin
of the settlement Real de las Palmas, today's city of Las Palmas de
Gran Canaria. Conflicts in the invading party led to the deposition
of Rejón as governor of the island. His successor, Pedro de Vera, sent
him back to Castile as a prisoner, but Rejón gained his freedom, returned to the Canaries and executed de Vera. Rejón's own life ended
in 1481 in an attempt to conquer La Gomera. He was murdered at the
behest of a rival conquistador, Hernán Peraza. The conquest of Gran
Canaria was completed two years later.

**Founder of
Las Palmas de
Gran Canaria**

ENJOY
GRAN CANARIA

Would you like to know where the Canafrios love to eat, hike or swim? We have put together the best addresses and tips for you. .

Accommodation

Hotels for All Tastes

Be it a beach hotel, a holiday flat in the second row or a holiday house in the green interior – Gran Canaria is prepared for everything. There is accommodation for about 160,000 visitors, starting with a simple room in a family-run bed & breakfast to a luxury suite in a five-star hotel. A large amount is in apartments and bungalows. Camping, on the other hand, is not common.

Most visitors to the Canaries book package holidays from home including air travel, accommodations and maybe board. Those who look for accommodation themselves, be it online or when there, will generally pay more but not necessarily get a better room, since the large tour companies often reserve the best rooms for their customers. If you are not travelling during the high season from Christmas to Easter, you should not have any trouble finding a room on your own.

Book from home

Package holidays include a choice in the type of board. Some hotels on the Costa Canaria also offer **all inclusive holidays**, which have the advantage of predictable costs. But often the quality of the food, especially in the cheaper hotels, is less good. A room with breakfast allows a free choice of when and where to eat in the local restaurants but tends to be more expensive than half board or all inclusive.

? | MARCO ⊕ POLO INSIGHT

Campgrounds

Camping Temisas
Lomo de la Cruz between Agüimes and Santa Lucía
Camping Playa de Vargas
Carretera de Vargas s/n
www.campingplayadevargas.com
Camping Villamar
Playa del Asno
between Mogán and La Aldea

Hotels and apartment complexes are divided into **five categories**. The hotels are awarded stars, and the apartments are awarded keys. The standard is based on the quality of the interior and furnishings, not on the quality of the service and food.

Categories

Apartment complexes are common on Gran Canaria. They appeal mainly to self-caterers. An apartment generally includes a combination living and bedroom, and a kitchen.

Apartments and studios

The finest in wellness:
Hotel Villa des Conde Melonaras

The Country Alternative

The southern coast of Gran Canaria is getting tight. In the last 50 years extensive holiday resorts have been built on every beach and everywhere where it was possible to make beaches. But the island interior has hardly been touched by tourism. For some years Turismo Rural, a country tourism initiative, has been successfully routing at least a small segment of the visitors inland. Along with the rural setting many guests appreciate the quiet location away from the crowds and the good hiking possibilities nearby.

In the 1990s many of the houses in the mountains were left empty as a result of urban migration and were just waiting to be put to use in the service of tourism. In 1998 the first country house, Casa Rural El Palmito, was opened in Valsequillo. A short time previously the island parliament had passed a law to promote rural tourism and soon the first subsidies from the **EU structure fund LEADER** arrived. The rules are strict: Restoration using public funds is only possible if the traditional building style is kept. These are often houses with a special charm, which are located in very beautiful places. Choose between converted water mills, fincas in the middle of banana plantations or surrounded by orange or almond trees. But many of these houses are in remote areas and a rental car is necessary.

Country houses and hotels

Most of the **country houses** are for self-caterers. Along with sleeping and living quarters they have completely furnished kitchens; almost all of them have a terrace with a wonderful view and some with a barbecue grill. Size and comfort level varies. Smaller houses have just enough room for two to three people, but there are also larger ones with two or even more bedrooms.

For people who don't want to make their own beds or breakfast there are **country hotels**. A few have a restaurant attached and offer half board. The most attractive of these Hoteles Rurales are introduced in the travel section under the area where they are located, like Casa de Los Camellos (► Agüimes) and the country hotel Las Longueras im Valle Agaete (► Agaete). The Parador de Cruz de Tejeda (► Cruz de Tejeda) is even a mountain hotel with four stars – it lies in the geographical heart of the island at an elevation of 1,560m/5,150ft with a magnificent panoramic view of the surrounding mountain world.

INTERNET
www.grancanariafincas.com

SELECTION
The prices lie between €80 and €110 per night.

Casa Rural El Borbullón

El Mesón 22, Teror
Tel. 928 23 02 86
www.elborbullon.com
The colonial house with a typical Canarian inner courtyard is located about half a mile from the centre of Teror. The original architecture was retained to the last detail: thick stone walls, wood floors, pine timbering. The three apartments are extravagantly furnished with old vases, jugs and slightly kitschy pictures. The garden with a small pool offers wonderful relaxation.

Hotel Rural Las Calas *Insider Tip*

El Arenal 36, La Lechuza
(Vega de San Mateo)
Tel. 928 66 14 36
www.hotelrurallascalas.com
The colonial house from the year 1800 has a pleasantly quiet location. It is a typical stone and wood country house with a slight Arab influence visible in the door relief and the window bars. Some rooms are decorated with African sculptures; all nine have beautiful old furniture. Lemon and almond trees blossom in the garden depending on the time of year.

Casa Rural Finca La Salud

Barranco Seco de Telde 52, Telde
Tel. 928 67 73 40
www.fincalasalud.com
This vineyard with a sea view is surrounded by vines in one of the most beautiful canyons on the island. The buildings are listed monuments. Apart from the bodega with its tastefully furnished dining room there are two houses and a garden. The owners keep horses.

Casa Rural El Palmeral del Valle

El Valle 13, Santa Lucía de Tirajana
Tel. 928 33 02 62
www.santaluciarural.com
The former lodge for shepherds and farm hands is located in the valley of the village Santa Lucía. Palms, tropical fruit trees, olive groves and fields surround the property. The traditional style of building was followed strictly during the restoration. There are two bedrooms, a bathroom, a kitchen, a dining room and a large terrace with a pool.

El Caserío de San José de las Vegas

Camino Viejo de San José 25, San José de las Vegas (Santa Brígida)
Tel. 928 64 30 39
www.elcaseriodesanjose.com
Just lay in one of the lounge chairs in the garden and enjoy the atmosphere! The farm, which is surrounded by gardens, fields and palm trees, consists of two country houses in typical Canary style. There is also a fitness room, a pool, a pond and some fruit trees.

House with a Moorish touch: Las Calas

Children

Hits for Kids

As a holiday and beach destination Gran Canaria is ideally suited for families with children. The year-round mild climate guarantees fun on the beach all year; and if the 18°C/65°F warm Atlantic Ocean is too chilly in February, all of the larger hotels and holiday apartment complexes have heated pools. Away from the water there are many opportunities for filling the children's days with fun – on the southern coast the region between Costa Canaria and Costa Mogán with its large selection of theme parks and excursion venues could even be called a children's paradise.

Many of the artificially built beaches on the south coast are protected by breakwaters so that the surf is reduced and the water is almost completely calm. The beaches Playa de Mogán, Playa Taurito and Playa de los Amadores are well suited for children since they shelve quite gently. On the east coast, however, the Atlantic frequently shows its rougher side; it's best to leave these beaches to surfers of all kinds.

Fun on the beach

The selection of theme and water parks aimed at children as well as organised excursions is huge. But not all of them are worth visiting and many are very expensive. A day at a water park for a family of four can cost €85.

Theme and water parks

Most of the parks are in the south, while the north has few attractions to offer children. The water park Aqualand is a good alternative when the seas are rough. The theme park Holiday World with Ferris wheel and other rides is one of the biggest attractions, followed by the animal parks Los Palmitos in Maspalomas and Cocodrilos in Agüimes.

Kids almost always love a **boat trip** (►Excursions); in Puerto de Mogán the »Yellow Submarine« makes trips every hour (www.at lantidasubmarine.com; €29 per trip).

Excursions

Animal rides are also offered in several places: Near ►Fataga there are two **camel safaris**, as well as one by the dune lake near the lighthouse at Maspalomas. Horseback riding is available at Rancho Park (►Playa del Inglés).

A »**burro safari**« goes along paths through the farmland of Santa Lucía (www.burrosafari.com).

There are many places for the little ones to splash around

Attractions for children

ZOOS AND BOTANICAL GARDENS
Cactualdea
▶ La Aldea de San Nicolás: Cactus Park – the place for friends of prickly plants

Palmitos Park
▶ Maspalomas: subtropical animal park with dolphin, falcon and parrots shows, also about 1200 birds, reptiles, orang-utans, butterfly and orchid houses.

Parque de Cocodrilos
▶ Agüimes: small zoo with crocodile and parrot show

Jardín Canario
▶ Tafira: large botanical garden with Canarian flora. It has many endemic plants that can't be seen otherwise.

OPEN-AIR MUSEUM
Mundo Aborigen
▶ Playa del Inglés: in the footsteps of the Guanches in the open air museum Mundo Aborigen.

AMUSEMENT AND THEME PARKS
Holiday World
▶ Maspalomas: Ferris wheel, carousels, Mississippi paddle wheel-

This is fun: playing with daddy in the sand

er, roller coaster and many other attractions and shows

Sioux City
▶ San Agustín: artificial Wild West town with shows

WATER PARKS
Aqualand
Carretera Palmitos Park, km 3 (3 km/2mi north-west of Maspalomas)
❶ Jul/Aug. 10am – 6pm, Sept. until Jun 10am – 5pm, admission €25, children (3-12 years) €18
www.aqualand.es
Aqualand (previously Aqua Sur) on the road to Palmitos with its about 30 waterslides, wave pool and water channel on which you can take an »air mattress cruise« is one of the biggest water parks on the Canaries. Many guests think that the somewhat worn down park is too expensive since lockers, lounge chairs and sun umbrellas cost extra. The food is not cheap either.

GO-KART
Racing Kart Maspalomas
Carretera Palmitos Park, km 2 (2km/1¼mi north-west of Maspalomas)
❶ daily 10am – 11pm; price for 10 minutes €17, children €13.
www.racingkartmaspalomas.com

Along with karts for adults, teenagers and children, they also rent racing karts and double karts; observation terrace with restaurant.

Gran Karting Club
Tarajalillo, San Agustín Carretera del Sur, km 46
❶ daily 11am – 10pm, in winter until 9pm.
Adults: €18, children €9
www.grankarting.com
Go-karts for all ages: there is a children's track with mini karts for children from the age of 5; for children from 10 years there are »mini-bikes«; for ages 12–16 there is a junior track and older go-kart guests even have a 1650m/1800yd-long track.

MINIATURE GOLF
San Valentin Park
Playa de Inglés, Calle Timple, near the junction of Avenida de Tirajuna and Avenida de Gran Canaria, daily 9am – 11pm

Las Caracolas
Puerto Rico, on the northern edge of Playa de los Amadores, daily 10am – midnight
A new course decorated with sculptures of water sprites, seahorses and seashells.

Festivals · Holidays · Events

Religion Live

Canarios know how to enjoy themselves; the calendar is well-filled with festivals and events all year. Religious festivals are very important. Las Palmas has also made a name for itself with its cultural festivals. But the most Canarian fiesta of all is carnival, which is celebrated at least as extravagantly as it is in Rio or along the Rhine River.

Every town has its own fiesta in honour of the local patron saint. In the summer months there is always a festival going on somewhere. The **fiestas** all have more or less the same pattern. The religious part comes first, a church service and then a procession (**romería**) on streets decorated for the event with local people wearing elaborate costumes. Then the secular events and entertainment follow: Folklore groups dance and sing, a fair and sporting events like the »lucha canaria« take place. The climax is the »verbena«, a dance at night that lasts into the morning hours. The festival often concludes with fireworks. If the saint's feast day falls in the middle of the week, the festival is usually moved to the preceding or following weekend so that at least two nights are free for celebrating. Festivals often even last for several days.

Canarians love to celebrate

> **MARCO ● POLO TIP**
>
> ! *Festivals and dates* **Insider Tip**
>
> An up-to-date calendar of events including the best island festivals, but also exhibitions, sporting events, concerts, theatre and much more is available in three languages under www.turismodecanarias.com

A large palette of cultural events is on offer especially in the city of Las Palmas.

Cultural festivals

The year starts off with the Festival de Música de Canarias, which is held in January and organised together with the neighbouring island of Tenerife. Internationally famous symphony orchestras and soloists perform in the Auditorio Alfredo Kraus. In April cinema fans meet at the International Film Festival of Las Palmas (www.lpafilmfestival.com); from March until June the Teatro Pérez Galdós is the setting for the opera festival. In July the International Jazz Festival welcomes bands from America and Africa; in November the WOMAD World Music Festival takes place in Parque Santa Catalina.

Carnival in Las Palmas is like carnival in Rio de Janeiro

Exciting and Colourful Fiestas

Be it carnival, saints' or flower festivals, fiestas are celebrated elaborately and with great enthusiasm on Gran Canaria.

Virgen de Pino

The most important island festival takes place in September in **Teror** around the pilgrimage church. Up to 80,000 pilgrims from all parts of the islands flock to the mountain village for the Fiesta de la Virgen del Pino every year, many on foot but most of them with some vehicle, which regularly causes chaotic traffic conditions. The pilgrimage's origins go back to an event that took place in 1481 when the Virgin Mary is said to have appeared to a shepherd boy in the crown of a tree. The festivities in honour of the Virgin of the Pines take up a whole week and are accompanied by folk music and dancing in local costumes. The high point is on September 8 when the honoured figure of Mary is carried through the streets in a festive procession.

Almendro en Flor

Fiestas del Almendro en Flor, the almond blossom festival, is celebrated without religious background in **Tejeda**. The festival dates are chosen according to when the almond trees blossom and are made public a few weeks beforehand. It generally falls on the first or second Sunday in February (tourist information offices will know the exact dates). Here as well folklore, costumes and timple

Parades and street parties are part of the fiestas on Gran Canaria

Greetings from Rio on the Gran Cabalgata, the largest carnival parade in Las Palmas

music play a role. In the village street, which is decorated with palm branches, craftsmen show how baskets and brooms used to be made, paella is cooked in large pans and regional almond specialties are offered everywhere. Tejeda is, incidentally, not the only place to honour the almond. **Valsequillo** generally celebrates its own almond blossom festival a week before or after Tejeda. But the festivals in both villages cannot quite do without the church; at least a mass is celebrated in honour of the almond.

Carnival

No other festival is celebrated as elaborately on Gran Canaria as carnival, and that with at least as much enthusiasm as it is in Mainz, Cologne or Rio de Janeiro. The preparations begin already months in advance when professional designers or mask makers design fanciful costumes, choreographers

and composers come up with new dance steps and songs for the many carnival groups from the various parts of the city. The large events, like the election of a carnival queen, take place at the giant open air stage in Santa Catalina Park. The Drag Queen Gala, a scurrile homo and hetero show, is the absolute highlight of the carnival. The grand finale of the carnival is the burial of the sardine; a burial procession accompanies a giant paper maché fish to the beach at Canteras and burns it there with loud wailing and fireworks. The festivities in **Las Palmas** last three weeks and exact dates as to when and where events are held can be obtained from the tourist offices or online (www.lpacarnaval.com). Things don't end on Ash Wednesday on Gran Canaria. After the carnival in Las Palmas things only get rolling in the south of the island, in **Maspalomas** and **Playa del Inglés**.

Calendar of events

PUBLIC HOLIDAYS
1 January
New Year (Año Nuevo)
6 January
Epiphany (Los Reyes)
1 May
Labour Day (Día del Trabajo)
30 May
Canary Island Day (Día de las Islas Canarias)
25 July
(Feast of the St James) Santiago Apóstol
15 August
Feast of the Assumption of the Virgin (Asunción)
12 October
Discovery of America; national holiday (Día de la Hispanidad)
1 November
All Saints' Day (Todos los Santos)
6 December
Constitution Day (Día de la Constitución)
8 December
Immaculate Conception (Inmaculada Concepción)
25 December
Christmas (Navidad)

MOVABLE HOLIDAYS
March/April: Good Friday (Viernes Santo)
June: Corpus Christi (Día del Corpus)

JANUARY
Cabalgada de los Reyes
On the evening of 5 January the arrival of the Magi is celebrated in Las Palmas.

JANUARY/FEBRUARY
Festival de Música de Canarias
Internationally known orchestras and soloists take part in the festival of classical music. Performances take place in the Auditorio Alfredo Kraus in Las Palmas. www.festivalcanarias.com

FEBRUARY/MARCH
Carnival
Carnival is celebrated extravagantly in many towns. The centre is Las Palmas.

Fiestas del Almendro en Flor
Almond blossom festival in Tejeda and Valsequillo

Festival de Opera
Right after the music festival the opera festival takes place in the capital. www.operalaspalmas.org

MARCH/APRIL
Semana Santa
Holy Week sees numerous processions and other religious as well as secular events.

Fiesta de Ansite
On 29 April in Santa Lucia, this festival commemorates the last resistance of the original Canarians against the Spanish conquerors at Fortaleza de Ansite.

MAY
Fiesta del Albaricoque
The apricot festival in early May signals the beginning of the apricot harvest with dancing, fireworks and a craft show.

MAY/JUNE
Corpus Christi
Corpus Christi is celebrated with processions and elaborate carpets of flowers and volcanic earth; the celebrations are especially impressive in Las Palmas and Arucas. So that everyone can take part, it is celebrated a week later than the actual date of Corpus Christi.

JUNE
El Día de San Juan
24 June, the feast of St John, is the founding day of Las Palmas. It is celebrated every year with many events.

JULY
International jazz festival
in Auditorio Alfredo Kraus in Las Palmas

Fiesta de Nuestra Señora del Carmen
Feast of the patron saints of Las Palmas, Gáldar and La Aldea de San Nicolás, celebrated on 16 July with boat parades.

Fiesta de Santiago Apóstol
From 15 to 30 July in San Bartolomé de Tirajana the feast of St James is celebrated.

AUGUST
Bajada de la Rama *Insider Tip*
This is one of the leading folklore festivals on the Canaries and is celebrated in Agaete from 4 to 7 August. The »lowering of the branches« goes back to an ancient Canarian custom in which their god is beseeched to supply enough water for the harvest.

Today it is still customary to climb into the hills, bring back a pine branch and beat the water with it at the beach.

SEPTEMBER
Fiesta de la Virgen del Pino
Pilgrimage on 8 September in Teror. Many towns have made this a local holiday.

Fiesta del Charco *Insider Tip*
The »pond festival« takes place on 10 September in La Aldea de San Nicolás. Great fun to be had by all (► MARCO POLO tip, p. 159).

OCTOBER
Fiesta de la Naval
In the harbour of Las Palmas on 6 October the Spanish victory over the fleet of Sir Francis Drake in 1595 is celebrated.

Fiesta de Nuestra Señora de la Luz
Pilgrimage and procession to the sea in Las Palmas on the second Saturday in October

NOVEMBER
Womad Festival
For four days world music stars perform in Parque Santa Catalina in Las Palmas. www.womad.org/festivals/canaries

DECEMBER
Fiestas de Navidad
The exhibition of nativity scenes in Ingenio is worth seeing (► MARCO POLO tip, p. 157).

Food and Drink

Much More than Just Fish

No matter what your opinion is on Canarian cooking, it is definitely unique. In most of the restaurants and at the hotel buffet however you won't see much of it, apart from the obligatory »Canary evening«. That is a pity because some of the local specialties are definitely worth tasting. But you can find them in the capital city Las Palmas or in simple country restaurants.

The hotels have adapted to the tastes of the mainly central and northern European guests and serve international cuisine. Occasionally »papas arrugadas con mojo«, small potatoes with a salt crust and a spicy sauce, might appear. Typical Canarian food can be found away from the tourist centres, but don't expect too much: The cooking is not very sophisticated. Dedicated gourmets will not have it easy, as there are no cooks decorated with Michelin stars on the Canary Islands yet. Canarian cuisine is simple, farm cooking that lives from what the land and the sea have to offer. But you might be surprised at how good the freshly cooked fish and in part hearty meat dishes taste together with Canarian potatoes from the latest harvest. Canarian cooking has clearly been influenced by the Spanish mainland: lots of olive oil, garlic and many herbs and spices. Many of the Spanish who emigrated from the mainland brought their own regional dishes with them. So Basque, Catalan or Galician restaurants can be found in the capital as well as in the holiday centres.

Simple home cooking

MARCO POLO INSIGHT

Triumph of the potato

Before the potato reached the European mainland in the 16th century it was already in use on the Canary Islands. Today more than 30 varieties of potatoes are cultivated here. Incidentally, the popular spud is called »papa« on the Canary Islands and »patata« on the Spanish mainland.

Canarian cooking lives from fish and meat, so vegetarians will have a hard time in traditional restaurants. Even in a chick pea or bean soup little pieces of meat can be found, but the viscid vegetable soup (Potaje de verduras) offered in many places is usually completely vegetarian. The holiday resorts are better prepared for vegetarian guests. Italian, Indian and Thai restaurants always have a good selection of vegetarian dishes.

Vegetarian cooking?

Canarian cooking has many surprises in store

Gofio – Hearty and Healthy

Gofio is one of the few traditional foods that was able to prevail on the Canaries despite pizza, pasta and paella. But it is difficult to find in the hotel kitchens, which have adapted to Central European tastes.

That might have something to do with the taste, which takes some getting used to. But anyone who knows Italian polenta or Tibetan tsampa will like gofio. You will find the dish anywhere Canarians are: at home, in the mountains or the rural towns of Gran Canaria's green north. But the nourishing dish is also served in many excursion restaurants.

Production

It is very easy to produce. Grain - along with barley wheat and corn are main types – is roasted in a drum-shaped oven at a temperature of about 150°C/300°F, which allows the typical aroma to develop. Then the grain needs to be ground to a fine flour. The early Canarians and later the Spanish settlers used simple grinding stones as they can be seen in the ethnographical museums on the island. The whole grain is ground, including the bran and the germ, which makes gofio a whole grain food according to modern food diets. It contains neither preservatives nor other additives. Gofio is not only rich in fibre, it also has a lot of B vitamins and minerals. The large amount of complex carbohydrates makes gofio meals very filling.

Preparation

Originally the roasted flour was kneaded to a firm dough with the addition of water or goat's milk and eaten by itself. Today it is often still eaten as an appetiser in this form. But with a little imagination there is no limit to what can be done with gofio, like gofio bread or pancakes. Gofio gives Canarian soups and stews their texture, and it can be sweetened as well.

Some restaurants serve mousse de gofio as a dessert. Gofio is then combined with ground almonds, sugar, some milk and stiffly beaten

»Guanche muesli« Gofio

egg yolk, after which whipped cream is carefully folded in.

A tasty breakfast is also easy to prepare. Gofio is combined with mashed bananas and the juice of one orange, and then flavoured with honey and lemon juice.

Shopping

Gofio is available in every supermarket on Gran Canaria in many varieties. Freshly ground gofio can also be bought in the Molino de Gofio in Vega de San Mateo (Calle del Agua 9), for example.

Restored Gofio Mills at Work

Some restored old gofio mills are open to visitors, like in San Bartolomé de Tirajana (La Hacienda del Molino, Calle Los Naranjas 2) and in Firgas (Calle El Molino 3).

Gofio mill in Vega de San Mateo

Typical Dishes

… that have prevailed despite the internationalisation of cuisine, mainly in restaurants that have not yet been discovered by tourists – mostly in rural restaurants and at excursion sites.

Papas arrugadas: Small potatoes cooked in sea salt are the main side dish of the Canarian kitchen. They are served mainly as a side dish to fish or rabbit. The trick in cooking them is to leave them in the pot until the salt water has evaporated. The salt crystallises on the potatoes as a white crust on the somewhat wrinkled skin. The potato is eaten with the skin.

Tortilla: Tortilla, a round potato omelette fried in oil, is a Spanish national dish. It is made of potatoes, eggs, olive oil and salt, often with a great variety of vegetables. Of course, every chef in every restaurant or bar and every Spanish housewife claims that he or she serves the best tortilla.

Conejo en salmorejo: Rabbit is very common on the Canaries and is served in pretty much every country restaurant. Cut in small pieces, the meat is marinated overnight in white wine, olive oil, garlic and spices and cooked in a ceramic pot the next day. In the past, wild rabbits shot by amateur hunters were used, but most of today's rabbit meat comes from New Zealand.

Mojo: The salt-crusted potatoes are never served without mojo. Mojo consists of oil, local herbs and spices and lots of garlic. The two main kinds are »mojo rojo« with red paprika and some chili as well as the green variety »mojo verde« with coriander leaves. Red mojo is eaten with meat dishes, and green mojo with fish.

Paella: This Spanish specialty cannot be left out on Gran Canaria. This rice dish is prepared in a large pan and originally comes from the region of Valencia. Characteristic of paella is the rice that has been coloured yellow with saffron, but in cheaper eateries yellow food colouring is often used instead of the expensive spice. Because the preparation is complicated, good restaurants only prepare it when two or more people order it.

Bienmesabe: The name of this dessert means literally »tastes good to me«, and it's no wonder that a sweet with such a name is the most popular on the Canaries. This almond pudding is made by peeling and grating almonds, cooking them briefly with lots of sugar and egg yolk, and flavouring the mixture with cinnamon and grated lemon peel. Almost as much sugar as almonds is used.

Drinks
The local springs produce excellent **mineral water** (agua mineral). It is available as carbonated (con gas) or non-carbonated (sin gas) mineral water. The spring at Firgas produces a very good island mineral water, which is available in practically every supermarket and many restaurants.

Beer (cerveza) is often drunk with meals. Many imported beers are available and many restaurants have German or Danish beer on tap, but the Canarian beers are also good. The Tropical brewery is located on Gran Canaria, Dorada on Tenerife.

Wine is the second most popular beverage among the Canarians. On Gran Canaria only a few hundred acres of vineyards remain, near Tafira. The wine is of average quality. The supermarkets sell wines from Lanzarote and Tenerife, mostly simple table wines.

A meal is usually finished off with **coffee**. It is served as »café solo« (black), »café cortado« (with a little milk) or »café con leche« (coffee with more milk). Another variation is »carajillo« (black coffee with a shot of brandy or rum).

EATING IN A RESTAURANT

Restaurant, bar or bar restaurant?
There is a large selection of restaurants in the tourist centres on Gran Canaria; recommended restaurants are listed under »Sights from A to Z« at the respective location. Restaurants in Spain are classified not with stars but with forks (1–3), but the forks do not reflect the quality of the food – the criteria for **classification** are the range of choice, the interior furnishings, etc. The food in a simple restaurant with only one »fork« can be as good as or even better than the food in a restaurant with three »forks«. Moreover, few restaurants make use of the official forks. Along with **restaurants**, which can be expensive (especially in the tourist centres), there are other ways to satisfy your hunger. In a **bar** – nothing more than the local pub – there is always something to snack on, as a large selection of tapas is usually available. These snacks are eaten while standing at the bar or seated at a little table, if available. A »**bar restaurant**« has more tables and a larger selection – drinks and tapas are served at the bar and meals at the tables. Often »raciones«, a double portion of tapas, are served.

> ! MARCO ⊕ POLO TIP
>
> *Eat late* **Insider Tip**
>
> The noon meal is usually eaten between 1 and 2pm. The evening meal is also eaten late. Canarios hardly ever go to a restaurant before 8pm. Hotels and restaurants have adapted to guests from Great Britain and Germany and serve the evening meal from 6pm.

Marisquerías
Fish and seafood restaurants are called marisquerías in Spanish. The name comes from Spanish mariscos (seafood). They are usually lo-

cated near the water or the harbour and have an especially varied selection of everything that is caught or raised along the coast. The price of the fish is usually calculated by weight and is served »a la plancha«, from a hot platter. A large platter of mixed fish is almost always served as a specialty, but also fish soups and rice dishes with crustaceans. Hardly any meat dishes are served, and you will look in vain for pasta or pizza.

There are a few firm restaurant rules: Never sit down at a table with a stranger. The question »Is this seat available?« is simply not asked. But do not sit at a vacant table either (in southern Gran Canaria with mainly international guests this rule does not apply in simple restaurants). Wait at the doorway of the restaurant. The head waiter will come quickly, ask for the number of people in your party and suggest tables. Then you will be taken to the table and given menus.

Choice of seating

The Bill is never split in Spanish restaurants and bars. One person always pays for everyone. If the group moves from one bar to the other, you take turns footing the bill. It is not divided down to the last cent, **generosity** is expected – with the tip as well. It will be difficult as a foreigner in a group of Spaniards to try to pay for the bill. Someone else is always quicker. The bill is requested casually. It will arrive on a small plate, and the waiter will leave again. Someone will casually reach for the bill, glance at it and place cash or a credit card on the plate. The waiter will return just as casually and take the plate while murmuring »gracias«. After a while he will return and place the plate with the change in front of the payer with another »gracias«. In turn, that person ignores it for a few seconds, then pockets the change and leaves the tip on the plate. The waiter will only pick up the tip when all the guests have left the table.

One for all

Shopping

Art and Bird of Paradise Flowers

Gran Canaria is not really a shopper's paradise. The shopping centres (centros comerciales) in the tourist areas, especially in the south, only have the usual cheap goods for sale. But there are exceptions. Anyone looking for quality and style can't avoid Las Palmas, where the island's largest selection of goods by far is available. Authentic Canarian crafts have also found their niche.

In the capital city **Calle Mayor de Triana** is one of the most popular shopping streets. The first shops there were opened in the mid-19th century when traders and businessmen from around the world landed in the newly built harbour Puerto de la Luz of Las Palmas. Their shops made the Triana, along with the side streets, to the liveliest shopping district of the city at that time. That has not changed, even though it has not been easy for the district to keep up with the newly built shopping centres in other parts of the city. Many of the shops in the side streets are empty. But there is no place in Las Palmas for strolling like the car-free Triana, and even the locals know that. The nicely restored Art Nouveau façades make a beautiful setting. *(Shopping streets in Las Palmas)*

While the Triana hosts many small shops, the **Avenida Mesa y López** invites browsing through the large fashion and department stores. You will find textiles, shoes and accessories here, including international branches offering exclusive designer fashions. The **El Corte Inglés** in Mesa y Lopéz is also the department store with the best selection on the whole island. The largest Spanish department store chain started out as a tailoring business for children's clothing in Madrid in 1890 and first made a name for itself with clothing inspired by English fashion (El Corte Inglés means »English cut«). The seven-storey temple to consumerism is not exactly cheap, but everything is a bit more exclusive, and the services leave nothing to be desired. The gourmet floor in the basement is pure pleasure.

The seal of quality **FEDAC** (Fundación para la Etnografía y el Desarrollo de la Artesanía Canaria) marks crafts that are guaranteed not to come from the Far East but only from Gran Canaria. The foundation, which is operated by the island government has made it a goal to promote traditional crafts. The craftsmen that have been brought together by the foundation covert he whole spectrum of Canarian crafts. Pottery and ceramics are still made in part in the old traditional way without a pottery wheel. Baskets are made from palm leaves and *(Authentic art)*

Sunday market in Teror

Dulcería Nublo bakery in Tejeda

cane; mortars like the ones used in Canarian kitchens to make mojo are made from wood. Typical are timples, small stringed instruments as found at every festival. The Canarian knives (cuchillo canario), used by farmers in former times, are special. The artistically carved handles are made of goat horn and brass and are popular collectors' items. Drawn work embroidery, which requires hours of work, is also available; the mountain village Vilaflor is known for this craft.

FEDAC has two shops of its own on the island, one in Las Palmas (Calle Domingo Navarro 7), the other one in Playa del Inglés in the Yumbo Centrum right next to the tourist office. Fairs also offer the craftspeople a chance to show their work directly. The fairs are held in Las Palmas in Parque de San Telmo (from 2-5 January) and at Faro Maspalomas (generally in August). In order to interest more people in the crafts, the profits are used to finance free training courses.

Alcohol and tobacco

The Canary Islands have been a free trade zone since 1852. However, the lack of customs duty does not necessarily mean that prices are low, although tobacco products and spirits are cheaper than at home. Banana cordial and rum from the distillery in Arucas can be found in almost every souvenir shop.

The rum is best sampled after a tour of the distillery (►Arucas). As far as wine is concerned, the winegrowers on Gran Canaria do not produce quite as good a quality as those on Tenerife or Lanzarote; the

Casa del Vino in Santa Brígida (Calle Calvo Sotelo 26) gives an overview of what's available. Canarian cigars mainly come from the neighbouring island La Palma.

For anyone who has taken a liking to Canarian cooking needs to stock up on gofio and mojo; they can be bought in the supermarkets. There are also specialties made with almonds, which are mainly made in Tejeda. Goat cheese and especially flower cheese (Queso de flor) from ▶ Santa María de Guía are the best choices for cheese products.

Culinary souvenirs

Flower shops will pack strelitzia (bird of paradise flowers) for air transport, so that memories of the Canary flora linger for a few days at home. Last minute purchases of strelitzia are possible at the airport. Seeds are also available for some of the local plants, like the dragon tree.

Flowers

Most shops are open Mon – Fri 9am – 1pm and 4pm – 8pm, Sat 9am to 1pm. In the tourist centres some shops open longer, and even on Sundays.

Opening hours

El Mirador Shopping Centre is located on the edge of Las Palmas, has a view of the sea and any amount of shops

Papayas, Black Pudding and Lots of Knick-knacks

There are almost as many markets on Gran Canaria as there is sand in the dunes of Maspalomas. There is one on almost any day of the week in various locations. Not all of them are worth visiting. Some are geared only towards tourists, others only towards residents. The lively Sunday market in Teror is highly recommended, where a colourful variety of visitors meets around the pilgrimage church.

The Tuesday market in Arguineguín is well visited as is the Friday market in Puerto de Mogán. It is especially busy in high season so that moving through the aisles is only possible at a snail's pace. Cheap textiles are sold, African traders sell handbags and leather goods. But really unusual wares are hard to find.

The flea market in Las Palmas is different. Here there are also many Africans who sell made-to-look-old masks, drums, costume jewellery and sunglasses. There are also stands with second-hand goods like CDs, DVDs, household articles and many more or less useful knick-knacks. What is interesting is the multi-cultural bustle, which is best watched from the terrace of the Art Nouveau cafés on the square.

Farmer's markets

Visitors to the mountain town **Vega de San Mateo** will find a large covered market there. The Mercado del Agricultor is one of the best places to buy fresh groceries. Only fruits and vegetables grown on the island are sold here, everything that the season has to offer. What with the mild climate, this can be a lot, no matter what time of year you're there. In the summer mangos, peaches and apricots fill the stands; in the winter they are replaced by citrus fruits, avocados, papayas, cherimoyas and other exotic fruits. There is also a flower market with potted plants and cut flowers.

Make sure to try the cheese specialties at one of the stands. Goat cheeses are offered in various degrees of ripeness, from cream cheese (queso fresco) to hard cheese (queso duro) that has been ripened for at least two months. The cheeses weigh up to three kilos (over six pounds) and are rolled in gofio or rose paprika, which gives them their own unique taste. There is often also a lightly smoked variety. The mild and creamy flower cheese from Santa Maria is a specialty only produced on Gran Canaria. The juice from a wild artichoke variety is used to make the milk curdle for the cheese. But this delicacy is not to be found on the breakfast buffets in the holiday resorts.

While the farmer's market in San Mateo sells mainly food the Sunday market in **Teror** is a mixture of crafts, jumble and clothing. There are also sellers of local specialties like chorizo de Teror, a spicy paprika sausage, or morcilla, a slightly sweet black sausage spiced with raisins, almonds and cinnamon that presents an unusual taste for central Europeans. The historic setting in the old city gives the market its atmosphere.

Arguineguín
Plaza Negra
Tue 8am – 2pm

Puerto de Mogán
Fri 9am – 2.30pm

Las Palmas
Flea market Parque de San Telmo
Sun 8am – 2pm

Vega de San Mateo
Mercadillo de Agrícola
Sat 8am – 8pm, Sun 8am – 2.30pm

Teror
Sun 8am – 2pm

The farmer's market in Teror

Waves, Wind and Hiking

Gran Canaria would be wasted on a holiday spent entirely on the beach. Hiking, biking, golf – the island is a paradise for sports lovers who appreciate an unbelievably varied and large selection. Many of the larger hotels have tennis courts and fitness rooms for guests interested in sports; some resorts even have their own golf course and golf school. And of course the island offers no lack of activities in, under and on the water.

BEACHES

Gran Canaria's most beautiful beaches are in the south near Maspalomas or Playa del Inglés. The quality of the water here is excellent. In the tourist centres topless sunbathing is common, but this is bound to attract attention on beaches frequented only by the local people. Nude bathing is tolerated on more remote beaches. Nudists should go to the dunes near Maspalomas or Playa del Inglés.

Beach paradise

Guests at the hotels around the former fishing village of Arguineguín have to make do with a tiny beach; the well-kept swimming pools look more attractive.

Arguineguín

North-west of Las Palmas lies the 3km/2mi-long, light sand **Playa de las Canteras**, one of the largest urban public beaches in the world. Rock reefs form a barrier against the surf and swimming here is safe. Even though the beach and the promenade are well cared for, it is impossible to forget that the beach is in a city: At weekends it is overcrowded, but the northern end of the beach offers quieter places at a sandy or rock cove.

Las Palmas

An 8km/5mi-long, well-tended beach of white sand stretches from the lighthouse at El Oasis to Playa del Inglés. It is bordered by impressive dunes that are under nature protection. This fascinating coastal scenery is **Gran Canaria's main attraction**. In the winter months masses of sun-starved Europeans come here. A never-ending line of beachcombers walks along the edge of the water then – all day, every day. In many places loungers, sunshades, paddleboats, surfboards, etc. can be rented; there are countless simple snack bars along the beach.

Playa del Inglés/ Maspalomas

Gran Canaria is a great place for sports: both on land and water

Show what you can do

Puerto de las Nieves
Puerto de las Nieves is the only place in north-western Gran Canaria with an adequate beach. The stretch of dark sand is about 100m/100yd long and 25m/25yd wide, and mainly used by local people.

Puerto de Mogán
Puerto de Mogán has a small beach of light-coloured sand. Breakwaters make it possible for children to splash around safely. Alternatives are **Playa del Taurito** to the east, which is now surrounded by resort facilities, or **Playa de Veneguera**. This dark and rocky beach has been earmarked as the site of another development.
The ultimate beach experience can be found at **Playa de Güigüí** (▶MARCO POLO Insight, p. 214), which is only accessible on foot or by boat.

Puerto Rico
The beach at Puerto Rico does have one huge advantage: The sun is usually still shining here when Maspalomas or Playa del Inglés are

already covered by clouds. Since that is often the case in the winter, this beach can get crowded then. Even at other times the 400m/450yd-long artificial beach seems to be paved with beach loungers. Swimmers share the water with numerous surfers, sailors and yachts. Rock reefs prevent the surf from getting too powerful. **Playa de los Amadores** west of Puerto Rico provides some relief from the congestion. This artificial beach is one of the most beautiful on the island.

MARCO ⊕ POLO TIP

Insider Tip

Water sports with a difference

Puerto Rico is the centre for water sports on the island. Sailing and surfing are on offer, of course, but as an alternative how about a banana boat ride or jet skis? Paragliding over the water is also a favourite activity. Information on the beach at Puerto Rico.

Compared to the adjacent Playa del Inglés, the **beach of San Agustín** is more modest. But the almost 1km/½mi long beach is a good alternative. A promenade connects Playa de San Agustín with the somewhat smaller **Playa de las Burras**.

San Agustin

SPORTS ACTIVITIES

Gran Canaria is the cradle of Spanish golfing – the first Spanish golf club was opened in 1891 in Las Palmas. The course lies right next to Caldera Bandama and has some of the most charming landscapes on the island. With the development of the south into the tourist centre, golf then moved there into the sun-spoiled part of the island. Of the meanwhile eight courses five are on the Costa Canaria. Golf lessons are offered by Meloneras Golf and the El Cortijo Club de Campo near Telde.

Golf

Ideal conditions for deep-sea fishing can be found just two miles off the coast of Gran Canaria. Boats start regularly especially from Puerto Rico and Puerto de Mogán; previous experience is not necessary.

Deep sea fishing

Because of the topographical conditions with mountains up to 2000m/6600ft, cycling on Gran Canaria is something for fit people. Bear in mind that the island has no bike paths. But there is not much traffic on the narrow mountain roads and the island also has some off-road trails on offer with spectacular downhill sections. The main season for biking is the winter since the summer temperatures can get hot. Several biking stations on the Costa Canaria offer guided tours for racing bikes and mountain bikes with a shuttle service into the mountains to save some of the ascent. For those who did not bring their own bikes there are professionally maintained rental bikes and e-bikes.

Biking

The mountains in the island interior are a real challenge for bikers

Horseback riding

There are several riding stables on Gran Canaria that rent to tourists, offer riding lessons or organise trips on horseback.

Sailing, windsurfing

Winds are strong along some parts of the coast; beginners might not find the sailing easy here. Sailors and windsurfers find ideal conditions on the south and south-west coast of Gran Canaria.
Sailing lessons are given in Puerto Rico. Surfboards can be rented in Playa del Inglés, San Agustín, Puerto de Mogán and Puerto Rico. Surfing for experienced windsurfers is at Pozo Izquierdo near El Doctoral. Beginners find suitable conditions in the summer in Bahía Feliz and Playa del Aguila.

Diving

Diving conditions around the Canary Islands are ideal. There are ten diving schools on Gran Canaria, most of them in the south or south-west of the island. They offer beginners' and advanced courses in many of the hotels. They also organise diving trips to the underwater park at Arinaga with its beautiful sea flora and fauna.

Many large hotels have excellent tennis courts, most of them with floodlights. There are usually tennis teachers available.

It's not necessary to be active in every kind of sport; watching can be fun too. In Pozo Izquierdo the world's elite of surfers meets every summer for world cup races. Spectators can watch the spectacular jumps and loops from a safe distance; with wind speeds of up to 90 km/h Pozo Izquierdo is an excellent speed location. The surfer beach on the east coast is basically the home of surfing pro Philip Köster. The son of German immigrants grew up on Gran Canaria and became world champion in 2011 at the age of 17 in the discipline wave-riding. The Danish-Dutch world champion Bjørn Dunkerbeck also learned his trade on Gran Canaria. The boat races in the bay of Las Palmas also draw crowds of spectators. The boats sail under a lateen sail (vela latina), a typically Canarian boat class with overly large tri-angular sails relative to the size of the boat. Small and larger regattas take place on many weekends from April until October.

Golf can be played all year round

Beautiful Trails Through the Mountains

Gran Canaria does not have to hide behind the favourites Tenerife and La Palma as far as hiking is concerned; the island is no longer a secret among hikers. The »miniature continent« has surprises in store in the mountains with landscape dominated by bizarre rock formations.

Gran Canaria's network of hiking trails is well developed and can offer tours in all degrees of difficulty. Recently some of the camino reales (royal roads) that were built after the Conquista by the Spanish crown and various old roads that connected villages and were grown over by vegetation have been restored and were given uniform signs. Country hotels and numerous fincas in the mountains make good starting points for hikers. For those who prefer to be independent a rental car is unavoidable.

Anyone staying in the Maspalomas/Playa del Inglés area can reach various starting points by bus. The most important connection for hikers is line 18, which leaves from the Maspalomas lighthouse for Vega de San Mateo several times a day. It stops at San Bartolomé de Tirajana, Ayacata, Cruz Grande, Tejeda and Cruz de Tejeda, all good places from which to start on half-day hikes.

Hiking in groups

Anyone who does not want to strike out on his own can join an organised hiking tour. Some well-known tour organisers offer hiking weeks that include the airplane flight and accommodations on Gran Canaria, also hiking trips across the island with stops in different places. A guided hiking tour has the advantage of being able to hike in very beautiful places and have a bus waiting to transport the group back to its base. It is also beneficial to have a knowledgeable tour guide along who can give information on the local sights, flora and fauna. Instead of a package hiking tour, it is also possible to book day hiking tours with local travel agents.

Every Sunday the group Montañero goes on a guided hike. The tours are generally between 12 and 20 km (7 and 12 mi) long with varying degrees of difficulty. The group usually stops for a picnic at a place with a good view. The starting point is the Mobil petrol station in Arguineguín at 8am; participants pay a fee to cover transportation.

Hiking regions

Thanks to its varied landscape, lush vegetation and excellent climate, the island's interior is ideal for hiking. Various hiking tours are described in the section »Sights from A to Z«. ►Barrancos of Agaete, Arguineguín and Guayadeque are especially suited for hiking. A walk around ►Caldera de Bandama is not difficult. A well-built trail leads to the foot of ►Roque Nublo (►MARCO POLO Insight , p. 218); the short climb to the cultic site at Roque Bentaiga requires sure-footedness. ►Fataga and Mogán are also good starting points for a tour. Anyone who wants to combine swimming and hiking should follow the route to Playa de Güigüí (►MARCO POLO Insight , p. 214). Further suggestions for individual tours can be found in good hiking guidebooks (►Literature).

One week of hiking

Samsara Tours offers Hiking Weeks for dedicated hikers. A variety of tours is available, and their website is a good place to start gathering information about hiking on Gran Canaria. Samsara is dedicated to showing the other side of the island to people ready to explore it on foot.
Tel. 0034 928 27 30 2
www.walking grancanaria.com

LOCAL ORGANISERS

Free Motion
Playa del Inglés
Avenida Alfereces Provisionales s/n
(in Hotel Sandy Beach)
Tel. 928 77 74 79
www.free-motion.net

Happy Biking
Playa del Inglés, Avenida Italia 2
(Hotel IFA Continental)
Tel. 928 76 68 32
www.happy-biking.com

Montañero
www.trekkingmogan.com

Hikers at La Aldea de San Nicolás

Information sport and outdoors

CYCLING
Both of these agencies rent mountain bikes and other bikes, and organise guided tours of varying degrees of difficulty.

Happy Biking
Hotel IFA Continental
Avenida Italia 2
Playa del Inglés
Tel. 928 76 68 32
Fax 928 76 68 43
www.happy-biking.com

Free Motion
Hotel Sandy Beach
Avenida Alfereces Provisionales
Playa del Inglés
Tel 928 77 74 79
www.free-motion.net
This biking and hiking centre also has branches in Meloneras (C.C. Oasis Beach) and Puerto de Mogán (Hotel Cordial Mogàn Playa).

DIVING
Diving Center Nautico
IIn the IFA Interclub Atlantic Los Jazmines 2, San Agustín
Tel. 928 77 81 68
www.divingcenter-nautico.com
The diving centre offers an extensive selection of courses suitable for children as well.

Sun Sub
In Hotel Buenaventura Playa Plaza de Ansite s/n, Playa del Inglés
Tel. 928 77 81 65
www.sunsub.com
The courses for children and teenagers are organised according to age groups. Most of the diving is

done on the reef off Pasito Blanco.

Top Diving
Puerto Escala Puerto Rico
Tel. 928 56 06 09
www.topdiving.net
Boats take divers to sites, including the shipwrecks off Puerto de Mogán.

GOLF
Real Club de Golf Las Palmas
Carretera de Bandama s/n
Las Palmas
Tel. 928 35 01 04
www.realclubdegolfdelaspalmas.com
18-hole golf course in the club founded in 1891. Golfers can enjoy the wonderful views from the course.

El Cortijo Club de Campo
Autopista del Sur, km 6,4 bei Telde
Tel. 928 71 11 11
www.elcortijo.es
18-hole course with very old palm trees.

Maspalomas Golf
Avenida Touroperador Neckermann s/n, Maspalomas
Tel. 928 76 25 81
www.maspalomasgolf.net
This 18-hole course is located in the dunes of Maspalomas near the ocean.

Salobre Golf & Resort
Autopista GC-1, km 53
Urb. El Salobre/Maspalomas
Tel. 928 01 01 03

www.salobregolfresort.com
18-hole course with a view of the mountains and the sea.

Anfi Tauro Golf
Barranco del Lechugal Valle de Tauro s/n, Mogán
Tel. 928 90 80 00
www.anfi.com
A 18-hole course with beautiful lakes

RIDING
El Salobre Horse Riding
Calle Islas Malvinas 3
El Saolbre/El Tablero
Tel. 616 41 83 63
www.elsalobrehr.es
The small riding stable, about 15 minutes by car above Maspalomas, offers excursions for young and old; for interested guests there is free transport from and to the hotel in the Playa del Inglés/Maspalomas region.

Pretty Horse
Carretera de los Palmitos s/n
Maspalomas; Tel. 928 14 72 33
www.pretty-horsegc.net
The stables are located on the road to Parque Palmitos, rides and lessons are offered.

TENNIS
Tennis Centre Maspalomas
Avenida Touroperador
Tjaereborg 9
Tel. 928 76 74 47
Tennis and squash are available on public sand and hard courts.

WINDSURFING
Club Mistral
Autopista del Sur, km 44
Bahía Feliz; Tel. 928 15 71 58

www.club-mistral.com
The well-known surfing centre on the beach of Bahía Feliz offers courses for beginners and advanced surfers. They also organise trips for surfers to the nearby Salinas de Arinaga known for its strong winds.

Centro Internacional de Windsurf
Playa Pozo Izquierdo
Tel. 928 12 14 00
www.pozo-ciw.com
Surfing centre with an attached hostel, restaurant, pool and internet access

There's often a good wind off the southern coast of Gran Canaria

Just Don't Hurt Him!

Almost every town of any size on Gran Canaria has fields where »lucha canaria« (Canarian wrestling) matches are held. Another less well-known Canarian sport is »juego del palo« (stick fight).

The two »pollos« (fighting cocks) take their starting position. Each bends forward, places his right foot slightly forward and bends his legs while grabbing the rolled up trouser leg of his opponent with his left hand. At the same time the two participants shake hands with their right hands. Then the referee gives the signal, and the fight begins. Manolo grabs his opponent, the tanned Antonio, by the rolled-up pants and tries to throw him to the ground over his hip. But Antonio has seen through it and is able to resist this hip throw. The two men gasp, stamp their feet, pull and grab each other. Then Antonio grabs his opponent's shirt with his right hand and pulls Manolo towards himself; he lifts him up and throws him with a loud shout over his left shoulder. Manolo lands with a dull thud on his back on the black sand. The point goes to Antonio.

Wrestling Canary-Style

Some historians presume that Canarian wrestling originated in **ancient Egypt**. Others think that »lucha canaria« was invented by the ancient Canarians. In the 15th century, the Spanish chronicler Alvar Garcia de Santa Maria reported that wrestling was very popular among the early Canarians as a noble and chivalrous kind of martial art. Its primary aim was not to defeat the opponent but to make up

after the match with a peaceful embrace. »Lucha canaria« is still very popular on the Canaries, taking second place after football. There are wrestling clubs and grounds in every sizeable town, and matches are held regularly. The **tournament rules** made in 1872 are still in use. Thus only two teams compete against each other, each team consisting of twelve wrestlers (recently including women), of which each member of each team wrestles against one member of the opposing team. The barefoot wrestlers wear sturdy shirts and pants that have been rolled up over the knees. The opposing »luchador« has to be thrown within two minutes. To do this almost everything is allowed: The wrestlers may push, pull, yank, lift or throw; hitting, kicking, punching, twisting and painful grips are not allowed. Only the body can be attacked, never the head. Each match lasts three rounds, and the winner is the one who throws his opponent twice. The **winner** then wrestles the winner of another match and can only wrestle three other opponents after his first one. The team that gets twelve points with a two-point lead over the other team in the two-hour tournament is the winner. Incidentally, it is considered to be good sportsmanship for the winners to say at the end that the other team won.

A Matter of Agility

Another less well-known Canarian sport is »juego del palo«, a **stick fight** or stick fencing. Here two opponents simulate attack and defence with a 2.5cm/1in-thick, shoulder-high stick (palo), which they grip with both hands. Real experts can judge the simulated hits, thrusts and stabs, which are made with minimum physical effort, so well that they stop only millimetres from the opponent's body. The worst thing that can happen to a duellist is to lose his stick. This guarantees dishonour and shame. Before the Spanish conquest of the Canaries, the stick fights were part of a dangerous duel, for example, between the chiefs of opposing tribes. The Spanish quickly prohibited the Canarians from carrying arms.

It was only at the end of the Franco era in 1975 that the Canarians became more conscious of their own native ancestry, history and culture, and thus resurrected stick fighting. The winner of the »juego del palo« is chosen by intuition. What matters is not winning, but the elegance of movement and adherence to rules and rituals.

Lucha canaria: the best fighters are very popular on the island

TOURS

Our tours take you to the island's natural and cultural highlights – like the Barranco de Agaete in the illustration – and we also show you the best places to take a break.

Tours on Gran Canaria

All but one of these tours through the island's most beautiful towns and natural landscapes begin in the tourist centres on the Costa Canaria. All are day trips and include recommendations on where to eat and take breaks en route.

Tour 1   Around the Island

Gran Canaria is not large – it is possible to drive around the island in one day. But this doesn't leave much time for more than a quick stop at the various sights.
►page 114

Tour 2   Fascintaing Mountains

The most beautiful spots in the »other« Gran Canaria away from the beaches and tourist centres can be seen on this tour.
►page 118

Tour 3   Through the South on the Trail of the Guanches

This route will introduce you to the culture of the Guanches, the original Canarians, thereby exploring southern Gran Canaria with its deep barrancos.
►page 120

Tour 4   Highlights in the North

Those familiar with the south of the island will be surprised at the lush green of the north. Take this tour on Sunday in order to visit the local markets.
►page 122

The main attraction of Playa del Inglés is the beach

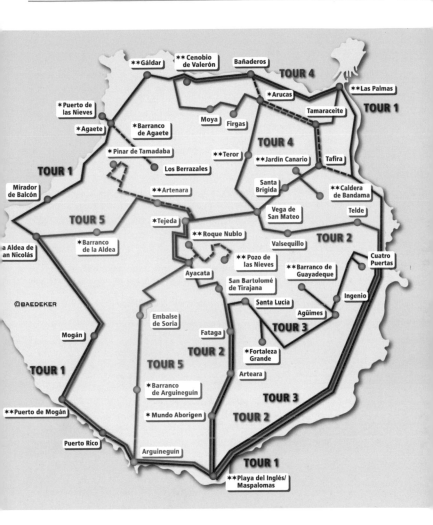

Tour 5   **By Jeep into Secluded Country**
Even if the roads have improved considerably, this tour into the interior always includes a touch of adventure.
▶page 123

Holiday on Gran Canaria

The right place for a holiday

Most guests come for the sun and sand. They find this most often in the south and south-west, which, unlike the more cloudy north, are ideal for swimming all year round. By far the largest tourist centres are **Costa Canaria**, known for the holiday resorts Playa del Inglés, Maspalomas and San Agustín, and **Costa Mogán** between Arguineguín and Puerto de Mogán. But don't expect to find island culture here, since almost all the holiday resorts in the south only sprang up as part of the tourism boom of the last 50 years.

The right means of transport

The public **bus network** on Gran Canaria is excellent. Buses from Costa Canaria and Las Palmas run to many of the attractions and make day trips possible. But in order to explore the more remote west coast and the central mountains a **rental car** is necessary. The roads along the coast are excellent except in the west, and there is a motorway from the capital to the holiday resorts in the south. But the mountain roads in the interior are narrow and winding and best left to experienced drivers. 4-wheel-drive vehicles are necessary for off-road tours.

TOURIST CENTRES

Costa Canaria

If you are not bothered by an artificial-looking resort, you will enjoy **Playa del Inglés**. Mile-long beaches, a large selection of sports and other activities as well as a variety of great nightlife are the main attractions of this holiday resort. The nearby **Maspalomas** and the newer town **Costa Meloneras** to the west are more luxurious. The exclusive hotels and comfortable bungalow villages are not as close together; they are a good choice for people looking for peace and quiet. **San Agustín** east of Playa del Inglés is also more tranquil. Many of the hotels here are not new and the beach is not as wide either, but San Agustín lives from loyal guests who do not need the best of everything when on holiday. **Playa de Aguila** and **Bahía Feliz** on the edge of San Agustín attract young surfers.

Costa Mogán

The largest and most popular tourist site on Costa Mogán is P**uerto Rico**. Not everyone likes the hive-like apartment complexes that stretch up the cliffs, but the area is spoilt with sun and the sheltered location make the harbour the largest centre for water sports in the Canary Islands. The relatively small beach, however, cannot keep up with the tourist crowds in the high season. The nearby **Playa de los**

The dunes of Maspalomas: you can walk and walk and walk …

Amadores, where several luxury resorts were built recently, relieves the congestion. Of the resorts north-west of Puerto Rico, **Puerto de Mogán** is considered to be one of the most successful examples of holiday architecture. The area around the yacht harbour is a beautiful place to stay, but the »Venice of Gran Canaria« is generally flooded by day-trippers.

Las Palmas   Anyone looking for local Canarian and Spanish culture will find it in the capital city of Las Palmas. The city has an excellent public beach and a large selection of hotels in all categories, but is not very quiet. The colonial old quarter with its interesting museums, attractive festivals and its carnival has a broad selection of culture and entertainment.

Turismo rural   The mountains offer holidays of a different kind. Rural tourism (turismo rural) is a movement that has restored country estates and hotels in the interior; these are ideal bases for nature-loving guests and hikers who want to discover the breathtaking mountains and lakes. This is the right place to spend the nicest weeks of the year away from crowds (►MARCO POLO Insight, p. 70).

Tour 1   Around the Island

Start and finish: Playa del Inglés
Duration: 1 day
Length: 212km/127mi

This drive around the island is almost a must for first-time visitors to Gran Canaria, for it gives a good impression of the island's varied landscape. Of course, there is little time to tour the individual attractions at length.

Leave ❶**Playa del Inglés** or Maspalomas heading west. Pass the fishing village of Arguineguín on a good coastal road to ❷**Puerto Rico** with its artificial beach. The western point of the large tourist region in southern Gran Canaria is ❸**★★Puerto de Mogán**. A stroll through Gran Canaria's »Little Venice« is a must! The coastal road ends in Puerto de Mogán. Continue on the road GC 200 northwards through the fertile Barranco de Mogán. On both sides of the road small houses with gardens cling to the slopes of the mountains. Another 8km/5mi from Puerto de Mogán lies the town of ❹**Mogán**. The main road now runs north-west and begins to climb. Vegetation becomes sparse. About 10km/6mi beyond Mogán a rock wall on the right shimmers in many colours. It is called Azulejos. From Toco-

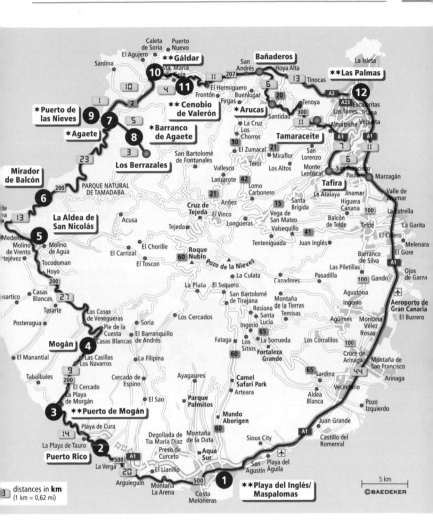

distances in km
(1 km = 0,62 mi)

domán the area is again populated, and the plains with alluvial land and an ample water supply around **⑤ La Aldea de San Nicolás** have the right conditions for productive agriculture. There are windmills to pump the water to the surface, but since the underground water table is sinking, not many of them are still running. For a long time La Aldea de San Nicolás' only contact with the outside world went through Puerto de la Aldea. Beyond this little port the GC 200 runs mostly along the coast again. The main road offers several magnificent views; a stop at ❻**Mirador de Balcón** is a must. Along this part of Gran Canaria's coast there are steep cliffs to the ocean and countless curves along the 40km/25mi from La Aldea de San Nicolás to ❼*****Agaete**.

Side trip to
Barranco de
Agaete

The town is located at the mouth of the ❽*****Barranco de Agaete** and is considered to be the most fertile part of the island. A drive to the former spa Los Berrazales (8km/5mi one way) goes through lush tropical and subtropical vegetation.

In the centre of Agaete a road turns off westwards to ❾*****Puerto de las Nieves** (1km/0.5mi); from the once quite bizarre rock Dedo de Dios (finger of God) a sizable piece broke off during a storm in 2005. But the detour is still worth it to taste freshly caught fish in one of the many excellent restaurants. Leave Agaete on the GC 2 to the northeast (if you are interested in making a detour to Cueva de las Cruces, take the old country road GC-293 and you will reach the small caves after 5km). The new road will reach ❿*****Gáldar** after 9km/5.4mi. Stop here for a stroll through a typical Canary Island town. If there is enough time, visit the archaeological park *Cueva Pintada in the old city.

Side trip to
La Guancha

Gáldar was already settled in pre-Spanish times, as the housing remains and graves of La Guancha show. It is located 2km/1¼mi north of Gáldar near the town of El Agujero. There is a signposted road on the western edge of Gáldar and a sign at the church in Gáldar to El Agujero.

Gáldar and the town of Santa María de Guía, 2km/1¼mi to the east, have practically merged. Guía, as it is called for short, lived mainly from bananas. Just beyond Guía leave the GC 2 and continue the trip around the island on the winding old coastal road. This road leads to ⓫*****Cenobio de Valerón**, one of the most interesting early Canarian sites. The mountain with its cave complex offers a fantastic view of the Cuesta de Silva coastline. The region was named after Diego de Silva, who tried to land here during the Spanish conquest in the 15th century. The old coastal road winds along the mountain slopes and meets a more modern road at San Felipe. The cliffs are less steep here than in western Gran Canaria and there are only a few pebble or sand coves. The fertile land in the delta of the barrancos is mainly used to cultivate bananas.

Alternative
route via
Arucas and
Tafira

For those who do not want to stop in Las Palmas on this tour, we recommend turning off the east-west route at Bañaderos to avoid the chaotic traffic of the capital and to enjoy the beautiful landscape on this alternative route. Arucas with its huge neo-Gothic church, Tamaraceite and Tafira – where the Jardín Canario is worth a visit for an impression of the overwhelming variety of plant life on the Canary

Gáldar nestles at the foot of Pico de Gáldar

Islands – finally lead to Marzagán. From there the motorway is a quick connection to the south of the island.

The coastal road to the north reveals the less pleasant side of the city. There are industrial sites and poorer residential areas along the coast, but the centre of ⑫**Las Palmas** makes a different impression. The many attractions and opportunities to shop make it an inviting place to stop. One of the good restaurants in the island capital is an ideal place to end the day. In southern Las Palmas, in the old quarter of Vegueta, the motorway begins and leads back to the tourist centres in the south.

Main route via Las Palmas

Tour 2 Fascinating Mountains

Start and finish: Playa del Inglés
Duration: at least 6 hours
Length: 130km/78mi

This tour to the central mountains is without question the most beautiful on Gran Canaria. In order to see as much as possible of the landscape, make the trip in good weather. It pays to start early to beat the clouds that form due to the trade winds.

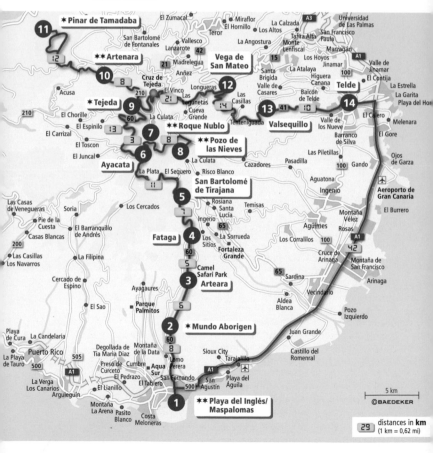

Leave ❶**Playa del Inglés** via the suburb of San Fernando and follow the signs northwards to Tunte or Fataga / San Bartolomé de Tirajana. You will soon leave the houses behind and be captivated by the mountains. There are constantly changing views of the barren and bizarre landscape. After 6km/3.5mi a stop at ❷***Mundo Aborigen** is worthwhile; it is a theme park on the early Canarian peoples. The first town, ❸**Arteara**, appears after 10km/6mi. The countryside gradually gets greener; there are small oases, palm trees and occasional lemon or orange groves. There is a camel safari here as well as a new and very informative archaeological park on the Guanches. The road continues north and soon the first houses of ❹**Fataga** appear. The town is picturesque with its many palm trees. 8km/5mi north of Fataga lies ❺**San Bartolomé de Tirajana**, the administrative centre for southern Gran Canaria. The area is agricultural and the major crops are varieties of fruit. The fruit is mainly used to produce liqueurs and cordials.

About 10km/6mi beyond comes the tiny village of ❻**Ayacata**. A road turns off here towards the east to the striking monolith Roque Nublo and to Pozo de las Nieves. From a parking lot a few miles further on it is possible to make the short climb up ❼****Roque Nublo**. Then continue the trip towards the east to the summit of ❽****Pozo de las Nieves**, Gran Canaria's highest peak (from Ayacata 9km/5.5mi one way). On clear days there is a fantastic view of the island from the peak of the »well of snow«.

Side trip to Roque Nublo and Pozo de las Nieves

The next part of the tour, to Tejeda, also has some interesting views. The route to the picturesque mountain village of ❾**Tejeda** has many curves, and the village is a popular photo motif. From here Cruz de Tejeda, the highest point on the pass (1,490m/4,888ft), is another 7km/4mi away. There is almost always lots of activity around the cross. Fruit and souvenirs are sold from stands and various restaurants encourage visitors to stop.

Turn off shortly after Cruz de Tejeda towards the »cave village« of ❿****Artenara** amidst a wonderfully untouched landscape. There are two restaurants here with views for an enjoyable break. ⓫***Pinar de Tamadaba** Tamadaba is an inviting place to hike and picnic. The distance from Cruz de Tejeda to Pinar de Tamadaba and back is 50km/30mi, to Artenara and back about 38km/22mi.

Side trip to Pinar de Tamadaba

The main route runs from Cruz de Tejeda towards the east to ⓬**Vega de San Mateo**. Turn off onto the GC 41 in the town. The route leads through small villages to ⓭**Valsequillo**. The fields around the town are used in part for dry farming. In January and February, when the almond trees are blossoming, the area is especially beautiful.

Then it is a quick 11km/7mi from Valsequillo to ⑭**Telde**, the island's second-largest city. The Iglesia de San Juan Bautista is well worth a visit. Those less interested in art will soon leave the bustling town behind and take the motorway back to the south.

Tour 3   # Through the South on the Trail of the Guanches

Start and finish: Playa del Inglés
Duration: at least 5 hours
Length: 125km/75mi

Tour 3 explores several interesting archaeological sites from the time of the early inhabitants of the Canary Islands. The theme park Mundo Aborigen depicts the life of the early inhabitants. This tour also leads to many natural wonders.

For this tour take the road that runs from ❶**Playa del Inglés** northwards into the mountains. The theme park ❷***Mundo Aborigen** is only 6km/4mi away and gives an interesting picture of the life of the early islanders. The next stop is ❸**Arteara**. A very narrow lane after the hamlet leads to a cemetery from early Canarian times, which can be explored along paths. The next part of the trip has many impressive views of the grandeur of the mountains. Drive through the palm-shaded village of ❹**Fataga** and after 8km/5mi turn off right towards ❺**Santa Lucía**. The mosque-like dome of the village church can be seen from far off. The restaurant Hao with a little museum attached is a good place to take a break.

2km/1¼mi beyond Santa Lucía a road turns right off the GC 65 towards La Sorrueda (signed Ansite). Drive through the hamlet with its pretty palm trees. The road ends about 3km/2mi after leaving the main road at a parking lot. From here it is just a short walk uphill to ❻***Fortaleza Grande**. These rocks were sacred to the Guanches and the site of the last decisive battle against the Spanish conquerors. Return to the main road and drive 22km/12mi to ❼***Agüimes**, where the central square with its ancient trees is very pretty. At the northern edge of town follow the signs to ❽****Barranco de Guayadeque**, an impressive gorge with lush vegetation. Note the caves which were used by the Guanches as homes. To spend a little time in one of these caves, try one of the two restaurants in Barranco. A visitor's centre about 3km/2mi beyond Agüimes on the left has more background information on Guanche culture.

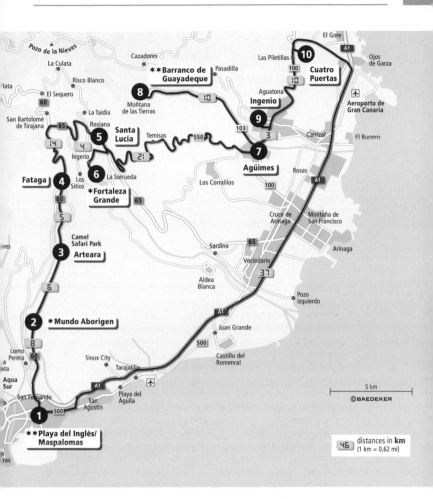

Follow the same road back through the barranco. After 7km/4mi (from the end of the barranco) keep left and drive to ➒ **Ingenio**. The craft shop here with drawn-work embroidery is more interesting than the little rock museum. The GC 100 connects Ingenio with Telde. After 7km/4mi a lane turns off to the ➓ **Cuatro Puertas**. You can drive within about 200m/200yd of the cave with its four large entrances. On the southern slope there are more caves that were inhabited by the Guanches. Return to Playa del Inglés via the GC 140. After 4km/2.5mi it meets the Las Palmas – ➊ **Playa del Inglés** motorway.

Tour 4 Highlights in the North

Start and finish: Las Palmas
Duration: at least 5 hours
Length: 120km/70mi

This tour goes to the north with its rich vegetation. There are pretty little towns and interesting sights on the way. The roads are in part winding, so the tour takes a relatively long time.

Leave ❶****Las Palmas** on the GC 100 towards ❷**Tafira**. The many villas set in large gardens show that this is the area where Gran Canaria's wealthy residents live. Don't miss visiting the ❸****Jardín Canario** below Tafira Alta. Then follow the main road, GC 100. In Monte Coello turn off left towards Pico de Bandama. The observation point on the peak offers an excellent view as far as Las Palmas and down into the ❹****Caldera de Bandama**. At the foot of Pico de Bandama a road runs south to Campo de Golf and on to La Atalaya, which is on almost every organised island tour. About 3km/2mi to the north of La Atalaya rejoin the GC 15. Follow it for 2km/1¼mi to ❺**Santa Brígida**, an attractive town of villas. The next town of any size is ❻**Vega de San Mateo**, which is especially busy on Sundays because of the livestock market. In Vega de San Mateo turn onto the GC 42 towards ❼****Teror**, which many people consider the prettiest town on Gran Canaria. When walking around the town note the many balconies with artistic woodcarving. The next stop is ❽***Arucas** north of Teror. After touring the elaborately decorated neo-Gothic church, a drive up to Montaña de Arucas is worthwhile. Arucas' local mountain offers a good panoramic view (restaurant).

Shortening the tour If you tire of the endless winding roads or are familiar with the north from other visits, return to Las Palmas from Arucas via Tamaraceite. The drive offers impressive views of the capital and Isleta off the coast.

The main route runs from Arucas westwards to ❾**Firgas**, which is known for its mineral spring and offers charming water steps lined with tiled benches. The lush and blooming vegetation in the area is also interesting, a result of the plentiful water supply. From Firgas take the same road back to Buenlugar, and from there west to ❿**Moya**, which is known for its mineral spring and offers charming water steps lined with tiled benches. The lush and blooming vegetation in the area is also interesting, a result of the plentiful water supply. From Firgas take the same road back to Buenlugar, and from there west to ⓫****Cenobio de Valerón**, the »monastery of Valéron«. The cave complex,

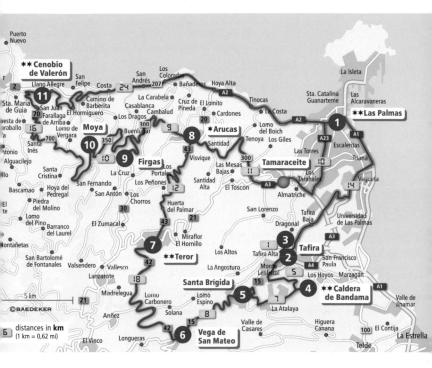

which consists of almost 300 caves, is located underneath a basalt arch and probably represents the most impressive remains of the Guanches. The road offers magnificent views of the section of coast called Cuesta de Silva. After a few miles it meets the GC2, which runs along the coast and back to the island city of ❶****Las Palmas**.

By Jeep into Secluded Country   Tour 5

Start and finish: Playa del Inglés
Duration: at least 5 hours
Length: 160km/96mi

Even though the winding road in the interior of the island is paved, except for a short section, it is in such bad condition that it is generally impassable in a normal vehicle. After a rainy period – especially in the winter – a Jeep might have problems, too. The road is often very busy at weekends!

From ❶ **Playa del Inglés** take the coast road heading west. At the fishing village of ❷ **Arguineguín** take the well-surfaced road north into the interior through the ❸ *****Barranco de Arguineguín**, passing the town of Cercado Espino and then winding up to ❹ **Embalse de Soria** (Soria Reservoir). From the Casa Fernando, the popular holiday restaurant in Soria, the road runs along the west shore of the reservoir and after half a mile turns into an unpaved, adventurous track, which meets the paved GC-605 again after a few miles. Keeping to the right at ❺ **Ayacata** it joins the main road through the interior. Follow this north and enjoy the many changing views of the mountains. Just beyond ❻ *****Tejeda** at Cruz de Tejeda turn off left towards ❼ *****Artenara**. After seeing the cave homes and the cave church try one of the two terrace restaurants here, which have a mag-

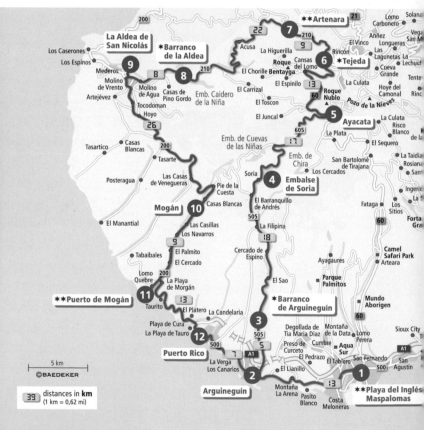

nificent view of the highest peaks of the island. From Artenara drive 4km/2.5mi westwards and turn off left towards La Aldea de San Nicolás. Now comes the most beautiful part of the entire route. It leads through secluded mountains on a narrow and winding road. The road through ❽ *****Barranco de la Aldea** passes several reservoirs and finally reaches ❾ **La Aldea de San Nicolás de Tolentino**. To return to the starting point follow the main road from here southwards via ❿ **Mogán,** ⓫ ****Puerto de Mogán** and ⓬ **Puerto Rico.** This route is described as part of the trip around the island (▶p. 114). One of the restaurants in the yacht harbour of Puerto de Mogán makes a good place to end the day.

SIGHTS FROM A TO Z

Magnificent dunes, great beaches, aromatic pine woods, bizarre rock formations and pretty coastal villages like Puerto de Mogán are what characterise the third largest Canary island.

✷ Agaete

✦ B 2

Elevation: 41m/133ft above sea level
Population: 5,800 (entire district)

Agaete lies in north-western Gran Canaria at the foot of Mount Tamadaba and is the capital of the district of the same name. Many tourists come here on trips to the fertile Barranco de Agaete.

The residents still live mainly from agriculture. In the past agricultural products were shipped from the nearby harbour, ▶ Puerto de las Nieves. Agaete's white houses give it a friendly appearance; it is a rural town that has not lost its authenticity. The plaza in front of the Iglesia de la Concepción is the focal point. Old and young gather here under shady trees. It is a good place to start a short tour of the town. Narrow lanes and alleys, and houses with pretty wooden balconies give the town its atmosphere.

WHAT TO SEE IN AGAETE

Iglesia de la Concepción
The simple Iglesia de la Concepción was built in the late 19th century to replace an earlier church. Every year during the **Bajada de la Rama** (4 – 7 August) the church is the centre of the town's activities. The festival is held to ask Nuestra Señora de las Nieves for enough rain for the next months.

Huerto de las Flores
Follow Calle Huertas, which starts at the church plaza, a short distance to the **flower garden** Huerto de las Flores. The small, somewhat overgrown garden has impressive examples of Canarian and tropical plants, including sapodilla and camphor trees.
❶ Wed – Sun 11am – 4pm

AROUND AGAETE

Cueva de las Cruces
Leave Agaete and drive on the old road GC-293 towards Gáldar; after 5km/3mi on the right is the Cueva de las Cruces (= **Cave of Crosses**). Its name is supposed to have come from the crosses that were carved into the cave walls by the Spanish conquistadors. Scientists believe that the caves were adapted to the needs of the early Canarians. Thus the hole in the roof of the cave served as a chimney. There is another theory that the caves were not used as living quarters but only made later in the process of building roads in the area.

Paradise: Barranco de Agaete is very fertile

One of the most beautiful barrancos on the island stretches south-east from Agaete. Many day-trippers come at weekends and generally stop at one of the restaurants on the main road to the barranco. On other days the picturesque valley offers rest and seclusion. Barranco de Agaete has a lush, partially tropical vegetation due to the generous water supply and the shelter offered by the steep valley walls. Lemon, orange, mango and avocado trees flourish between palms. The farmers in this area are especially proud of their coffee plants.

*Barranco de Agaete

From Agaete the road into Barranco de Agaete passes farms and holiday accommodation. After 8km/5mi comes the village Los Berraza-

Los Berrazales

Agaete

WHERE TO EAT
Dulcería La Esquina €
Plaza Tenesor
The room of the small pastry shop is decorated with posters from the local fiesta; people come here to enjoy a bocadillo (sandwich) or coffee and croissants.

El Perola €
Plaza de Tomás Morales 9
Tel. 928 55 44 30
A bar that modern times seem to have passed by without leaving a trace. The shelves, which reach the ceiling, are full of wine and cordial bottles that have seen better days.

WHERE TO STAY
Finca Las Longueras €€

Valle de Agaete; tel. 928 89 81 45
www.laslongueras.com
The »red house« was built in 1895 in the middle of an extensive orange plantation. It has 1 suite and 9 double rooms, as well as a separate house. Cosy courtyards and a swimming pool are inviting places to relax. A rental car is necessary because of the remote location.

les. When no tour buses stop, time seems to have stood still here. Los Berrazales was known as a **spa** in the past. The iron-rich spring water was considered to have health benefits. In the meantime it has proved more profitable to bottle the water and sell it as mineral water. Little is left to remind visitors of the former spa; some of the houses stand empty. The paved road, which is hardly ever used, ends just above a closed former spa hotel. A path leads uphill from here and the valley ends after about 1.5km/1mi. The houses of El Sao can be seen above the steep valley walls.

Agüimes

✴ C 4

Elevation: 286m/943ft above sea level
Population: 30,000 (entire district)

Agüimes is located about halfway between Las Palmas and Maspalomas and is generally only a stop on the way to Barranco de Guayadeque. A pity really, since the rural town has a charming old town and an informative history museum.

The locals derive their income mainly from agriculture, concentrating on tomatoes. Cacti are also grown in large numbers here. The plants flourish here in alkali-poor soil and excellent climatic conditions. It takes about three years until the cacti are large enough to export.

WHAT TO SEE IN AGÜIMES

Agüimes has an old city that is well worth seeing, with many mostly single-story houses. The town was established in 1486 shortly after the conquest of the idland, which makes Agüimes one of the oldest towns on Gran Canaria. The centre of the historic quarter is taken up by **Plaza del Rosario**, which is shaded by large Indian laurel trees. The city once grew up around this square.

*Casco Histórico

The parish church is located on the east side of Plaza del Rosario. Building of the church began in the late 18th century, but was only completed in the mid-19th century. Its large dome is reminiscent of oriental structures. Some of the statues of saints inside are attributed to Luján Pérez. The church was declared one of Spain's national monuments in 1981.

Iglesia de San Sebastián

Evening atmosphere in the lanes of Agüimes

Agüimes

INFORMATION
Oficina de Información Turística
Plaza de San Antón
Tel. 928 55 44 30

WHERE TO EAT
Hornos de la Cal €€€
Playa de Arinaga
Avenida Lopez de Orduñez s/n
Tel. 928 73 80 71
www.restaurantehornosdelacal.com
The Marisquería on the Risco Verde
north-east of Arinaga has one of the
most unique dining rooms on the island.
It is located in the chimney of a former
limekiln, where a few tables have been
set up in the upper floor. When the
weather is sunny guests are served at
rustic wooden tables set up on the terrace where they enjoy portions of fish,
which is sold by weight.

La Farola €€€–€€€€
Calle Alcalá Galiano
On the Arinaga jetty; tel. 928 18 04 10
This well-known seafood restaurant specialises in lobsters and black rice. The
seating is right along the jetty in a nauti-
cal atmosphere; it pays to make reservations on the weekend.

Tagoror €€
At the end of Barranco de Guayadeque
Tel. 928 17 20 13
Huge cave restaurant with a terrace and
a good selection of tapas. The rest of
the menu is more international than
Canarian. Bus tours often stop here.

La Tarteria €
Plaza del Rosario 21; tel. 928 78 77 38
After a stroll around town this small cafeteria on the plaza in front of the parish
church is a good place to stop for cake
or freshly pressed fruit juice.

WHERE TO STAY
Hotel Rural Casa de los Camellos € – €€
Calle Progreso 12; tel. 928 78 50 03
www.hecansa.com
A former camel station near the church
with twelve comfortable and individually
furnished rooms. The little country hotel
with a large courtyard is run by a school
for hotel management.

Calle El Progreso The street that runs off Plaza del Rosario is one of the most homey old town streets on the island. The low houses are built with sculpted natural stones and painted in warm pastel tones. It takes only a few steps to reach a former camel station that has been converted into a comfortable country hotel. Follow the street to Plaza de San Anton. There are two bars on the plaza as well as a small tourist information office.

Museo de Historia The museum in the former bishop's palace gives an overview of the customs and various old trades and crafts on Gran Canaria in eight rooms with photo displays explained in three languages, including burning lime, fishing, milling and of course farming. Displays inclu-de farming implements and domestic tools, old saddles and harnesses, weaving looms and shuttles for weaving. Room 5 with the theme of superstition and witchcraft is interesting. It is explained, for example, that a woman can more easily become pregnant by eating a teaspoonful of roasted frog's meat. According to another old custom the new mother was supposed to dance on the ninth day after giving birth to prove that she was healthy. There is also advice on how not to become pregnant. An outer staircase leads from the inner courtyard, which is planted with cacti, to the upper floor. This floor is used by local artists for revolving art and photo exhibitions.

❶ Tue – Sun 9am – 5pm, admission charge €2.50

✷✷ BARRANCO DE GUAYADEQUE

North of Agüimes, Barranco de Guayadeque is a nature reserve because of the many endemic plants that grow here. The valley is especially beautiful in spring, when everything seems to be blooming everywhere. Some grain and vegetables are grown on small fields full of poppies. If it weren't for the tour buses and tourists in hire cars, the place would look as if time had stood still one hundred years ago.

Tagoror, a bar in a cave

Barranco de Guayadeque has one other unique characteristic: In the steep walls of the valley there are many **caves**. Some of these caves are natural and some are man-made; they were used as living quarters and burial sites by the pre-Hispanic inhabitants. Some of the caves are still occupied; others are difficult to reach due to landslides. This is probably why so many artefacts, including pottery, clothing, bones and mummies, were found here.

Centro de Interpretación de Guayadeque

On the road leading into the barranco the Centro de Interpretación de Guayadeque was recently constructed into a rock wall. Along with the pre-Spanish cave culture it also has information on the volcanic origins, flora and fauna of the canyon. There are not many exhibits, however, only some copies of early Canarian ceramics; but the early Canarian mummy in the glass display case is authentic. The historical photographs are also interesting; they show Spaniards who had moved into and made themselves at home in the caves dug into the cliffs by early Canarians.

❶ Tue – Sat 9am – 5pm, Sun 10am – 3pm, admission €2.50

Cueva Bermeja

About 2.5km/1.5mi after the visitor's centre comes the cave village Cueva Bermeja. The village got its name because the caves were dug into the reddish canyon wall. A flagged walk leads up to the caves. Some of them are inhabited while others are used as stables or for storage. In any case please respect the privacy of the residents and be content with a quick look from the street. There is a cave chapel right on the street with niches for three statues of saints and a chancel that was also carved out of tuff stone. There is a cave bar to the right of the chapel.

Further into the barranco there is a picnic area in an area that is especially pleasant when the almond trees are blooming. 500m/1,600ft further on comes the cave restaurant Tagaror, which is big enough to serve several busloads of guests at a time.

Insider Tip

Restaurant Vega, located 100m/330ft above it where the paved road ends, is less crowded. From there it is possible to take a short walk to the top of Sendero Montaña las Fierras. The walk leads past cave cottages and further into the end of the canyon for magnificent views of the unusual mountains.

Hike the barranco

The starting place for a hike into the barranco is at the northern edge of town at the country road GC-100 towards Ingenio. Leave the road here onto GC-103 (Calle La Orilla) and 300m/1,000ft further pass the turn-off to the Casco histórico. After another 400m/1,300ft leave the road after the town sign for Agüimes to the left on a path that is paved at first (hiking sign). The path follows the left edge of Barranco Guayadeque and ends at the cave dwellings of Cueva Bermeja after 6km/3.6mi.

AROUND AGÜIMES

Do not expect too much if you plan to visit Parque de Cocodrilos: Various kinds of deer, dwarf donkeys, ponies, ostriches, baboons, crocodiles and other animals live here, but much too close together. There is also a crocodile and parrot show several times a day. It is worth mentioning that the privately owned zoo is a refuge for animals that have been abused elsewhere. To get to the zoo drive from Cruce de Arinaga (6km/3.5mi south-east of Agüimes) towards Los Corralillos; the zoo is on the right-hand side of the road. Buses also run from some of the hotels in the south to the zoo.

Parque de Cocodrilos

❶ Mon – Fri, Sun 10am – 5pm, admission €9.90

From Cruce de Arinaga drive 5km/3mi east to the **fishing village** of Arinaga. Arinaga has one of the few remaining desalination works on Gran Canaria. **Playa de Arinaga** is sheltered in a broad bay and attracts mainly the locals; surfers consider it to be a good shallow surfing area.

Arinaga

The town itself is not very attractive with its gridded streets and unimaginative apartment buildings. But a 10-minute walk from the Muelle de Arinaga along the beach promenade eastwards to Risco Verde is possible. At the foot of the oddly shaped promontory **Museo de la Cal** informs on the production of lime here from the 16th century. It was not just used to whitewash houses, but also as mortar. In the late 18th century the demand for the sought-after raw material grew sharply when the harbour of Las Palmas was being built. One of the kilns has been turned into a museum (free admission during the daytime), another kiln serves as a restaurant. From the lime museum the promenade leads up onto **Risco Verde**, which offers a great view of the barren coast and the Montaña de Arinaga (199m/650ft). The walk can be continued on the well developed path from Risco Verde to **Faro de Arinaga**, which can be seen in the distance. The light house has been standing since 1892. In 1984 a new light house was built to replace it. After years of decline it has been restored recently and soon the old light house and keeper's house will be the home of a restaurant and fishing museum.

Lomo de los Letreros is a mountain range near **Barranco de Balos**, only a few miles west of Agüimes. The name »Los Letreros« (»the inscriptions«) reveals why visitors and souvenir hunters have been coming to the 300m/1,000ft-long cliff for years. Simple but sometimes quite bizarre human figures were carved into the rock and later discovered here. The figure of a boat with a curved prow has attracted a lot of attention, as it is the first sign that the early Canarians had boats. Simple geometric patterns, spirals and circles have also been found here. You will not see much of this today without an ex-

Lomo de los Letreros

perienced guide, since the carvings are worn away by wind and weather, and many tourists felt that they had to leave their own marks behind. The area is fenced off. However, if you want to try your luck, leave Agüimes on the GC 550 towards Santa Lucía; after about 3km/2mi a road turns off to the left towards the hamlet Los Corralillos (it curves back to Cruce de Arinaga). 1km/0.5mi after Los Corralillos follow the path on the right on foot down into Barranco de Balos.

Arguineguín

✦ D 2

Elevation: Sea level
Population: 12,000

The days as a quiet fishing village are long gone. Only 12km/7mi west of the tourist centre of Maspalomas, Arguineguín is still typically Canarian, with lots of activity on Tuesdays during the weekly market.

Insider Tip

Coming from Maspalomas, Arguineguín does not look very attractive at first with the cement factory dominating the scene, but the picturesque **fishing port** is different. Excursion boats depart from here, and there are regular connections to Puerto Rico and Puerto de Mogán. Restaurants in every class from simple to luxurious line the port road. Many of them have a wonderful view of the harbour and the sea. While holiday-makers – including many long-term guests – have to make do with tiny beaches and a not very attractive setting, they appreciate the fact that the place was not planned on a drawing board.

AROUND ARGUINEGUÍN

Patalavaca

Arguineguín and Patalavaca are connected by a promenade. The main road does not hint at the exclusive hotels that line the coast here – especially the La Canaria. Here you can eat in a restaurant away from the usual tourist crowd. The white sand on **Playa de la Verga** to the west was imported from the Caribbean.

*Barranco de Arguineguín

Driving to Barranco de Arguineguín and on to the centre of the island is a popular weekend pastime for Canarians. Many jeep safaris offer this tour as well. The route from the traffic circle in Arguineguín via Barrancillo Andrés and Cruz de San Antonio to Ayacata is paved now, but in view of the narrow road with many curves it is only me-

Arguineguín

SHOPPING
Mercado
Around the harbour   **Insider Tip**
Tue 8am – 2pm
The selection is huge: fruit, vegetables, fish and meat, but also crafts, clothing and much more.

WHERE TO EAT
La Charca €€
Calle Juan Juanez
Tel. 928 73 53 25; closed Wed.
Fish restaurant with specialties including Sama a la Sal (Dentex in salt crust). Usually full on Tuesdays during the market. The tables on the terrace give a good view of what goes on there.

Cofradía de Pescadores €€
Avenida del Muelle (at the harbour)
Tel. 928 15 09 63; closed Mon.
The fish lands on the table right from the boat; open from noon straight through to the evening.

Casa Fernando € – €€
Embalse de Soria
(below the town wall)
Tel. 928 17 23 46
Daily 10am – 6pm
Day-trippers meet in the bar for typical Canarian cooking.

WHERE TO STAY
Aparthotel Dorado Beach €€€
Avenida Canarios 1
Tel. 928 15 07 80
www.bullhotels.com
Sound three-star hotel with almost 200 rooms on nine floors, all with an ocean view. Only all-inclusive, including the spa, fitness room and sundeck with whirlpool on the roof.

ant for experienced drivers. It is only passable in a Jeep and the rough trail between Soria and Cueva de las Niñas continues to be adventurous. The 50km/30mi from Arguineguín to Ayacata (including a side trip to **Embalse de Soria**) takes at least two hours without longer stops.

From Arguineguín drive east on the paved road into the barranco. The lower part of the valley is dry and no one lives there. But the higher the elevation, the more settlements appear until they actually merge with each other. The area is agricultural, producing citrus fruits, papaya and wine.

After the hamlet of **Cercado Espino** the road gets narrower and the barranco ends soon afterwards. The road then winds up the mountain. Just 8km/5mi after Cercado de Espino the road divides, the right branch leading to the picturesque Soria Reservoir after 2km/1¼mi, the paved road ends high above the picturesque western shore (the jeep trail starts there). The dam Embalse de Soria was completed in 1971, but the reservoir has never been completely full. The area offers excellent hiking. For **Presa de la Cueva de las Niñas** go back towards Barrancillo Andrés to the fork in the road, turn right and con-

From Arguineguín small and winding roads lead into the mountains and to Embalse de Soria

tinue northwards. The beautiful view of the reservoir surrounded by pine forests compensates for the drive. There are picnic areas for those who want to rest awhile. From the Cueva de las Niñas reservoir the drive continues on the well-developed GC-605 to **Ayacata**, where there are several bars for taking a break.

✷✷ Artenara

✦ B 3

Elevation: 1,251m/4,104ft above sea level
Population: 1,200 (entire district)

The landscape around the mountain village of Artenara in north-western Gran Canaria is still relatively untouched. Artenara is the highest settlement on the island. Tourists come here to visit the cave church and to get an impression of the local culture.

At first glance Artenara seems no different from any other Canarian mountain village. But a closer look reveals that many of the residents still live in caves. These »caves« have been given normal house façades. Life in the village is not primitive: TV antennas are visible on many of the houses, and the kitchens have modern appliances.

WHAT TO SEE IN ARTENARA

To reach the **cave church**, Iglesia de la Virgen de la Cuevita, follow the street opposite the church in the centre of town (near the Casa Consistorial) uphill. It ends just a few feet in front of the cave church, which can be recognised by the bell above the entrance. The church is dedicated to the Virgin of the Cave, the patron saint of cyclists and folk musicians. No one knows the exact age of the church, but it was probably only carved into rock a few decades ago.

Iglesia de la Virgen de la Cuevita

The life-sized statue of the Basque **philosopher Miguel de Unamuno** stands on the lookout platform named after him. This is located only a few steps from the village square in Calle Párroco Domingo Báez (opposite house number 6). In his travelogue »Por tierras de Portugal y de España« the head of the University of Salamanca described the mountain world of Gran Canaria extravagantly as a »stone thunderstorm«. In fact the panorama leaves nothing to be desired.

*Mirador de Unamuno

Artenara

INFORMATION
Oficina de Turismo
Calle Párroco Domingo Báez 13
Tel. 928 66 61 02

WHERE TO EAT
La Esquina € – €€   **Insider Tip**
Town centre, near the church
Tel. 928 66 63 81; closed Mon.
The terrace offers a sensational view of the mountains. Canarian food.

La Cilla €€
Camino de la Cilla 9;
Tel. 609 16 39 44
This panorama restaurant reopened in 2011 after being closed for seven years.

It is a short distance from the town centre but easily reached on foot from the square. Just walk towards the statue of Christ on the hill, a 50m/150ft long pedestrian tunnel runs through the hill. The Canarian cooking is not outstanding, but the view can't be beat.

WHERE TO STAY
El Pajar €
Calle Párroco Domingo Báez 22
Tel. 902 15 72 81
The spacious cave dwelling has a living room, three bedrooms, kitchen and a terrace with a small garden. Situated right on the mountainside, it has a wonderful view of the Caldera of Tejeda.

In Artenara the »Fiesta of the Cave Virgin« is celebrated
enthusiastically in late August

Mirador de la Atalaya   From the road to Cruz de Tejeda there is a good view back to the village church of Artenara, with the Roque de Bentaigo behind it. The plaza is decorated with a rusty iron sculpture; it was erected in 2007 in honour of the people who work for the environmental authority.

AROUND ARTENARA

*Pinar de Tamadaba   Tamadaba Forest lies at an elevation of 1,400m/4,600ft and can only be reached by car from Artenara (about 8km/5mi). The most beautiful, but somewhat sparse, pine forest on the island is a fitting reward for the drive on a winding road. A single lane runs around Pico de Bandera. You can park your car at Casa Forestal and hike for about 45 minutes to the fire watchtower (closed). There is a beautiful panoramic view all around from its base.

4km/2.5mi after Artenara on the road that connects it to Pinar de Tamadaba, a trail turns off to the south. It is relatively easy to drive up to **Acusa**, then the road winds steeply down the mountain. The beautiful and isolated mountain landscape can be seen when driving down. After a while the road passes the Embalse de Parralillo and then other reservoirs. After about two hours the houses of ▶**La Aldea de San Nicolás** appear.

MARCO ⊕ POLO TIP

! *Exploded* **Insider Tip**

GC 110 between Artenara and Valleseco has an astonishing view of the island's most recent volcano. Caldera Pinos del Gáldar was probably formed about 3,000 years ago by a massive explosion that blew the top of the volcano away and left the impressive crater. The observation point lies 1,510m/4,954ft above sea level and has a wonderful view of the north coast. On a clear day you might even see Pico de Teide on Tenerife.

* Arucas

⬦ B 3

Elevation: 250m/825ft above sea level
Population: 36,900 (entire district)

Arucas lies 17km/11mi west of Las Palmas. It is the third-largest town on Gran Canaria after the capital and Telde. The pretty old part of town is dominated by the large neo-Gothic parish church. Arucas is also the home of the only rum distillery on Gran Canaria. It is open for tours.

Agriculture thrives here, as the town is located in one of the most plentifully watered parts of the island. After the Spanish conquest sugar cane was planted, but was no longer profitable after the 17th century. In the early 20th century agriculture concentrated on bananas. While the area prospered for some decades with this monoculture, it suffered when Canarian bananas became increasingly difficult to market. Large areas of the banana plantations were abandoned in the early 1980s, and the fields were converted to fruit, vegetable and flower farms.

The Arucas area was settled before the Spanish came; the early Canarians called the settlement »Arehucas«. On the nearby Montaña de Arucas a decisive battle between the leader of the early Canarians,   **History**

Arucas

INFORMATION
Oficina de Turismo
Calle León y Castillo 10
Tel. 928 62 31 36
www.arucas.org

SHOPPING
Mercado
Saturday is market day in Arucas; the market takes place on Plaza de la Constitución and the surrounding streets.

WHERE TO EAT
Mesón de la Montaña €€€
Montaña de Arucas   **Insider Tip**
Tel. 928 60 14 75
The drive up to the volcano crater is worthwhile for the view alone. Local people enjoy this restaurant as well. The cooking is Canarian and international.

Café El Parque € – €€
Plaza de San Juan 2
Tel. 928 60 25 90

Tapas and small meals are served in an art nouveau building from 1907. The quiet terrace faces the northern entrance to the cathedral.

Tasca Jamón-Jamón € – €€
Calle Gourié 5
Tel. 928 60 34 97; closed Mon
This tiny bistro near the cathedral specialises in air-dried Iberian ham and also serves other tapas with their house wine.

Pizzeria Harimaguada €€
Calle La Heredad 2
Tel. 928 62 90 00
Closed Mon and Tue
The pizzas served in this pizzeria, which is located opposite the water works, all have early Canarian names. Tell them how many people and how hungry you are and they'll make your pizza and price accordingly. View of Montaña de Arucas from the terrace.

WHERE TO STAY
Hacienda del Buen Suceso €€ – €€€
On the Arucas – Bañaderos (1 km/0.5mi) road
Tel. 928 62 29 45
www.haciendabuensuceso.com
The hacienda's history goes back to 1572. The present owners have restored it with great care and turned it into a pretty finca in the midst of banana plantations. It has 18 individually designed rooms.

Doramas, and the leader of the Spanish, Pedro de Vera, took place in 1481. Only after Doramas was wounded in an ambush was Pedro de Vera able to kill him. The Spanish officially founded Arucas in 1505.

WHAT TO SEE IN ARUCAS

The pretty plaza is nicknamed Plaza de los Gansos (Lazybones Square), because the unemployed used to gather here in front of the Casa Consistoriales in order to apply for work. The two-storey town hall was built in an eclectic style on plans by the architect José López Echegarretta in 1875. The inner courtyard and the azulejos-tiled walls of the stairwell can be viewed during business hours.

Plaza de la Constitución

The park borders the plaza on the west. It is a fine botanical garden and once belonged to the Gourié family. At the entrance a tablet shows the location of various trees; along with an avenue of dragon trees there are soapberry, silk floss and cinnamon trees, among others, to be seen. Their former residence is now the Museo Municipal. On display are works by local artists like Santiago Santana (1909 – 1996), Guillermo Sureda (1912 – 2006) and Manolo Ramos (1899 – 1971). In the three rooms on the lower floor are sculptures by Abraham Cárdenes (1907 – 1971).

Parque de Municipal

❶ Mon – Fri 10am – 6pm, Sat 10am – 1pm

Diagonally opposite the town park in Calle de Francisco Gourié is a row of pretty 19th century townhouses. The Heredad de Aguas stands out the most. This neoclassicistic structure with an elaborately partitioned façade was designed in 1912/1913 by the architect Fernando Navarro, who also played a major role in the design of the Gabinete Literario in Las Palmas. The Arucas and Firgas waterworks is located in the building with a domed clocktower. The waterworks was significant in the agricultural development of the northern coast; it had irrigation channels, pools and dams built. The profits were used to build the local market hall and the Theater Pérez Galdós in Las Palmas.

Heredad de Aguas de Arucas Y Firgas

The rooms of the foundation are used for rotating exhibits of contemporary art. The tourist information office is located in the same street.

Fundación Mapfre Regua-narteme

❶ Calle León y Castillo 10, www.fundacionmapfrereguanarteme

Follow Calle León y Castillo and Calle Gourié, where there is a magnificent dragon tree in the inner courtyard of the Casa de la Cultura, to the massive Iglesia de San Juan Bautista. Because of its size and neo-Gothic style, the church, which is dedicated to John the Baptist, is often called a **cathedral**. Construction began in 1909 and the first mass was celebrated in 1917, but the last of the four towers was not completed until the 1970s. Local grey basalt was the main building material. It is especially resistant to weathering but is not easy to work. This makes the rose window above the main entrance all the

Iglesia de San Juan Bautista

more impressive. Note the colourful stained glass windows inside, and the reclining figure of Christ, which was made by the sculptor Manuel Ramos (1899 – 1971), a native of Arucas.

The production of **rum** has a long history in Arucas. Destilería Arehucas (on the edge of town going towards Guía) started out in 1884 as a sugar factory. Despite the decline of Canarian sugar cane (sugar cane is imported now), about 3.5 million litres of rum of various kinds are produced every year. »Ron Añejo«, a twelve-year-old rum, is considered to be exceptional. The distillery also produces a variety of »specialties«, like rum with honey (Ron Miel) or rum with milk and lemon (Leche Rizada). Free tours of the factory are available. The tour includes a display of oak barrels with the autographs of prominent guests such as Plácido Domingo and Juan Carlos I. There is also a tasting room where the different varieties of rum can be sampled.

*Destilería Arehucas

❶ Mon – Fri 1pm – 2pm in winter

AROUND ARUCAS

About 500m/1600ft outside of the town centre via the road to Bañaderas (GC-330) lies the Garden of the Marquesa. Also called Jardín de las Hesperides, this private garden was built from 1880 by the first Margrave of Arucas around the former summer residence of the nobel family; it is open to the public since 1985.

*Jardín de la Marquesa

It is surrounded by banana plantations and about twelve acres in size; the lushly planted park has about 500 different subtropical und tropical varieties from all five continents. Among the old trees, along with several varieties of palm trres, there is a 200-year-old dragon tree; it stands behind the cafeteria. The stately Norfolk pines are also worth seeing, as are jacaranda trees that bloom sky-blue in the summer, a calabash tree and a jackfruit tree from India.

The admission includes a guide booklet on plants, but it is a pity that not all of the plants have signs to identify them.

❶ Mon – Sat 9am – 1pm, 2pm – 6pm; admission €6
www.jardindelamarquesa.com

Just north of the town centre stands Montaña de Arucas (412m/1,352ft above sea level). A narrow road starts at the church (signposted) and ends on a large parking lot with a restaurant. There is a wonderful **panoramic view** from the top.

*Montaña de Arucas

While the cathedral of Arucas looks like it has always been here, it was only completed in the late 1970s

** Caldera de Bandama · Pico de Bandama

—————————— ⟡ B 4

Elevation: 569m/1877ft above sea level

About 10km/6mi south of Las Palmas, Caldera de Bandama is a reminder of the island's volcanic legacy. The almost perfectly round crater is the result of a massive eruption that took place about 5,000 years ago. From the nearby Pico de Bandama (569m/1,867ft) there is a wonderful view of the crater and the rooftops of the capital city.

Drive to the caldera via Monte Lentiscal, where a side road branches off the GC 15 and leads to the observation area (with cafeteria) on the peak of Pico de Bandama. On the way to the top there are beautiful views of Caldera de Bandama. The crater is about 1,000m/3,300ft across and 200m/660ft deep. There is an abandoned farm on its floor. Some of the surrounding fields are still in use, but it takes a lot of effort to farm here, since only a small path leads into the crater.

Hiking region Caldera Bandama

Insider Tip

The spectacular caldera can be explored on two relatively short hikes. Note that it is only open between 8am and 5pm. A trail that is steep in parts leads from the Bandama bus stop past an observation platform to the bottom of the crater; a small round path leads around the crater floor (whole trip there and back about two hours). The trail leads past the abandoned farm of the Dutchman Daniel van Damme, who settled in the crater in the 16th century and after whom the caldera was named. Another hike is possible by starting at the observation platform and walking around the edge of the crater; the trail leads through the Bandama Golf Course for a short distance. The golf course was established in the late 19th century by an Englishman and is the oldest in Spain. This hike also takes about two hours. The cafeteria in the golf hotel offers a chance to take a break.

Caldera de Bandama

WHERE TO STAY
VIK Hotel Bandama Golf € € €
Lugar de Bandama
Tel. 928 35 15 38
www.vikhotels.com

The little family-run hotel at an elevation of 400m/1,300ft is right next to the golf course. There is also a swimming pool, tennis court and riding stable (lessons upon request).

** Cenobio de Valerón

B 3

Opening hours: Tue – Sun 10am – 5pm,
April – September 10am – 6pm, admission €2.50

Cenobio de Valerón is one of the most significant archaeological sites on the Canary Islands. The cave complex has posed many riddles to archaeologists. Until well into the 20th century it was presumed to be a religious site for the early Canarians that was shrouded in myth.

Coming from Guía follow the winding coastal road marked »Cuesta de Silva« eastwards to Cenobio de Valerón. After a thorough restoration the caves have been open to the public again for a few years. The lighting for photography is best in the morning.

Cenobio de Valerón is a complex of 298 caves under a natural basalt arch that is about 30m/100ft wide and 25m/80ft high. In the soft tuff stone, which is easy to work even with simple tools, the early Canarians created caves on various levels and adapted natural caves. They were separated by wooden doors and connected by corridors and stairs. The complex eventually became a real cave palace. In one of the caves higher up simple geometric patterns are carved into the wall.

Cave palace

There has been much speculation in the past as to the purpose of these caves. Earlier historians called Cenobio de Valerón the **cave monastery of the harimaguadas**, holy virgins who lived here as priestesses. Another version has it that young women spent some time here before they got married. A rich diet was supposed to help them gain weight to ensure that they would have many offspring. Latest research has departed from these mythological explanations. It is possible that the cave palace was simply used to **store grain**.

Old sources have revealed that Cenobio de Valerón used to be decorated much more richly than it is today. Pedro Augustín del Castillo y Ruiz Vergara described it as follows: »When I had occasion to go to the Guía area, two of the town leaders asked if I would like to see one of the monasteries of these ancient people, which was located at a high and steep place above Barranco de Valerón. They guided me there at considerable risk. I admit that I was amazed at the structure. There was a large arch carved into a cliff – without sharp iron instruments, which the ancient people did not have, but only with flint splinters mounted on wooden handles that were used like axes and picks to work wood and cut down trees. Under the arch a corridor led inside and there was a large number of cells or rooms on both sides: one above the other and all with windows. On each side of the

Mysterious until today – the Cenobio de Valerón

entrance there was a kind of tower, which was accessible from inside and had windows facing the depths of the barranco.«

Tagoror   On the peak above Cenobio de Valerón there was a tagoror, a place of assembly. The stone seats can still be seen. The summit commands a wonderful view of the section of coast called **Cuesta de Silva**. It was named after Diego de Silva, who tried to land on Gran Canaria's north coast during the Spanish conquest.

Cruz de Tejeda

B 3

Elevation: 1,510m/4,983ft above sea level

Cruz de Tejeda marks the highest point on the pass in the centre of Gran Canaria (1,510m/4,983ft). Almost all tour buses stop at the stone cross.

This is a commercial and chaotic place. Fruit and sweets are on sale in stands, and before you can turn around you will have been photographed with a donkey – for a fee of course. Cruz de Tejeda is known for its grand mountain panorama. The Spanish poet and philosopher Miguel de Unamuno called the landscape a »petrified storm«. Only a few steps from the pass stands the **4-star Parador**, which was designed by Néstor de la Torre (▶Famous People) and his brother Miguel in the typical Canarian style. It was completely modernised and re-opened as a mountain hotel in 2009 after years of renovation. Next to it is the Terraza Mirador, an observation deck that is open to the public.

North-west of Cruz de Tejeda there is a **hiking trail** with beautiful views to the residential caves of Caballero (round trip about 2 hours 30 minutes).
From Cruz de Tejeda take the GC 150 towards Gáldar. After 150m/500ft comes a parking lot. From there take the left-hand trail

Hiking to Cuevas del Caballero

Cruz de Tejeda

Insider Tip

WHERE TO EAT
Asador de Yolanda €€
Tel. 928 66 62 76
The restaurant at Cruz de Tejeda is busy when the weather is good. It serves hearty grilled food such as lamb shanks with papas arrugadas and steamed vegetables, accompanied by local wines. The balcony on the first floor is a nice place to eat.

Roque Nublo €€€ – €€€€
Tel. 928 01 25 00
The Parador Hotel kitchen with upscale Spanish-international cuisine is open to

outside guests as well, the island menu is recommended. The guests dine under a high rustic wooden beam ceiling. The house bar is a good place for a café con leche or a snack on the sun terrace with its beautiful view.

WHERE TO STAY
El Refugio €€
Tel. 928 66 65 13
www.hotelruralelrefugio.com
The ten rooms in this country hotel with a pool are very popular among hikers. The restaurant serves good Canarian cuisine.

(signed PR GC-01) to the water reservoir. After a steep start the panoramic route meets the GC 150 again after about a half hour. Follow it to the left to **Mirador de las Palomas** and continue on the paved path. After 15 minutes follow the intersecting trail to the left to **Cruz de los Morriscos**. It takes about ten minutes from the crossing to Cuevas del Caballero. The entrances to the caves are closed off but the magnificent panorama including the Roque Nublo and Roque Bentaiga rising up out of Caldera de Tejeda is well worth the hike.

Fataga

C 3

Elevation: 680m/2,231ft above sea level
Population: 1,000

Fataga is a pretty, typically Canarian mountain village in the barranco of the same name. It is worth stopping here on a trip from the tourist centres in southern Gran Canaria to the central mountains.

There is enough water in and around Fataga to farm small fields. Orange, almond and apricot trees flourish here. One of the area's specialties is »tarta de almendras«, a sweet and rich but delicious almond cake. The apricot harvest in early May begins with a festival every year. The high points are a bicycle race and fireworks at midnight.

There are no special sights in Fataga, but the atmosphere is worth taking in. It is best to leave the car on the main road near the late 19th-century church and take one of the narrow streets into the centre. There are pretty white houses with lush floral decorations to delight the eye. A few bars or restaurants offer refreshments and meals.

AROUND FATAGA

Arteara

The route from Fataga and the village of Arteara 5km/3mi to the south leads through pretty countryside. Palms sway in the wind between fields. Arteara is the starting point for small camel safaris (on the right-hand side of the main road when coming from Fataga). Another attraction is the **Parque Arqueológico de Arteara** with paths leading through an ancient Canarian cemetery. The more than 800 burial sites, many of which are now only recognisable to experts, were made between 500 BC and c AD 1700. Open to the public.

Fataga

WHERE TO EAT
El Albaricoque € – €€
Tel. 928 79 86 56
The menu is not very exciting: snacks and tapas. But the terrace has seating with a wonderful view. There are also two simple rooms to rent.

WHERE TO STAY
Hotel Rural Molino de Agua €€
Tel. 928 15 59 25
www.elmolinodeagua.com
This pretty country hotel with 20 individually furnished rooms is 1km/0.5mi north of Fataga near the GC-60 (km 31). Molino del Agua also has a terrace restaurant.

It is possible to walk from Fataga to Arteara. There is a path parallel to the road. At first it runs east of the main road; later it switches to the west side. Leave the main road at the southern edge of Fataga and turn off to the right (coming from Maspalomas) onto the paved way that is marked »Los Llanos«. It leads past the cemetery and then zigzags down the hill. When the path branches keep left. After about one hour you will come to the driveway to a farm. Follow it to the right and soon you will be back on the Maspalomas – Fataga road. Follow the road for a short distance and then turn off to the right on a path marked »Presa de Ayagaures«. It passes the **Arteara reservoir** and leads to the bottom of Fataga canyon. Soon the aforementioned camel safari station appears.

Hike to Arteara

Firgas

✳ B 3

Elevation: 500m/1,650ft above sea level
Population: 7,600 (entire district)

Firgas is located about 25km/15mi west of Las Palmas in fertile green countryside. There was already a settlement here in the 16th century. Mineral water is bottled here and sold on the whole island.

Firgas consists of simple country cottages that cover the hillsides. The Paseo de Gran Canaria is an attraction. The street with water cascades in the middle is bordered by seats clad with colourful ceramic tiles. Above them are the coats of arms of the 21 administrative districts of Gran Canaria. On Paseo de Canarias, the continuation of the cascade, are depictions of various Canarian landscape scenes.

Modern tile decoration on the Paseo de Gran Canaria in Firgas

Plaza San Roque   Firgas consists of simple country cottages that cover the hillsides. The **Paseo de Gran Canaria** is an attraction. The street with water cascades in the middle is bordered by seats clad with colourful ceramic tiles. Above them are the coats of arms of the 21 administrative districts of Gran Canaria. On Paseo de Canarias, the continuation of the cascade, are depictions of various Canarian landscape scenes.

From the plaza, which is surrounded by sycamore and Indian laurel trees you look down on the northern coast as if standing on a balcony; when the weather is clear you can even see Lanzarote and Fuerteventura. The parish church **San Roque** with its pretty bell tower stands on the site of a hermitage that dates back to 1502. The **town hall** opposite was built in the middle of the last century in traditional island-style architecture; the façade is made of blue stone from a local quarry; the balcony is made of teak wood. **Casa de la Cultura** from 1848, which stands only a few steps away, is also very decorative. It now houses the town library and is used for exhibits and theatre productions.

Firgas

INFORMATION
Oficina de Información Turistico
Calle El Molino 3

Tel. 928 61 67 47; www.firgas.es
The small tourist information office is
located in a gofio mill (16th century).

Mirador Montaña de Firgas

Follow the GC 30 further uphill to where the GC-306 branches off after 1.5km/1mi to the Mirador Montaña de Firgas. The top of the hill covered with eucalyptus trees offers a fine panoramic view of the towns Firgas, Moya and Gáldar to the north-west and Arucas and Las Palmas can also be seen.

Aguas de Firgas

In the town centre a street branches off to the Aguas de Firgas (approx. 5km/3mi). It ends above the mineral water plant, where more than 200,000 bottles are filled every day.

** Gáldar

B 3

Elevation: 143m/469ft above sea level
Population: 24,000 (entire district)

Gáldar, located in north-western Gran Canaria, is easy to reach on the coastal road from Las Palmas (28km/17mi). Since tourists generally only stop off in Gáldar on a tour of the island, the town has maintained much of its original atmosphere. Remains from pre-Hispanic times are a special attraction here.

At the foot of **Pico de Gáldar** (434m/1,424ft above sea level), the town is gradually merging with ▶Santa María de Guía. No matter from which direction you approach Gáldar, the mainstay of the local economy is evident: bananas wherever you look. However, the collapse of the market for Canarian bananas has left its mark in Gáldar as well. Many of the plantations have closed in the last years. Exotic fruits or flowers are grown on some of the fields while others are fallow. Unemployment is high in Gáldar.

History

The area around Gáldar was settled before the Spanish conquest. It was the seat of one of the island's two kings. The early Canarian settlement Agaldar was located around Cueva Pintada (see p.155) with more than 60 houses and artificially constructed caves. Agaldar was inhabited from the 6th to the 16th century. When Juan Rejón tried to conquer the island in 1478 for the Spanish crown, Tenesor Semidan ruled the north-western half of Gran Canaria from Gáldar. After the Spanish found him and some of his people hiding in a cave he surrendered. His forced baptism was effective: In later conflicts between the Canarians and the Spanish, **Tenesor Semidan** tried repeatedly to get his people to surrender and accept Christianity. Was this what earned the last guanarteme of Gáldar a monument? It was donated by the King Juan Carlos I on 24 July 1986 and stands only a few hundred metres east of the plaza in Gáldar.

WHAT TO SEE IN GÁLDAR

Plaza de Santiago Plaza de Santiago is the centre of town. It is a nice place to relax on benches under shady trees. A kiosk sells refreshments and there are many smaller shops and services in the neighbouring streets.

Iglesia de Santiago de los Caballeros Iglesia de Santiago de los Caballeros is located on Plaza de Santiago. Construction began in 1778 and the first service was held in 1826, but the church was not completely finished until 1872, almost 100 years after it was begun. The green **baptismal font**, which is now in the Museo de Arte Sacra (entrance on Calle Fernando Guanarteme), is supposed to have been brought to Gran Canaria from Andalusia in the late 15th century and was thus probably used for forcible baptism of the native Canarians. In the church there are some interesting statues of saints (including Incarnation of Christ and Virgin of the Rosary), which have been attributed to Luján Pérez.

Ayuntamiento The town hall is only a few yards from the church on the shady plaza; it is house number 1. When the offices are open (only mornings) it is possible to go into the courtyard and see the magnificent dragon tree (**drago**). It was planted in 1719; today there is hardly any room for its roots and branches in the courtyard.

Casa Museo Padrón The little museum in Calle Drago, north of Plaza de Santiago, is dedicated to a native of Gáldar, the painter **Antonio Padrón** (1920 – 68). Graphics, pictures and wood and stone sculptures by the artist, who was influenced by Expressionism and Cubism, are on display in his former home and studio. The rural culture of the farmers and fishermen was the central theme of Padrón's work.
❶ Mon – Fri 8am – 3pm, free admission

*Parque Arqueológico Cueva Pintada Cueva Pintada (»painted cave«), one of the early Canarians' major legacies, has been open to the public again for a few years. It is now part of an archaeological park with a museum, excavation sites and reconstructed early Canarian houses. Cueva Pintada was discovered

Gáldar

INFORMATION
Oficina de Turismo
Edificio Heredad de Aguas
Tel. 928 89 58 55

SHOPPING
Mercado
Calle Capitán Queseda;
Mon – Sat 8am – 2pm
Good and large selection of fresh regional products, including the tasty »queso de flor« from the neighbouring town of Santa María de Guía.

WHERE TO EAT
Marisquería La Fragata €€€
Sardina, an der Mole
Tel. 928 88 32 96; closed Wed.
The well-known seafood restaurant has a French owner. The daily selection swims in a large tank right at the entrance. The restaurant's name is also its theme: The interior decorations are from an old frigate.

Pizzeria Casa Nostra €€
Calle Capitán Quesada 1
Tel. 928 55 05 39
Closed Mon
Small old town pizzeria, which also serves risotto, fresh pasta and fish. Next to the casino on Plaza Santiago.

La Traba €€
Calle Fernando Guanarteme 1
Tel. 928 89 74 58
Chic bistro next to the church, serving tapas, croquettes and a Canarian tortilla filled with avocado and gambas. With Wi-Fi zone.

in 1873 but not restored until 1970 – 74. This valuable cultural treasure was closed to the public for decades to prevent it from being completely destroyed, but exact replicas could be viewed in Museo Canario in ▶Las Palmas. Because of its **cave paintings**, which are unique to Gran Canaria, Cueva Pintada has a special status among all the known caves. It measures about 5 x 4.5m (16 x 14ft) and is 3m/10ft high. The walls are decorated with colourful geometric patterns, including squares, triangles and concentric circles. Cueva Pintada's original function, whether as a burial site, residence or religious site, is unknown. The guided tours of the archaeological park begin with a visit to the museum, which displays many finds from early Canarian times. Two films bring the world of the early Canarians to life. The tour of the excavation site with early Canarian remains follows. A visit to Cueva Pintada and reconstructed early Canarian buildings and a farm complete the tour.

❶ Tue – Sat 9.30am – 7pm, Sun 11am – 6pm, last guided tour one hour before closing, admission €6

Replica of Cueva Pintada in Museo Canario in Las Palmas

AROUND GÁLDAR

*Sardina Just beyond the south-west edge of Gáldar a street branches off towards Sardina (6km/3.5mi from Gáldar). The little fishing village is a popular place for Canarian families to swim in one of the little sandy bays and eat in one of the good **fish restaurants**.

At weekends the coastal road is clogged, but during the week the picturesque scenery can be enjoyed in peace. Anyone who wants to stay longer can stop off in one of the apartment buildings with an ocean view. There are almost always vacancies, except during the summer holidays.

Faro de 3km/2mi away the Faro de Sardina offers an enchanting view of the
Sardina coast. There is a holiday resort beyond the lighthouse.

One of the major archaeological excavations on the Canary Islands is located about 2km/1¼mi north of Gáldar, on the coast near **El Agujero**. The hamlet consists of one row of houses along the coast, but there is plenty of activity at weekends. Local people enjoy the stony beaches. To the left and right of the main road between the houses there are a few remains of early Canarian houses, which were excavated in 1934 and show that the inhabitants lived in round or oval houses with an area of about 30 – 50 sq m (300 – 550 sq ft).

*La Guancha

Follow the road that runs parallel to the coast about 400m/1,300ft to the fenced, somewhat elevated burial site of La Guancha. Normally the gate is not locked and the grounds with several burial sites can be viewed at any time. The necropolises are round structures built of mortarless stone. Presumably the largest tumulus (at the highest point in the burial site) is the tomb of the nobility or ruling class. Here numerous smaller squares are grouped around two central stone chambers – possibly the burial place of the guanarteme. The chambers were once covered with stone slabs. When the necropolis was excavated in 1935, 30 mummies from the late 11th century AD were found.

Ingenio

C 4

Elevation: 339m/1,112ft above sea level
Population: 30,000 (entire district)

Ingenio is located just 30km/20mi south of Las Palmas, near Aeropuerto de Gando. Its name »sugar maker« tells us how the people supported themselves in the past. Today Ingenio is known for embroidery.

The town flourished in the 16th and 17th centuries from the production of sugar and later also rum. Today tomatoes are raised instead of sugar cane. Ingenio is a typical Canarian rural town with some colourfully painted houses. The centre of the small old town is the Plaza de la Candelaria, where the 18th century colonial-style parish church with its Moorish-style brilliantly white dome is located. Follow one of the narrow lanes from the church

MARCO ☉ POLO TIP

! *Christmas on Gran Canaria?* **Insider Tip**

You won't see many Christmas trees, but there are beautiful nativity scenes. One of the largest and most elaborate is in the Museo de Piedras in Ingenio. The Christmas story is displayed in miniature with much love for detail, from the stable in Bethlehem to the Magi. It can be seen every year from mid-December to 6 January.

Hemstitched embroidery is a real art – you can learn it in Ingenio

square to Parque Néstor Álamo. In the park, with its usually dry river bed, tall palm trees and various decorative plants, there is an old watermill from the time when sugar was still produced here. A model of a sugar cane press commemorates the past. It was set up in 1991 at the eastern edge of town on the road to Carrizal.

WHAT TO SEE IN INGENIO

The **Museo de Piedras y Artesanía**, the rock and Canarian craft museum, is located 2km/1.2mi before the northern edge of town. Old agricultural implements are displayed outside. The »museum« is primarily a shop for Canarian crafts. A **school for embroidery** is attached (open to the public). The rock collection has little to offer the uninitiated. Many of the exhibits are inadequately labelled or not at all.

❶ daily 9am – 6pm, free admission

La Aldea de San Nicolás

—————————————— ✳ C 2

Elevation: 64 above sea level
Population: 8600 (entire district)

La Aldea de San Nicolás lies in a fertile valley where many of the residents still live from agriculture. The water supply comes from several reservoirs in the interior, where the trade winds bring rain. Tomatoes, potatoes, bananas, papayas, avocados and mangos are grown.

Located in western Gran Canaria, 5km/3mi from the coast, La Aldea de San Nicolás is still relatively difficult to reach. In the past the harbour, Puerto de la Aldea, was almost the only means of contact with the outside world.

La Aldea de San Nicolás is an elongated village without a real centre. A few stone and earth houses from the 17th century, as well as balconied 18th century houses can still be seen. Between the whitewashed houses there are still a few windmills to pump groundwater to the surface, but the water has become too salty for most plants.

AROUND LA ALDEA DE SAN NICOLÁS

La Aldea de San Nicolás does not have much to attract visitors. A stop in Puerto de la Aldea is more interesting. This still quite rustic **fishing village** has a few simple restaurants that serve the seafood catch of the day. The good value they seem to offer is the only explanation for the many local guests at weekends. The pretty beach promenade is also popular among day guests. The **beach** near Puerto de San Nicolás is about 500m/550yd long, relatively stony and bordered by cliffs. Expect strong waves. Most of the visitors are anglers. A hike of several hours will bring you to **Playa de Güigüí** the most remote beach on the island (▶ MARCO POLO Insight , p. 214).

Puerto de la Aldea

Drive through the Barranco de la Aldea to get one of the most beautiful scenic impressions of Gran Canaria. Although the road is well surfaced, it is very narrow and winding (!); it runs eastwards through the barranco from La Aldea de San Nicolás. At first it passes farms and fields, then several reservoirs surrounded by steep cliffs. After about 20km/12mi the mountain road meets the road that connects ▶Artenara and Pinar de Tamadaba. Since the road is not used much, it is good for mountain bikers as well, but they should bear in mind that the differences in elevation along the route amount to about 1,300m/4,300ft. The lower part of the barranco, around today's La Aldea de San Nicolás, was among the most popular settlement areas in pre-Hispanic times. Many ceramic finds and remains of early Canarian walls were

*Barranco de la Aldea

> **Insider Tip**
>
> *Fun in the mud*
>
> **MARCO POLO TIP**
>
> On 10 September La Aldea de San Nicolás celebrates the Fiesta del Charco, the »pond festival«. It goes back to the year 1766. The bishop at that time came for a visit and arrived at a bad moment: He caught men and women swimming almost naked in the pond. That could not go unpunished and the whole village was excommunicated. Today the festival is more decent: No one swims naked, but everyone has a great time! There is also a contest at some point: The person who catches the most fish in the pond wins.

discovered here. The individual sites are not marked and hard to find without an experienced guide.

Cactualdea lies on the road to Mogán, about 4km/2.5mi south-east of La Aldea de San Nicolás. As the name already hints, it's all about **cacti**. About 12,000 different varieties of cacti grow on the grounds, where there are also reconstructed Guanche caves. Small cacti are sold in a souvenir shop and a restaurant serves refreshment.

Cactualdea

❶ daily 10am – 6pm, admission €6

The road along the west coast is itself worth seeing because of the elaborate engineering. The best part of the GC 200 runs from La Aldea de San Nicolás to Agaete.
The most spectacular stops are **Mirador de Balcón** and **Andén Verde**, two observation points with a marvellous panorama of the wild and romantic coast.

Panoramic coastline

** Las Palmas

————————————— ✦ B 4

Elevation: 0m – 210m/0 – 690ft above sea level
Population: 383,000

Las Palmas de Gran Canaria is the uncontested metropolis of the Canary Isles. The capital of the eponymous province is bursting with urban life, which however includes permanent traffic jams and mass tourism on the outskirts. But the renovated old quarter, quality museums and the pulsing entertainment district of Santa Catalina make a visit to the island capital an absolute must.

Las Palmas is located on the northern point of the island. The city stretches along the coast from north to south for about 14km/8mi. The foothills of the central mountains form the border to the inner part of the island. The peninsula **La Isleta** (»the islet«) has been part of the city since the 20th century. La Isleta was once really an island, but a neck of land developed into a land bridge to Gran Canaria. With its official total of 383,000 residents (the real number is probably much higher) Las Palmas is by far the largest city on the Canaries and the eighth-largest city in Spain. It has always been a major economic, traffic and trade centre and owes its economic status to the **port** (Puerto de la Luz). Its strategic position at the intersection of shipping routes between Europe, Africa and South America turned

Important harbour

View from AC Hotel Gran Canaria to the city district Santa Catalina

MARCO ⊕ POLO TIP

! *Guagua Turística* **Insider Tip**

For anyone who wants to get through the big city traffic without much stress: From the bus terminal San Telmo and Parque Santa Catalina an open double-decker bus leaves every 30 to 60 minutes starting at 10am (Guagua Turística) for a city tour. The day ticket allows you to get on or off at 20 different bus stops.

it into one of the largest ports on the Atlantic. The city is especially proud of the **university**, which was founded in 1990. The residents of Gran Canaria fought for it for many years. Until 1990 anyone who wanted to go to university had to go to Tenerife or the Spanish mainland. Thousands of visitors from all over the world – sailors and tourists – give Las Palmas an international atmosphere. The city has almost 100 hotels, but the number is decreasing, as many foreign tourists come to the somewhat loud and chaotic city for a day, but spend the rest of their holiday in Gran Canaria's sunny south.

History   The city was founded on 24 June 1478 by **Juan Rejón**, who conquered Gran Canaria from here on the orders of the Spanish king. Since there was an unusually large number of palm trees in the place that the Spanish conquistadors had chosen for their administrative seat, it was named **Ciudad Real de las Palmas** (»royal city of the palms«). After the island was placed under Spanish rule in 1483, the time had come to move the bishop's seat from Lanzarote to Las Palmas in 1485. The town grew quickly. By 1487 about 3,500 people lived here; along with the Spanish there were many Genoese and Portuguese. The city profited from trade between Europe and the New World because of its location. Whether or not **Christopher Columbus** (►Famous People) really stopped on Gran Canaria in 1492 when he crossed the Atlantic for the first time and stayed in Casa de Colón, which was named after him, has not been definitely proven.

In the 16th century the city had to defend itself repeatedly; it repelled attacks by the English, French and Portuguese seafarers again and again. The most difficult battle was probably in 1599 when the Dutch fleet admiral **Pieter van der Does** tried to take Las Palmas with about 10,000 men. Las Palmas flourished in the 17th and 18th centuries. Beautiful buildings were built in the Vegueta district, some of which still exist.

However, Las Palmas really took off when the port was established in the late 19th century. While only 16,000 people lived there in 1860, in 1900 there were already almost 50,000 residents. Las Palmas expanded in all directions; the old quarter Vegueta merged with Puerto de la Luz and many residential areas were established above the coast. When tourism began to grow in the 1950s a building boom began along Las Canteras beach. New hotels sprang up.

Highlights Las Palmas

▶ **Playa de las Canteras**
Stroll along the almost 3km/2mi-long promenade by one of the most beautiful beaches in the world.
▶page167

▶ **Parque de San Telmo**
Take a break on the palm-shaded terrace of the beautifully tiled Art Nouveau café.
▶page174

▶ **Vegueta**
The old city with the cathedral and Columbus' house still emanates a colonial atmosphere.
▶page174

▶ **Museo Canario**
The Idol of Tara stands out in the leading Canarian collection.
▶page182

Las Palmas has been the **capital** of the island since 1820. When the Canaries were divided into two provinces in 1927, Las Palmas became the capital of the eastern province Las Palmas de Gran Canaria. In 1994 a modern convention centre was built at the trade fair site.

Las Palmas' city districts all have a character of their own and there is no real city centre. The area around **Parque de Santa Catalina** and along Las Canteras beach is the most touristy area. The tall round Hotel AC Gran Canaria and the post-modern government building Torre Woermann are the landmark of this district. Immediately to the east of Parque de Santa Catalina is the **port**, which has expanded to take in large parts of the Isleta.

City districts

Most of Las Palmas' attractions are in **Vegueta**, the oldest part of the city. Folk festivals and processions take place at Plaza de Santa Ana, its focal point. In the surrounding streets there are many beautiful old houses with artistic wooden balconies and quiet patios.

To the north the district of **Triana** adjoins Vegueta. The pedestrian zone Calle de Triana with many shops is the centre.

Las Palmas' most luxurious district is **Ciudad Jardín** (»garden city«) at Parque Doramas. Many luxury villas are surrounded by lush gardens in the side streets of this district. The residents' fear of burglars is evident in the alarm systems and barred windows. The satellite towns and the slums on the outskirts of Las Palmas stand in stark contrast to the exclusive Ciudad Jardín and the shopping districts with their extensive selection of goods. The city has grown in the past decades without any planning whatsoever. Depressing housing was built quickly to provide living quarters, but many people can't even afford to live in these grey dormer ci-

Santa Catalina / Ciudad Jardín

INFORMATION
Patronato de Turismo
Calle Triana 93
Tel. 928 21 96 00
www.laspalmasgc.es
www.grancanaria.com

Information kiosks
In Parque San Telmo opposite Ermita de San Telmo, at Paseo de las Canteras opposite Hotel Meliá Las Palmas and in Parque Santa Catalina.

PARKING
Parking in Las Palmas is extremely limited. It is best to go to one of the central parking garages, in the old town at Teatro Pérez Galdós or in Santa Catalina district at the Edificio Elder.

BUS/TAXI
There are good express bus connections to the capital from the tourist centres in the south, as well as a good network of city buses. Line 1 runs back and forth every few minutes between Teatro Pérez Galdós and the port. Taxis are reasonable; there are about 40 taxi stands in the whole central part of town.

SECURITY
Las Palmas is considered to be the most

In the market in Vegueta

dangerous city on the Canary Islands, but this doesn't mean that a robbery takes place on every street corner. During the day the city is no less safe than any central European city. At night it is best to be careful in the port district or Barrio Santa Catalina.

SHOPPING

Insider Tip

Anyone who comes to Las Palmas to shop should go to Avenida de Mesa y López, where there are large department stores and branches of large shoe and fashion chains. Smaller boutiques can be found in the pedestrian zone Calle de Triana, which runs through the district of the same name. There are book and antique shops in the side streets. In Santa Catalina district electronics shops run by Indian immigrants sell watches, stereo equipment and computer equipment – it pays to compare prices.

Shopping centre El Muelle
At the harbour
Give in to your consumer instincts in the large shopping centre at the port. This modern retail paradise has diverse cafés and restaurants, cinemas and discos along with its more than 100 shops.

Mercado del Puerto
At the port, near Castillo de la Luz
Mon – Sat mornings
Groceries, clothing, souvenirs.

Mercado de las Palmas
Calle Mendizábal, Vegueta
Mon – Sat 8am – 3pm
Fruit, vegetables, fish, meat, fresh every day

Mercado Central
Calle Galicia; Mon – Sat, 7am – 2pm

The largest food market in the city, with two floors

Flea market
At Parque San Telmo
Every Sunday morning.

FEDAC
Calle Domingo y Navarro 7
The embroidery, basketry and wrought iron in the FEDAC shop are guaranteed to come from local workshops.

NIGHTLIFE
Where to go
Especially around Parque de Santa Catalina or along the beach promenade there are bars, pubs and clubs.

Auditorio Alfredo Kraus
Paseo de las Canteras
Tel. 902 40 55 04
www.auditorio-alfredokraus.com
The best address for musical events from pop to classical.

Casino Las Palmas
Calle Simón Bolívar 3
Edificio Saba (Parque Santa Catalina)
Tel. 928 23 48 82

Pequeña Habana
Calle de Fernando Guanarteme 45
Fri – Sun 10pm – 4am
One of the most popular clubs in town; only Latino music.

WHERE TO EAT
❶ El Novillo Precoz €€€
Calle Portugal 9
Tel. 928 22 16 59
www.novilloprecoz.es
The many regular guests know that there's no better place in Las Palmas for

grilled meat. Excellent quality has its price, of course. But for that you don't just get a piece of meat, but rather you can choose between three different ways of grilling: »a la brassa« (on glowing coals), »a la ceniza« (in ashes) or »a punta de llamas« (over tongues of flames). Eating meat well done is almost a sacrilege; the chef recommends no more than »punto« (medium). Reservations recommended!

❷ La Casa Roja €€
Paseo de las Canteras/corner of Calle Luis Morote
Tel. 928 27 62 49
The popular Italian restaurant is located in the mezzanine of a colonial-style house. There are a few tables right on the promenade too.

❸ La Marinera €€€ Insider Tip
Paseo de Las Canteras
Tel. 928 46 88 02
This popular fish restaurant is located on the land spit La Puntilla at the northern end of Playa de las Canteras. The menu has everything that the Atlantic Ocean has to offer: parrot fish, comb grouper, dentex, etc., are calculated by weight. Gofio is served as an appetiser. During the day you can watch surfers from the large terrace.

WHERE TO STAY
❶ Santa Catalina
€€€ – €€€€
Calle León y Castillo 227
Tel. 928 24 30 40
www.hotelsantacatalina.com
The Spanish King stays in a suite in the Santa Catalina when he visits Gran Canaria. Other famous people like Plácido Domingo and Prince Charles have followed his lead. This typically Canarian house was built in 1953 in place of the hotel that opened in 1890. It is now the city's top address. The terrace café under the hotel arcades offers colonial ambience, a 2,800 sq m/30,000 sq ft spa guarantees relaxation and a casino provides entertainment.

❷ Reina Isabel €€€€
Calle Alfredo L. Jones 40
Tel. 928 26 01 00
www.bullhotels.com
Five-star hotel on the beach promenade with 208 rooms and 16 suites. It has a large swimming pool on the roof terrace and several restaurants. The café terrace has a spectacular view of the sea.

❸ Atlanta €
Calle Alfredo L. Jones 37
Tel. 928 27 80 00
www.atlantacanarias.com
This lower mid-range city hotel is in Santa Catalina district, about 50m/50yd from the beach. The 47 functionally furnished rooms and 20 apartments all have satellite TV, telephone and a safe. The central location means that it's not necessarily quiet!

❹ AC Hotel Gran Canaria €€€
Calle Eduardo Benot 3
Tel. 928 26 61 00
www.marriott.de
This circular high-rise hotel dominates the tourist district Santa Catalina. It is 23 storeys high and thus offers a spectacular view from the upper floors, but the view can also be enjoyed from the roof terrace with a pool and the restaurant.

ties. The poorest of the poor live in slum-like squalor in huts of wood and corrugated iron, for example on Isleta. No wonder that crime in Las Palmas has grown dramatically (don't leave anything in your car!).

WHAT TO SEE IN SANTA CATALINA

Construction of the Puerto de la Luz (▶ MARCO POLO Insight , p. 168), the port of light, began in the late 19th century; it was designed by the engineer **León y Castillo**. Puerto de la Luz has the sixth-largest annual turnover of all Spanish ports, but in terms of traffic is even more important: About 14,000 ships call here every year. Large cruise ships and ferries sail from the **Muelle de Santa Catalina** near Parque de Santa Catalina, transporting passengers and cars between the Canary Islands as well as to the Spanish mainland. Fishing boats dock here, too. But the actual fishing harbour is **Muelle Pesquero**. **Muelle de la Luz** is mainly used by freighters. The 3.5km/2mi long **Dique Reina Sofia** is at the eastern edge of the port. Large tankers and cruise ships stop here.

Puerto de la Luz

Near Muelle Pesquero at Calle de Juan Rejón the Castillo de la Luz rises above green lawns. The small, almost square fort was built in the 16th century to protect the city from pirate raids. It was burned down in 1599 in the attack by Pieter van der Does. Today it is used for cultural events.

Castillo de la Luz

Only a few hundred metres west of the fort on the way to Las Palmas beach stands the Mercado del Puerto, a 100-year-old market hall with an interesting iron construction.

Mercado del Puerto

Playa de las Canteras, one of the longest city beaches in the world, is more than 2.5km/1.5mi long and located in the north-west of Las Palmas. Its name (»canteras« means »quarry«) is a reminder that sandstone was taken from here for centuries for the cathedral of Santa Ana and other buildings. Reefs off Playa de las Canteras protect the beach from strong surf and make it possible to swim here safely. Considering its location the beach and the water are very clean: Playa de las Canteras was given a European Blue Flag award. It gets full on the weekends when thousands of local inhabitants come to relax on the beach. Playa de las Canteras is bordered by **Paseo de las Canteras**, a beach promenade with hotels, cafés, restaurants and shops. Island tourism began here in the 20th century.

****Playa de las Canteras*

From early December until Epiphany (January 6) the Belén de Arena, a nativity made of sand, located even with Plaza Saulo Torón at the

Belén de Arena

Puerto de la Luz

The harbour of light is one of the most important harbours in southern Europe and West Africa. It is indispensable for trade between these two continents and America. It was built between 1883 and 1902 on plans by the Canarian engineer Juan de león y Castillo as a replacement for the old harbour Muelle de San Telmo in Triana. The harbour also plays a large role in tourism as a port of call for cruise ships.

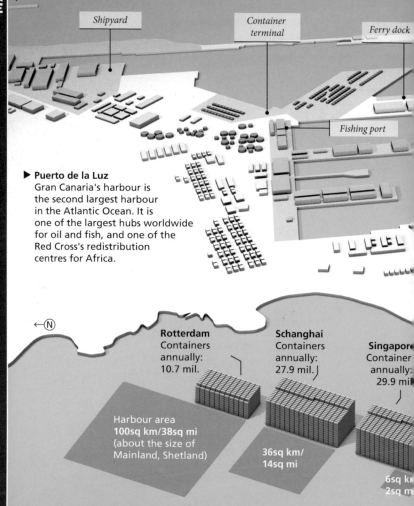

Shipyard

Container terminal

Ferry dock

Fishing port

▶ **Puerto de la Luz**
Gran Canaria's harbour is
the second largest harbour
in the Atlantic Ocean. It is
one of the largest hubs
worldwide for oil and fish,
and one of the
Red Cross's redistribution
centres for Africa.

←Ⓝ

Rotterdam
Containers
annually:
10.7 mil.

Schanghai
Containers
annually:
27.9 mil.

Singapore
Containers
annually:
29.9 mil.

Harbour area
100sq km/38sq mi
(about the size of
Mainland, Shetland)

**36sq km/
14sq mi**

**6sq km
2sq mi**

LANZEROTE

FUERTEVENTURA

LA PALMA

TENERIFE

GRAN CANARIA

○ Las Palmas

Atlantic Ocean

LA GOMERA

EL HIERRO

MOROCCO

50km/
31mi

*Container
terminal*

Ferry dock

*Marina/
Yacht harbour*

©BAEDEKER

The harbour in numbers

Ships total	9,000
Fishing boats	600
Fish loads	1,000 tons
Oil	1,5 mil tons
Landing stages	14km/8mi
Cranes	21
Tourists (ferry, cruise, yacht)	1 million

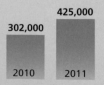

Gran Canaria
Containers
annually: 1.3 mil.

Cruise ship passengers

425,000

302,000

2010   2011

**2sq km/
0.7sq mi**

Las Palmas • Santa Catalina/Ciudad Jardín

Where to stay
1. Santa Catalina
2. Reina Isabel
3. Atlanta
4. AC Hotel Gran Canaria

Where to eat
1. Novillo Precoz
2. La Casa Roja
3. La Marinera

1. Casa Museo Pérez Galdós
2. Teatro Pérez Galdós
3. Gabinete Literario
4. Casa de Colón
5. Palacio Episcopal/ Casa Regenta
6. Casa Consistorial
7. Museo Canario

500 m
©BAEDEKER

northern end of Playa de las Canteras, attracts thousands of visitors. On an area of about 600m²/6,400sq ft several sand artists create an impressive nativity scene.

Playa de las Canteras ends in a rocky promontory at its northern end. A colourful wind vane on Plaza de la Puntilla turns softly in the wind; under it is a parking garage. Small fishing boats are beached in front of it. The Puntilla offers a wonderful view of the gently arced bay, accented by the Torre Woermann skyscraper and AC Marriott Hotel. Auditorio Alfredo Kraus can be seen at the southern end of Playa de las Canteras. And the fish restaurant on the Puntilla serves excellent food.

> **! MARCO ⊕ POLO TIP**
>
> *Sailing à la Canaria* **Insider Tip**
>
> Between April and October there are small and not so small Vela Latina regattas in Las Palmas every weekend. Vela Latina is a typical Canarian boat class with triangular lateen sails. The colourful event can easily be watched from the coast road near Real Club Náutico.

A few steps behind La Puntilla the peninsula La Isleta begins, which is bordered by a rough lava coastline. There's not much to discover in the impoverished neighbourhood where harbour workers and immigrants from Africa and Asia live in simple homes.   **La Isleta**

The **cultural and convention centre** at the south-west end of Playa de las Canteras is named after a native of Las Palmas, the tenor Alfredo Kraus (▶Famous People). The imposing complex was built in 1997 to plans by the Catalan architect Oscar Tusquets Blanca. Imitating a medieval castle, the building stands out for its austere geometric architecture and is crowned by a small, round lighthouse. In the two concert halls, the Sala Sinfónica with 1,656 seats and the smaller Sala de Camára, about 100 concerts, from classical to pop and jazz, are held every year.   **Auditorio Alfredo Kraus**

The centre of the tourist district in Las Palmas is Parque de Santa Catalina. On the shady pedestrian square there are several cafés, and street vendors sell their wares. Local people play chess and dominoes during the day, and in the evenings concerts often take place on an outdoor stage; the carnival queen is crowned here, too. The Casa del Turismo here has tourist information and brochures.   **Parque de Santa Catalina**

Visitors to the Science and Technology Museum, which was opened in 1999, in Parque de Santa Catalina (Calle Emilio Castelar 6) can find out how glass is made, air traffic is controlled or ships are navigated. There are also historical exhibits, including a train from the year 1885.   **Science and Technology Museum**
❶ Tue – Sun 10am – 8pm

MARCO ⊕ POLO TIP

! *Colourful folklore* Insider Tip

The folklore show in Pueblo Canario (every Sunday at 11.30am) is performed for tourists, but it still gives an impression of the old dances and songs of the island – and the colourful costumes are delightful. The show is free.

The circular **Hotel AC Gran Canaria** is the city's landmark and can be seen from far away. The panorama restaurant Bitácora has the best view of the city.

❶ Tel. 928 24 49 08, on the 24th floor

The 60m/200ft high office building ***Torre Woermann** has dominated the skyline of Santa Catalina since 2005. It was designed by the Spanish architects Iñaki Abalos and Juan Herreros and the 2000sq m/21,000sq ft of greenish yellow glass covering is arresting. The deconstructivist building is an outstanding example of modern architecture on the Canaries. The multifunctional building houses the administration offices of the island government (Gobierno Canario), among other things.

Centro de Arte La Regenta Contemporary art and photography is exhibited in revolving shows in the art centre in Calle León y Castillo 427 on two floors. The art forum was established in 1987 and is housed in a former tobacco factory; it is financed by the Canarian government.

❶ Tue – Fri 10am – 8pm, Sun 10am – 3pm, free admission

WHAT TO SEE IN CIUDAD JARDÍN

*Parque Doramas Take a taxi for the 2km/1¼mi between Parque de Santa Catalina and Parque Doramas. Walking through the drab streets clogged with traffic is not much fun. Parque Doramas is the centre of the high-class district called **Ciudad Jardín**. Wealthy Canarians live here in ostentatious villas set in lush gardens. Parque Doramas was named after the early Canarian king who ruled over the eastern part of the island. He was defeated in unfair combat with the leader of the Spaniards, Pedro de Vera (▶Arucas). With their leader gone, many of the early Canarians are said to have killed themselves by jumping off a cliff into a deep barranco. A modern monument on the eastern edge of the park commemorates this event. Typical Canarian flora grows in Parque Doramas, including several beautiful dragon trees. There are also fountains and a pool with Koi carp.

Hotel Santa Catalina Hotel Santa Catalina fits well into its surroundings. It is hard to believe that it was completed as recently as 1953. It replaced a hotel that was built by English investors in 1890 (see p.166).

Pueblo Canario Pueblo Canario (= Canarian village) was built next to Parque Doramas as an example of Canarian architecture. It was inspired by the

Playa de las Canteras gets crowded on weekends

watercolour paintings of the artist Néstor and begun in 1939. In the courtyard there are souvenir shops, the entrance to the Museum Néstor and a café. It is a refuge from the noise of the city.

Museo Néstor is located in Pueblo Canario. The museum was opened in 1956 and displays works of the Canarian painter Néstor Martín Fernández de la Torre (1887 – 1938; ▶Famous People); the furnishings of his studio are also on display. Many of Torres' major works are strongly influenced by Symbolist art.

Museo Néstor

In room 1, Wedding Poem and the self-portrait of Néstor de la Torre are among the most important works. The pictures in room 2 were made between 1934 and 1938 in order to provide models of typical Canarian architecture for the tourist industry. The paintings in room 3 all have the Atlantic Ocean as their theme; they were painted between 1913 and 1924. Room 4 is devoted to portraits, room 5 to drawings from 1934 to 1938, room 6 to sketches from 1913 on Mozart's opera Don Giovanni. In room 7 there are sketches of decorations and costumes for various ballets; room 8 has some studies of plants. The pictures in room 9 are on the theme of Earth. Room 10 has drawings and sketches of Néstor de la Torres' main works from his whole life.

❶ Tue – Sat 10am – 8pm, Sun 10.30am – 2.30pm, admission €2

WHAT TO SEE IN TRIANA AND VEGUETA

Calle Mayor de Triana

The southern extension of Calle de León y Castillo, Calle Mayor de **Triana**, is a **pedestrian zone** ideal for strolling. It is the main street of the area called Triana and has always been the city's business and shopping area. Art Nouveau buildings give the street its unique flair. Among the prettiest façades are **Casa Negrín**, which was designed by Fernando Navarro and built in 1907, and on the left **Casa Melián**, which was built a year later.

**Parque de San Telmo

Insider Tip

Calle Mayor de Triana runs past **Parque de San Telmo**. A tiled Art Nouveau pavilion from 1923, now a café, is a good place from which to watch the activity all around while seated under tall palm trees. The large building on the west side of the plaza houses the military headquarters of the Canaries. In this neo-classical building **General Franco** called for the deposition of the government in Madrid in 1936.

Ermita de San Telmo

The Ermita de San Telmo stands at the southern end of the park. The chapel was built in the late 17th century and dedicated to the patron saint of fishermen. Note especially the panelled ceiling inside in the Mudejar style. The many votive pictures in the chapel are mostly offerings from sailors who were spared from drowning at sea.

Museo Pérez Galdós

Calle Cano 6 – the street runs parallel to Calle Mayor de Triana – is the birthplace of the writer **Benito Pérez Galdós** (▶Famous People). He was born in the house in 1843 and lived there as a boy.

It is a typical 19th-century Canarian house with a picturesque courtyard. The museum that now occupies it has an interesting collection of works, Pérez Galdós' private library and a large number of personal items. In the study a life-sized wax figure of the most famous Canarian poet is seated at the desk.

❶ Tue – Fri 9am – 9pm, Sat 9am – 6pm, Sun 10am – 3pm, free admission

*Plaza Cairasco

Plaza Cairasco in the south-west of Triana district is named after the poet Bartolomé Cairasco de Figueroa (1540 – 1610); his bust is in front of the Gabinete Literario described below. Mature trees, many benches, a sidewalk café and magnificent buildings around the

Triana / Vegueta

WHERE TO EAT
❶ *Amaiur* €€€ – €€€€
Calle Pérez Galdós 2
Tel. 928 37 07 17
www.restauranteamaiur.es
Closed Sun
One of the island's best restaurants,
with suitably elegant atmosphere:
bright, high rooms in an old townhouse.
Basque cuisine is served midday and
evenings from 8.30pm.

❷ *Casa Montesdeoca* €€€
Calle Montesdeoca 10   **Insider**
Tel. 928 33 34 66   **Tip**
www.casamontesdeoca.com
Closed Sun
Unique atmosphere: Eat in one of the
rooms of a wonderfully restored Canarian house or on the patio. Spanish
cooking.

❸ *El Herreño* €€
Calle Medizábal 5
Tel. 928 31 05 13
Probably the best chance to try typical
Canarian tapas and taste real gofio. The
traditional restaurant lives up to its
name, »the man from El Hierro«, with
wines and cheese from this little Canary
island.

El Herreño: perfect Canarian cuisine

WHERE TO STAY

❶ Madrid €

Plaza de Cairasco 4
Tel. 928 36 06 64
www.elhotelmadrid.com
Half of the 40 simply furnished rooms
have a shower and toilet; the ones without a bath are very reasonably priced.
The hotel is appreciated mainly for its
central location in the old city. The attached café-restaurant is also popular
among non-residents.

❷ Parque €€

Calle Muelle de Las Palmas 2
Tel. 928 36 80 00
www.hparque.com
This simple mid-range hotel hosts many
business travellers as well. It is centrally
located at Parque San Telmo just a few
steps from the bus terminal. But the side
facing the park is not exactly quiet; the
rooms toward the back are better for
sleeping.

square make Plaza Cairasco a charming place to rest in the bustle of
Las Palmas.

Gabinete Literario

Gabinete Literario was built in 1842 as a theatre, but closed soon due
to lack of funds. Only a few years later the Gabinete Literario, which
was founded in 1844, rented it and later bought it. The city's oldest
cultural club sponsors exhibitions and musical evenings. It is still
used for cultural events. The building originally had a classical façade
and was redecorated in the present style after World War II. There is

Insider Tip

a café restaurant on the ground floor; guests can enjoy small meals
under the arcades of the Gabinete Literario.

Iglesia de San Francisco

Plaza de Cairasco is next to Plaza de San Francisco. Here stands the
church Iglesia de San Francisco, which was built in the 17th century
and expanded to three aisles in the 20th century.
The Baroque main entrance dates from 1683. Inside note the Mudejar ceiling and several wooden statues by Luján Pérez. The most valuable work is a figure of Mary: The **Virgin of Solitude** (Virgen de
la Soledad) is supposed to have the facial features of Isabella of Cas-
tille (1451 – 1504). It is possible that the queen herself gave the statue to the Franciscans.

Teatro de Pérez Galdós

East of Plaza de Cairasco, near the motorway that runs along the ocean, is the Teatro de Pérez Galdós, named after the famous novelist
(▶Famous People) who was a native of Las Palmas. The theatre was
built in 1919 to plans by Miguel Martín Fernández de la Torre. The
foyer is decorated with paintings by his brother Néstor de la Torre.
The large hall seats 1,400 people. The theatre is generally only open
for performances from September to December. From January to
April it is used for the music festival and opera festival. (Programme
information under tel. 902 48 84 88, www.teatroperezgaldos.es).

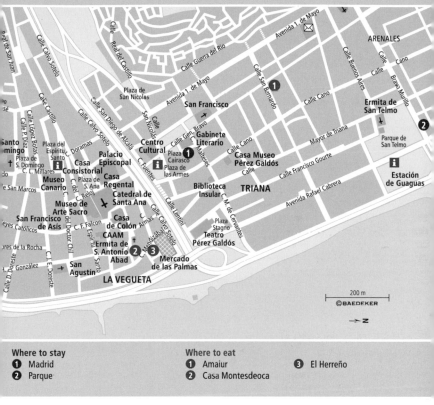

Las Palmas • Vegueta/Triana

ARENALES

Calle Guerra del Río

Avenida 1. de Mayo

Plaza de
San Nicolas

San Francisco

Ermita de
San Telmo

Parque de
San Telmo

Gabinete
Literario

Centro
Cultural

Palacio
Episcopal

Casa
Consistorial

Casa Museo
Pérez Galdós

Casa
Regental

Estación
de Guaguas

Museo
Canario

Catedral de
Santa Ana

Museo de
Arte Sacro

Biblioteca
Insular

TRIANA

San Francisco
de Asís

Casa
de Colón

CAAM

Ermita de
S. Antonio
Abad

Teatro
Pérez Galdós

San
Agustín

Mercado
de las Palmas

LA VEGUETA

200 m

©BAEDEKER

Where to stay
❶ Madrid
❷ Parque

Where to eat
❶ Amaiur
❷ Casa Montesdeoca
❸ El Herreño

When there is no performance, guided tours of the theatre are offered, including the stage.
❶ Mon – Sat 10am – 1pm, admission €5

Cross Carretera del Centro to reach Vegueta, Las Palmas' oldest neighbourhood. Mercado de las Palmas, opposite the theatre to the south, is accordingly the oldest of the city's four market halls.

Mercado de las Palmas

Vegueta is dominated by Catedral de Santa Ana. Its interior and exterior show that construction took centuries. It began in 1497 and was interrupted in 1570, but the completed Gothic part of the church could already be used for worship. In the late 18th century and early 19th century the classical façade was completed by the sculptor **Luján**

*Catedral de Santa Ana

Imposing: the Catedral de Santa Ana on the plaza
with the same name

Pérez (1756 – 1815). He also built the three-storey north tower with
its belfry and a small dome. The south tower was completed by 1857
as its counterpart.

The cathedral is divided into five aisles. Gothic ribbed vaulting is supported by slender columns. Valuable furnishings include a Baroque
high altar as well as several works by Luján Pérez, including the lady
of sorrows in the Capilla de los Dolores in the right-hand aisle. The
baroque statue of King Ferdinand III of Castile in the Capilla de San
Fernando is attributed to the Andalusian sculptor Luisa Roldán
(1652 - 1704). Saint Ana, patron saint of the city of Las Palmas is por-
trayed seated on a pedestal above the main altar. The crypt has a monument to the Canarian poet and historian José de Viera y Clavijo (d.
1813). In the side chapels are the tombs of various famous islanders,
including the engineer and port builder Fernando León y Castillo.
The cathedral can only be viewed during services or via the Museo
Diocesano de Arte Sacro.

❶ Mon – Fri 8am – 10am, Sat and Sun 8am – 9.30am and 6pm – 8pm

The Museo Diocesano de Arte Sacro is located in an aisle of the cathedral (entrance on Calle Espíritu Santo). Its treasures include statues, such as one by Luján Pérez, and a small picture gallery with the works of 16th-century Flemish painters as well as 17th- and 18th-century Canarian artists; it also has many gold and silver objects. From the Museo Diocesano de Arte Sacro it is possible to go into the quiet courtyard and the cathedral itself.

Museo Diocesano de Arte Sacro

❶ Mon – Fri 10am – 5pm, Sat 10am – 2pm

The cathedral's main façade faces the palm-lined Plaza de Santa Ana. It is bordered by imposing administrative buildings and residences and by bronze **statues of dogs**, a reminder of the origins of the island's name (▶p.13). However, the bronze figures have little in common with Canarian dogs, but were modelled on English dogs and set up about 100 years ago. During the feast of Corpus Christi, Plaza de Santa Ana is decorated with a beautiful carpet of flowers.

Plaza de Santa Ana

Opposite the cathedral is the **city hall**, the Casa Consistorial. The main façade of the mid-19th century building is topped by a balustrade. Figures of early Canarians and Spaniards stand on the corner columns The city coat of arms dominates the centre of the building.

The military commander lives in **Casa Regental** next to the city hall on the north side of the square. It was built in the mid-17th century and a classical upper storey was added in 1805.

> **MARCO ⦿ POLO TIP**
>
> ! *Great view* Insider Tip
>
> The panoramic view from the observation platform on the south tower of the cathedral is worthwhile; the lift gets you there in just seconds. Not only the old city and Plaza de Santa Ana below can easily be seen, but also the harbour.
>
> Mon – Fri 10am – 4.30pm, Sat 10am – 1.30pm

A few metres further on the north side of the square is the bishop's palace (**Palacio Episcopal**). Only a Gothic entrance remains of the original 16th century building.

Casa de Colón, near the back of the cathedral, was rebuilt in 1777 in typical Canarian style and was once the seat of the island's viceroy. It owes its name to **Columbus** (▶Famous People), who is supposed to have stayed in the previous building during a short stop on Gran Canaria. As part of the preparations for the 500th anniversary of the discovery of America in 1992, research was done. It emerged that, if Columbus stopped on Gran Canaria at all, he docked in the port of Las Palmas in order to repair the rudder on the Pinta in August 1492. A small marble tablet on the side of the house facing Pasaje Pedro de Algaba points out that the great explorer is supposed also to have stopped at Las Palmas in 1493 and 1502, as well as in 1492. It is certain,

**Casa de Colón

Casa de Colón owes its name to Columbus – but it is not certain if he stopped here

however, that Casa Colón is the birthplace of another famous person. A plaque on the wall of the house indicates that Alfredo Kraus (▶Famous People), an opera tenor with Austrian roots, was born here in 1927.

The attractive house with beautiful wood balconies and richly decorated stucco entrances now holds a museum (entrance on Calle Colón) with exhibitions on Pre-Columbian America; Columbus and his Travels; The Canary Islands as a Stage on the Way to the New World; and Origins and History of Las Palmas. A depiction of a cabin on Columbus' ship La Niña is especially interesting. The museum also displays paintings of the 17th to 19th centuries, most of which are on loan from the Museo Prado in Madrid. The two patios are pretty, the smaller one has a Gothic fountain.

❶ Mon – Fri 9am – 7pm, Sat 10am – 6pm, Sun 9am – 3pm, free admission

**Centro de
Artes
Plásticas**

Opposite Casa de Colón in Calle Colón 8 there are rotating exhibits of modern art.
❶ free admission

The Darkest Hour of Puerto de la Luz: the Sinking of the »Sudamérica«

Every year about 14,000 ships call at Puerto de la Luz, the »harbour of light«. Fortunately there have been few accidents. Puerto de la Luz experienced the darkest day of its 100-year history just five years after being opened, when on 13 September 1888 the Italian passenger steamer »Sudamérica« was rammed by another steamer while trying to enter the harbour and sank within minutes.

On this day at 5am three ships were approaching the harbour of Las Palmas from different directions: the 1,258-ton Italian passenger steamer *Sudamérica* with 260 passengers and a crew of 69 on board, which had just crossed the Atlantic after visiting Buenos Aires in Argentina and Montevideo in Uruguay; the steamer *La France* (4,600 tons) coming from the port of Marseille with 1,300 passengers, and finally the Spanish mail ship *Habana*.

Inevitable Collision

The *Sudamérica* appeared north of the city and then approached the harbour directly without reducing speed, while *La France* approached from the south heading straight for the Italian ship. Only the *Habana* had reduced speed and stayed away from the two steamers.

The sea was calm, the sun rose slowly in the east and there was not a cloud in sight. But at this moment a collision was already inevitable.

Panic on Board

The French ship rammed into the port side of the Italian ship with immense force. Woken by this massive collision, many passengers of the *Sudamérica* tried to get on deck, even though they were hardly dressed. Panic soon spread when they realized that the steamer was sinking, and their cries mingled with the shrill ship's siren, which the crew of the *Sudamérica* used to call for help.

A few boats that were waiting nearby for the arrival of the mail ship *Habana* came immediately for help, but since these boats had no means of lifting the endangered passengers from the ship, many people jumped from the deck. If they were lucky, sailors pulled them out of the water.

Help for a Few

Some passengers who did not manage to jump from the ship, or were afraid to do so, could no longer be helped. They were sucked under water by the vortex caused by the sinking ship. The passengers who were not able to get on deck suffered the same fate. However, the quick response of the small boats made it possible to save more than 250 people from drowning.

Ermita de San Antonio Abad	Columbus is supposed to have prayed in the Ermita de San Antonio Abad, located about 100m/100yd east of Casa de Colón, before setting off into the unknown. The chapel, the first Christian place of worship on the island, was built in the 15th century and completely restored in the 18th century.

Centro Atlántico de Arte Moderno (CAAM)

Only a few steps from Columbus' house in Calle de los Balcones 9/11 is the Atlantic Centre of Modern Art (Centro Atlántico de Arte Moderno, CAAM for short). While the façade is still original 18th-century work, the interior was completely restored in the 1980s. Exhibition rooms and offices on five storeys are grouped around a covered courtyard. This architectural style was intended to create a dialogue between traditional and modern styles. A collection of works by contemporary Canarian and Spanish artists is on display. There are also rotating exhibitions accompanied by courses and lectures. For visitors there is also a library, videotheque and a collection of periodicals.

❶ Tue – Sat 10am – 9pm, Sun 10am – 2pm, free admission

**Museo Canario

Museo Canario, the pre-eminent museum on the islands, is located on Calle Dr. Verneau 2, south of Plaza de Santa Ana. It opened in 1880 and was completely reconstructed in the 1980s. It is presently being expanded. It gives excellent Insight s into the life and **culture of the early Canarians**; the archaeological finds and anthropological exhibits are supplemented by models and graphics. One room holds a model of living quarters with utensils and various ceramic articles of the early Canarians. On display are also more than 1,000 skulls (including some on which brain surgery was performed), numerous skeletons and some mummies. A reconstruction of the **necropolis of La Guancha** (►Gáldar) shows how the dead were interred. An exact replica of the **Cueva Pintada** of Gáldar has also been reproduced in the Museo Canario. Among the many items of ceramics, jewellery and utensils, the stone hand mills and the so-called pintaderas are noteworthy. The exact purpose of the pintaderas is still not known. Since no two of these wood or ceramic »stamps« are alike, it is assumed that they were used to make a personal mark on objects. The best-known early Canarian work of art is the **Idol of Tara**. The 30cm/12in statue with grotesquely fat limbs appears female, even though it has no breasts (► ill. p. 42). The museum also has a reference library with about 40,000 books related to the Canary Islands or written by Canarian authors.

❶ Mon – Fri 10am – 8pm, Sat and Sun 10am – 2pm;
library: Mon – Fri 10am – 8pm, admission €4, www.elmuseocanario.com

Iglesia de Santo Domingo

A few steps south of the museum on Plaza Santo Domingo stands the church of Santo Domingo. It dates from the 17th and 18th centuries, and is one of the most beautiful in Las Palmas. Note the magnificent Baroque altars and several statues by Luján Pérez inside.

Maspalomas · Meloneras

D 3

Elevation: sea level
Population: 600

Maspalomas and Playa del Inglés together form the core of the Costa Canaria, the tourist region in southern Gran Canaria. The landmark of Maspalomas is its lighthouse, and the unique dunes to the east are one of the island's biggest attractions. In Melonaras west of the luxury hotels at the lighthouse another exclusive resort area was created.

Unlike the bustling ▶Playa del Inglés, Maspalomas is a quiet luxury-class holiday resort. Some of Gran Canaria's best hotel complexes and an exclusive golf course with every amenity are located here.

**They give the Costa Canaria its charm:
the dunes at Maspalomas**

It all began in the 1960s west of the mouth of Barranco de Maspalomas, which runs through the developed area. Along with a handful of four-star and five-star hotels the most luxurious resorts on Gran Canaria are here, set in a magnificent grove of palm trees. Behind them are the Campo de Golf and Campo Internacional. Some of the complexes are not close to the beach, so they try to compensate with a free shuttle service.

WHAT TO SEE IN MASPALOMAS

**Dunas de Maspalomas
An area of massive **sand dunes**, the only one of its kind on the Canary Islands, extends to the south of the tourist city. It is a long time since they were an untouched landscape – there are footprints everywhere – but the high shifting sand dunes make an impressive picture with their wind-formed, pale yellow shapes.

The sand consists almost completely of carbonates and comes from the sea. The highest dunes, some reaching 10 – 20m (30 – 65ft), are closest to the water. Some of the dune valleys further inland have vegetation, but only a small part of the original dry growth has remained. Tourism has its price.

In the late 1980s, however, Gran Canarians had a change of heart. Today 328ha/810 acres in the western part of the dunes are a nature reserve. Around the lagoon **Charca de Maspalomas** a new belt of sea grass is forming and many birds have discovered it as an ideal habitat, but the ecological balance in this area is still endangered.

> **?**
> **MARCO POLO INSIGHT**
>
> *Wandering dunes*
>
> The dunes of Maspalomas wander westwards ... The constant northeast Passat winds see to it that this mass of sand moves 2 to 5 m (6 to 16 ft) to the west every year until its weight and growth of vegetation stops the movement. This shift can take up to 500 years to complete.

**Playa de Maspalomas
The beach in front of the dunes is almost 4km/2.5mi long, from the mouth of Barranco de Maspalomas to Punta de Maspalomas, where it meets Playa del Inglés. This extensive beach is one of the most beautiful places for swimming on the Canary Islands. Paseo Marítima Oasis leads to Playa de Maspalomas. The Balneario Municipal here has showers, WCs and lockers. The only really busy part is the guarded section of beach by the hotels near the oasis. There is a **nude bathing zone** further to the east. Those who do not want to be disturbed retreat into the dunes.

Oasis de Maspalomas
The **Faro de Maspalomas** on the south-western edge of Maspalomas at the mouth of the barranco is the landmark of Oasis de Maspalomas. The lighthouse is 56m/184ft high and was the first building in

Maspalomas/Meloneras

Calderín

Palmitos Park,
Aqua Sur

Goya **Fataga**

EL TABLERO

Maldonado
Brasil
Joventud
Avenida del

Monterrey

Gaudí
Dalí

EL LOMO

San Salvador

Autopista G.C. 1

SAN FERNANDO

Autopista G.C. 1

Puerto Rico

de Trajana

Las Palmas

Centro
de Salud

Avenida Alejandro del Castillo

**Guardia
Civil**

Mercado
Municipal

Piscina
Municipal

Av. de Tunte

Casa de la
Cultura

SONNENLAND

Palmeral
5º Centenario

Estadio

Avenida de   Tejeda

Mílares
Carló

Escuela de Holiday
Turismo World
Ayuntamiento

G.C. 500

Ocean
Park

Cruce de
Laviuda
de Franco

Avenida del Gran Canaria

Agustín
Einstein

Policía
Local

Avenida del TUI

PLAYA DEL INGLÉS

EL HORNILLO

Mar
Tirreno

CAMPO
INTERNACIONAL

Av. T. Finnmatkat

Avenida

Avenida de Gran Canaria

Alfereces Provisional

G.C. 500

Av. de Cristóbal Colón

G.C. 500

Avenida del TUI

Barranco de Maspalomas

Faro 2

Avenida del Neckermann

Avenida

de Estados Unide

Avenida de

Avenida de Bonn

G.C. 500

Neckermann

MASPALOMAS

5

Club
de Golf

6

Campo de Golf

Tirajana

Avenida de Alema

MELONERAS

Avenida del

Avenida de

Gran Canaria

Avenida de Alemania

Meloneras

Palacio
de Congresos

9

Reserva
Natural Especial

Pasao Costa Canaria

aya de
s Mujeres

8

Avenida de Cristóbal Colón

Estación
de Guaguas

Charca de
Maspalomas

Dunas de   Maspalomas

2

1

5 6

OASIS DE
MASPALOMAS

2

7

4

3

Plaza
de Colón

3 1

2

Plaza
del Faro

4

Playa
del Faro

Faro
Maspalomas

500 m

© BAEDEKER

Playa de Maspalomas

Océano Atlántico

Maspalomas

INFORMATION
Tourist information in Playa del Inglés (▶p. 199).

SHOPPING
The shopping centres Faro II and Varadero on the Costa Meloneras have a great variety of shops.

NIGHTLIFE
Maspalomas does not cater for nighthawks in the way that Playa del Inglés does. Anyone looking for entertainment should go there.

WHERE TO EAT
❶ L'Orangerie
€€€€
Avenide del Oasis in the Palm Beach Hotel
Tel. 928 72 10 32; open Mon, Wed, Fri and Sat from 6.30pm, reservations recommended
The best for ambience, service and food. Prices to match. The cuisine is French-inspired, the wine list simply excellent.

WHERE TO STAY
❶ Grand Hotel Residencia
€€€€
Avenida del Oasis 32
Tel. 928 72 31 00
www.grand-hotel-residencia.com
It is the only hotel on Gran Canaria that is a member of the exclusive Leading Hotels of the World. In a style influenced by colonial architecture, it is located in the midst of a magnificent palm garden near the Maspalomas dunes. Special attention is paid to an environmentally friendly hotel management. Excellent gourmet cuisine, exclusive spa.

❷ Riu Grand Palace Maspalomas
€€€€
Plaza de las Palmeras
Tel. 928 14 14 48
www.riu.com
The promise is in the name: This five-star hotel (local classification) of the RIU Group seems a bit like an oasis. The extensive park with old palm trees is open only to hotel guests. During the day residents meet at the large swimming pool or at the pool bar, in the evenings in the exquisite restaurant or for a drink at the bar; regular live music or shows.

❸ Palm Beach
€€€€
Avenida del Oasis
Tel. 928 72 10 32
www.hotel-palm-beach.com
The seven-storey semi-circular, five-star hotel is not very attractive from the outside, but after remodelling by the famous architect Alberto Pinto, the interior is quite elegant. There is a new and luxurious spa area.

❹ IFA-Hotel Faro
€€€
Plaza de Colón
Tel. 928 14 22 14
www.lopesan.com
The five-storey hotel at the Maspalomas lighthouse has bright and friendly rooms. The garden is quite small however and there is not always enough room for all sunbathers.

❺ Bungalows Dunas Maspalomas
€€   €€€
Avenida Air Marin s/n
Campo Internacional
Tel. 928 14 09 12
www.dunashoteles.com
262 bungalows scattered through nicely planted, extensive grounds. The next main road is far away. The magnificent dune beach of Maspalomas is only 1km/0.5mi away and a shuttle bus runs three times a day. There are also three pools for sunbathers.

❻ Bungalows Cordial Green Golf
€€
Avenida Tjaereborg 2
Campo Internacional
Tel. 928 77 39 49
www.cordialcanarias.com
Bungalow complex right next to the Maspalomas golf course. It is well suited for guests who want peace and quiet on their holiday. While each apartment is furnished for three people, they are not very spacious. Must be booked for at least 5 days.

this area. Its light can be seen for 25km/15mi. Oasis de Maspalomas is the most exclusive hotel area in the tourist city. Little has remained of the originally lush vegetation, except for what can be seen in the hotel gardens. A few palms have survived north of the hotels. **Paseo del Faro** runs parallel to the coast and is lined with restaurants and shops.

On the east side of Barranco de Maspalomas from a parking lot at Plazoleta Hernando Colón it is only a short walk to a large **camel station**. Half-hour rides into the dunes are offered. But some of the animals are in pitiable shape.
❶ daily 9am – 4pm, admission €12

Camello Safari

The area that borders the Maspalomas golf course on the north is called Campo Internacional. It consists of new bungalow settlements surrounded by green lawns. While the tourist centres and beach are a mile or two distant, many of the guests appreciate this very fact: The usual bustle is far away.

Campo Internacional

East of Campo Internacional the entrance to the small but fine botanical garden is on Avenida del Touroperador Neckermann. The park is about 12,000 m² in size and holds about 500 different **tropical and subtropical plants** to admire. Suitable to a botanical garden almost all of them are labeled with their scientific names. The garden was

*Parque Botánico de Maspalomas

only planted a few years ago, which explains the many relatively young trees. The attractions include various kinds of palms, including Bismarck, royal and bottle palms, there are also calabash and sausage trees. The pride of the garden is an African baobab tree. There is a small department for endemic succulents and euphorbiae, also decorative plants, fruit trees and cultivated plants.

❶ Mon – Fri 10am – 6pm, free admission

Mirador de Golf
The **observation point** on Plaza Hierro above the botanical garden gives a splendid view of the Maspalomas golf course and the expansive bungalow complexes of Campo Internacional. Enjoy the panorama at your leisure from the cafeteria terrace, with the tourist information office next door.

Holiday World
On the northern edge of Campo Internacional, Holiday World attracts young and old. The 1.4ha/3.5-acre site has a 27m/88ft Ferris wheel, a roller coaster, various carousels, scooter cars, a Mississippi paddle-wheeler on an artificial lake and a bowling lane. Tall palm trees, cacti and agaves as well as flowering plants, a biotope and fountains set the scene, and restaurants and pubs offer refreshments and food.

Admission to the extensive park grounds is free. Anyone who wants to ride the roller coaster or any other ride buys a magnetic card (tarjeta) for 5 to 20 €, from which every ride is deducted by the card readers. The magnet card is transferable and can be used for up to one month.

❶ Summer daily 6pm – midnight, winter Sun – Thu 5pm – 11pm, Fri and Sat 5pm – midnight, www.holidayworld-maspalomas.es

Aqualand
Ocean Park, north of the motorway on the road to Los Palmitos is a hit with kids. Turbo- and kamikaze slides, river rides, a wave pool and other attractions keep the parents entertained too. There is a pool for adults that is quieter than the big pool.

❶ daily 10am – 5pm, Jul / Aug 10am – 6pm, admission €25, children €18

WHAT TO SEE IN MELONARAS

The as yet relatively new resort area on the Costa Canaria is located west of the Maspalomas light house. The building started here in the mid-1990s, and the quarter with upmarket hotels, good food and uniquely designed shopping centres is a pleasant change from the in part worn-out infrastructure in Playa del Inglés or Puerto Rico. There is currently room for more than 6,000 guests in the luxury resort. The two flagships of this new urban area are the five-star resorts Villa del Conde and the only recently constructed Baobab Resort of the

Lopesan-Group. Other nearby upmarket hotels and the Lopesan 18 hole golf course attract wealthy guests. All of the hotels, of course, have generous spas.

The **ocean promenade** is the heart of the up and coming area. It begins west of the Maspalomas lighthouse and runs to Playa de Meloneras, about a 30-minute walk. The first hotel along the promenade is Hotel Lopesan Costa Meloneras, whose pools cascade down to the promenade in a small waterfall. The restaurants in front of the two shopping centres Boulevard El Faro and Varadero are always bustling. But the beach is stony here and not suitable for sunbathing. ***Paseo Meloneras**

In front of the Varadero shopping centre are the modest remains of an ancient Canarian settlement, consisting of three foundations of houses. The **archaeological site** right next to the ocean is unusual since the ancient Canarians preferred to settle in the mountains. The exact date of the fenced-in wall remnants cannot be determined at present; bone and tool finds cover the 7th to the 17th century. **Punta Mujeres**

The completely white Riu Palace Meloneras, the Clubhotel Riu Gran Canaria with ist blue and white tiled tent roofs and the colonially inspired Villa del Conde are the next hotels along the Paseo Meloneras. The Villa del Conde allows a view of the wave pool in the lower level. The grounds with the copy of the Agüimes parish church and buildings painted in soft pastel tones looks like a Canarian town. **Other very large hotels**

Just after the Villa del Conde the natural beach Playa de las Mujeres (women's beach), which is never crowded, invites a swim. The about 300m/1,000ft long strip of sand is interrupted by a few rocks. **Playa de las Mujeres**

Unlike Playa de las Mujeres, this is an artificially constructed beach and supplies sun umbrellas and lounge chairs; there are also lifeguards. Halfway between Faro Maspalomas and the yacht harbour Pasito Blanco is Playa de Meloneras, currently the western-most community on the Costa Canaria. Here Restaurants and bars line the promenade along the fine-sanded beach as well. The Meloneras Playa shopping centre however appears to have been a bad investment; until now most of the shops have remained empty. **Playa de Meloneras**

The new congress and event centre is located away from the ocean within walking distance of the large hotels, but looks a bit lost in the middle of an undeveloped area. Its crooked form marks it as a postmodern structure. The building has several halls that can be used for different kinds of events; sporting events (tennis Fed Cup), exhibits and fashion shows take place here. The Auditorio Las Tirajanas with room for 800 people has a stage for classical and pop concerts, and **Expo Meloneras**

Meloneras

SHOPPING
Compared to the unimaginative shopping centres in Playa del Inglés or Puerto Rico, the centros comerciales in Meloneras are not only more attractive, they also offer more quality, but at much higher prices. One of the best shopping centres is the C.C. Varadero.

WHERE TO EAT
❷ Bali €€ – €€€
Mar Mediterraneo 2
Tel. 928 14 33 71
www.restaurantebali.com
It opened in 1978 in Playa del Inglés and moved to its new location in 2011 in the 2nd floor of the Shopping Centre Oasis Boulevard in Meloneras. The Indonesian restaurant enriches the Costa Canaria with classic dishes like nasi goreng, gado-gado (vegetable salad) and babi guling (roast suckling pig). The Balinese rice table with its 17 different dishes offers a survey of Indonesian cooking.

❸ Grill Faro €€€ – €€€€
Paseo Meloneras
Shopping Centre Boulevard Faro
Tel. 928 14 53 79
www.restaurantegrillfaro.com
The popular grill restaurant lies on the ocean promenade within view of the Maspalomas lighthouse. Along with fish and meat from the grill, there is also rabbit, olives from Gran Canaria and goat cheese from Fuerteventura.

❹ Maximilians €€ – €€€
Paseo Meloneras
Shopping Centre Boulevard Faro
Tel. 928 14 70 34
This café restaurant on the Costa Melo-

neras promenade serves tasty sandwiches, tortillas and salads as well as good apple strudel, about 20 different coffee specialities or a Caribbean cocktail. Next door is a pizza and pasta restaurant with the same name.

❺ Pingüino Soul € _Insider Tip_
Paseo Meloneras
Tel. 928 14 21 81
Large ice cream shop in an excellent location on the promenade in front of Varadero Shopping Centre. Along with huge ice cream creations, the various unusual truffle praline specialties are worth trying.

❻ Rias €€€ – €€€€
Shopping Centre Varadero
Tel. 928 14 17 68.
Very popular fish restaurant. The owner has a second fish restaurant with the same name in Playa del Inglés (next to the Yumbo Centrum).

WHERE TO STAY
❼ Lopesan Costa Meloneras _Insider Tip_
€€€ – €€€€
Mar Mediterráneo 1
Tel. 928 12 81 00
www.lopesan.com
Location, size and architecture make this four-star resort of the Lopesan Group, which opened in 2001, a superlative hotel. 1,136 rooms and suites in all, several restaurants, bars and a shopping arcade are spread over 20 buildings surrounded by 76,000m²/820,000sq ft of grounds with wonderful pools and hundreds of palm trees. The rooms are light and with 35m²/370sq ft quite spacious. Extras include an extensive Spa Centre, two 18-

hole golf courses nearby. But the food and the very large dining rooms are especially enjoyed by all of the guests.

❽ Riu Palace Meloneras Resort €€€ – €€€€
Urbanización Meloneras
Tel. 928 14 31 82
www.riu.com
The comfortable four-star hotel with about 450 rooms was the starting point in the 1990s for the development of Costa Meloneras. The rounded four-storey main building with crenelated towers and two adjoining but somewhat lower wings and a pool is set right on the ocean promenade. There are shows in the evenings for entertainment. Nearby is the Clubhotel Gran Canaria, also part of the Riu Group, an all inclusive resort.

❾ Villa del Conde €€€€
Meloneras
Mar Medeterraneo 7
Tel. 928 56 32 00
www.lopesan.com
As soon as you enter the hotel through the ostentatius lobby – built like the Agüimes parish church – you feel like you're in a small town of its own. The 561 rooms and suites are spread over several buildings built in Canarian style. Even a plaza with terrace café was added. The pool landscape is spread over several levels, and you feel at home immediately in the indoor pool and beauty centre. From an architectural point of view Villa del Conde is certainly one of the best resorts on the island.

Lopesan Costa Meloneras

ballet. Open-air events are held under a giant sun sail with room for a further 800 spectators.

Pasito Blanco West of Maspalomas a cul-de-sac runs to the **yacht harbour** Pasito Blanco 4km/2.5mi away. There is normally a barrier, but visitors are usually allowed to enter. A seaside promenade will soon connect Playa de Meloneras with Pasito Blanco.

El Tablero El Tablero is located 4km/2.5mi north of the motorway, which forms a natural boundary to the tourist centres. This somewhat faceless village developed parallel to the growing tourism on the southern coast and is mainly a dormer village for the employees of the tourist industry.

**Palmitos Park Turn left just before the western edge of Maspalomas and follow the GC 503 north into the mountains to get to Palmitos Park (about 10km/6mi to Maspalomas). The gardens were planted in a steep-walled valley on more than 20ha/49 acres. While it was not spared from forest fires in 2007, it has since then been rebuilt. The park is home to 50 different varieties of palms, countless cacti and agaves. Along with a few gibbon monkeys there are about 230 species of birds. Ducks and swans swim on the pond in the centre of the park, and flamingos and peacocks strut around the lawns. The main attraction is the dolphin arena with room for 1500 spectators, where two shows with the intelligent ocean mammals are performed daily (1pm

! MARCO ⊕ POLO TIP

Casa de los Músicos **Insider Tip**

The pianist and conductor Justus Frantz has created a leafy paradise for himself in the hinterland of Maspalomas. The good news is that guests are welcome. The main house has two double rooms and two suites that can be reserved. Guests are welcome to use the sauna, pool and tennis court. The finca is located in the middle of an organic orchard and vineyard.
Information and reservations through
Finca Justus Frantz
Monte León 4
Tel. 928 14 22 18
www.fincajustusfrantz.com

In Palmitos Park dolphins are the stars

and 4pm). There are other animal shows with parrots and hunting birds. Visitors can watch hundreds of butterflies from all over the world fly around the **butterfly house**. There is also an **aquarium** with fish from local waters as well as tropical fish and freshwater fish. Buses leave regularly for the park from various stops in Maspalomas, San Agustín and Puerto Rico; buses from Maspalomas run at least every 30 minutes.

Insider Tip

❶ daily 10am – 6pm, admission €28.50

Maspalomas' upper-class neighbourhood is Monte León, about 7km/4mi north-west of the centre. Of the many magnificent villas here, some belong to celebrities. Among them is the pianist and conductor Justus Frantz, who has hosted such celebrities as Leonard Bernstein, Steffi Graf and German chancellor Helmut Schmidt.

Monte León

Mogán

✳ C 2

Elevation: 250m/825ft above sea level
Population: 23,000 (entire district)

Mogán at the upper end of the barranco of the same name is the administrative seat of the coast between Arguineguín and Puerto de Mogán. The district is one of the richest in Gran Canaria because of the tax income that the tourist industry generates – even though Mogán was a remote mountain village until only a few years ago.

The village has only 700 residents and nestles at the foot of high mountains; it is bordered by fertile farmland divided into small fields. Thanks to the plentiful water supplies in the area, many residents have been able to maintain lush gardens around their cottages. Lemons, mangos, aubergines, papayas and other tropical fruits thrive here. Flowers are grown in hot-houses for export.

AROUND MOGÁN

Azulejos From the main road that connects Mogán with ▶La Aldea de San Nicolás, about 10km/6mi beyond Mogán there is a cliff that radiates many colours. It is called Azulejos (»tiles«). Iron hydrate and

---

Mogán

WHERE TO EAT
Acaymo €€ – €€€
Barrio del Tostador 14
Tel. 928 56 92 63; closed Mon
The trip is worthwhile: outstanding Canarian food and a marvellous view of the valley from the terrace.

Casa Enrique €€ – €€€
Calle San José 7; tel. 928 56 95 42
Located on the main street in the centre of town, this restaurant serves typical Canarian cooking and small dishes. But the sidewalk is too narrow for sitting outside.

WHERE TO STAY
Finca in Mogán € – €€
between Mogán und Puerto de Mogán
Islas Canarias Reisen
Tel. 0049 2924 974 69 30 (Germany)
www.islas-canarias-reisen.de
The holiday house, furnished in Spanish country style, is located in the Barranco de Mogán and has two holiday flats that can be rented separately. The smaller one has one bedroom and is designed for two people; the larger one has a separate entrance and room for four people. The agent also has other fincas around Mogán.

other iron compounds make the different shades of green in the rock.

About 2km/1¼mi above Mogán a narrow road runs through remote, untouched mountain scenery to several reservoirs in the interior and then on to **Ayacata** (about 20km/12mi). There are also magnificent views back into the **Barranco de Mogán**. After countless curves and turns comes one of Gran Canaria's largest continuous pine forests. The relatively open forest extends from the Inagua (1,426m/4,678ft above sea level) in the west to Roque Nublo, the mountain in the clouds, in the east.

Detour to the interior

Moya

✳ **B 3**

Elevation: 488m/1,601ft above sea level
Population: 8,000 (entire district)

Moya, the administrative centre of Moya district, is situated in the foothills of the central mountain range about 30km/20mi west of Las Palmas. The Canarian physician and poet Tomás Morales (1883 – 1921) was born here. Near Moya the remains of an original laurel forest have been placed under strict protection.

Moya is a pretty mountain village set on a rock plateau. The most beautiful view of the town is from the GC 700, the road that connects Moya with Santa María de Guía. In the centre of the town the parish church stands on a shady plaza.

WHAT TO SEE IN MOYA

The Iglesia del Pilar was built in the mid-20th century. It has fine statues of saints and woodcarvings. There is a wonderful view of Barranco de Moya from behind the church.

Iglesia del Pilar

The birthplace of Tomás Morales, which is right next to the church, now houses a small museum with Morales' private possessions and a library. The rooms are also used for public events. Morales spent his childhood and youth in Moya. He studied medicine in Cádiz and Madrid and later worked as a doctor in Agaete. Morales' poetry describes the sea in lyrical verses.

Museo Casa Morales

❶ Mon – Fri 9am – 8pm, Sat 10am – 2pm and 5pm – 8pm,
Sun 10am – 2pm, free admission

AROUND MOYA

*Los Tilos de Moya — Most visitors come to Moya to visit the **laurel woods** (Los Tilos de Moya) in Barranco de Moya. At one time much of Gran Canaria was covered with woods like this one. To get there follow the main road from Moya towards Santa María de Guía. Turn off to the left at the sign »Los Tilos« and drive into the valley. On the valley floor the laurel woods border the road for about 200m/200yd. The dark green laurel leaves do not let much light through to the floor of the woods and there is a slightly musty odour. The surroundings hint at how lush the vegetation must have been here once.

San Bartolomé de Fontanales — The narrow road (only for very experienced drivers!) winds through Tilos de Moya and on through Barranco del Laurel (»laurel tree«). At the upper end of the barranco the hamlet San Bartolomé de Fontanales lies in luxuriant greenery. This is one of the rainiest regions of Gran Canaria.

Playa del Inglés

✦ D 3

Elevation: Sea level
Population: 6000

Playa del Inglés and ▶ Maspalomas have merged and are by far the largest tourist area on the island. There are more tourist centres to the east and west; all of them together are called the Costa Canaria.

Playa del Inglés owes its popularity to the broad beach that stretches southwards for 4km/2.5mi to Punta de Maspalomas. The beaches can always be reached by bus from hotels that are further away. There is a good system of public transport on the Costa Canaria, and a drive to Las Palmas 50km/30mi away takes only about 30 minutes on the motorway.

Spain's largest tourist resort — Don Alejandro del Castillo, Conde de la Vega Grande, the owner of this otherwise unusable land, got the idea of building a holiday resort there in the late 1950s. Until that time there was not even a fishing village in the south and only one small paved road went there. But the expansion soon began. The count, whose family tree went back to Maciot de Béthencourt (▶ History, Famous people), founded various construction companies and gained a monopoly over the water supply. By the late 1960s his investment was beginning to pay off: Tourists came in droves to the new hotels and apartments. Today

Playa del Inglés

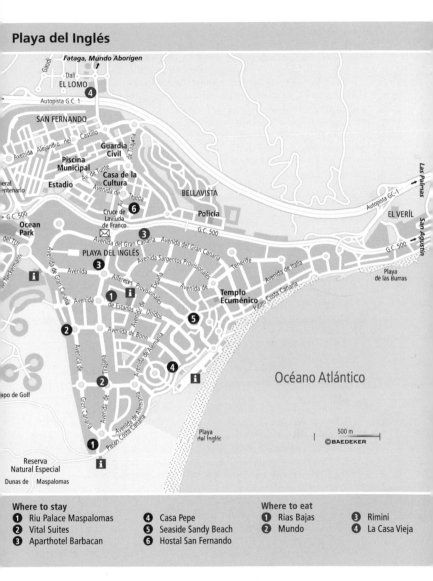

Fataga, Mundo Aborigen
Gaudí
Dalí
EL LOMO ❹
Autopista G.C. 1
SAN FERNANDO
Avenida Alejandro del Castillo
de Trajana
Guardia
Civil
Piscina
Municipal
Av. de Tunte
Casa de la
Cultura
Estadio
Avenida de Tejeda
eral
centenario
Cruce de
Laviuda
de Franco
Ocean
Park
✉
❻
BELLAVISTA
Policía
G.C. 500
Avenida del Gran Canaria
Avenida del Gran Canaria
❸
G.C. 500
❸
PLAYA DEL INGLÉS
ℹ
Avenida de Gran Canaria
Avenida
Avenida Sargentos Provisionales
Tenerife
Alféreces Provisionales
Avenida de Legata
Avenida de
❶
ℹ
Avenida de Estados de Unidos
Templo
Ecuménico
Paseo Costa Canaria
❷
❺
ℹ
Avenida de Bonn
Avenida de Alemania
del Neckermann
Avenida de Gran Canaria
Avenida de Trajana
Avenida de
❷
❹
ℹ
Océano Atlántico
Avenida de Gran Canaria
Avenida de Alemania
Paseo Costa Canaria
❶
Playa
del Inglés
500 m
© BAEDEKER
Reserva
Natural Especial
Dunas de Maspalomas
ℹ
Autopista GC-1
EL VERÍL
G.C. 500
Las Palmas
San Agustín
Playa
de las Burras

Where to stay
- ❶ Riu Palace Maspalomas
- ❷ Vital Suites
- ❸ Aparthotel Barbacan
- ❹ Casa Pepe
- ❺ Seaside Sandy Beach
- ❻ Hostal San Fernando

Where to eat
- ❶ Rias Bajas
- ❷ Mundo
- ❸ Rimini
- ❹ La Casa Vieja

Playa del Inglés and the surrounding communities have almost 150,000 hotel beds - the largest »tourist village« in Spain, and more are being added all the time.

Artificial holiday resort

At first glance it is evident that Playa del Inglés did not grow naturally. The city consists of nothing but large hotels, bungalow and apartment complexes, giant shopping centres, countless restaurants, cafés and discos – it could be anywhere. Depending on the season, the broad four-lane roads and large roundabouts either hardly cope with the traffic or seem to be abandoned. In the small side streets of Playa del Inglés it is easy to get lost because all the hotel complexes surrounded by flower gardens look alike. The local people live to the north of Playa del Inglés in **San Fernando**. You either love Playa del Inglés or you can't stand it.

> **MARCO POLO TIP**
>
> **Sightseeing on a mini-train** _Insider Tip_
>
> About every half hour a replica of a miniature Western train from 1864 runs through the streets of the holiday centre. It is a good way to get a first or second impression of Playa del Inglés. The »mini tren« is especially popular with children. Daily 10am – noon and 4pm – 8pm

Playa del Inglés

The uncontested focal point of Playa del Inglés is the **beach**. The »English beach« is named after British holiday guests who came to Gran Canaria more than a hundred years ago looking for relaxation. However, they went to Las Palmas since the southern coast was completely uninhabited. Today German guests are in the majority, at least during the winter. On sunny days, of which there are on average 300 every year on the Costa Canaria, tens of thousands of people swarm over the 4km/2.5mi-long super-beach. It is fortunately up to 300m/1,000ft wide in some places.

Paseo Costa Canaria

In Playa del Inglés the Paseo Costa Canaria borders the beach. The beach promenade has a wonderful view of the dunes, especially in the evenings. Stroll along the Paseo Costa Canaria to the east as far as ▶San Agustín, to the west to Costa Meloneras.

Reserva Natural

At the southern-most point there is one of the most beautiful views of the Maspalomas dunes from Hotel Riu Palace Maspalomas. Many holiday guests use this as a starting point for a walk through the dunes, which are as tall as houses. A small visitor's centre (Centro de Visitantes, unfortunately often closed) informs on the sensitive ecosystem.

Sport and fun

As would be expected of the largest tourist centre in Spain, the sports and entertainment attractions on the Costa Canaria are beyond measure. Equipment for all sorts of water sports can be rented at Playa del Inglés.

AROUND PLAYA DEL INGLÉS

*Mundo Aborigen

From Playa del Inglés drive north through San Fernando towards Fataga. The theme park and outdoor museum Mundo Aborigen is

Playa del Inglés

INFORMATION
Centro Insular de Turismo
Yumbo Centrum
Avenida España / corner Avenida de Estados de Unidos; tel. 928 77 15 50
Hours: Mon – Fri 9am – 9pm, Sat 9am – 1pm

PUBLIC TRANSPORT
The communities of the Costa Canaria are widely spread but connected by a dense network of public transport. A bus schedule of Global Bus Company is available in the information office in the Yumbo Centrum.

SHOPPING
Shopping Centres
There are several large shopping centres, including Kasbah and Yumbo. These expansive shopping zones not only have huge supermarkets, but also various shops and above all many restaurants. Prices can differ greatly from one shop to another. Groceries are cheapest in the supermarkets in San Fernando – the locals like to shop here too. The government-run FEDAC shop next to the tourist information in ther Yumbo Centrum has guaranteed authentic Canarian crafts.

Mercado
San Fernando; Wed, Sat 8am – 2pm
The weekly market also sells fresh groceries at relatively reasonable prices.

NIGHTLIFE
Playa del Inglés is known all over the Canaries for its extravagant club scene.

The Beckham Bar in Playa del Inglés is absolutely »in«

Shopping centre in the tourist area

Nightlife is concentrated on the shopping centre Kasbah. The not-so-young crowd prefers the clubs in Centro Comerciales Cita. As the night advances, Yumbo Centrum turns into the largest gay venue of the Canary Islands. About 30 night bars, pubs, sex shops and dark rooms open on the upper floors.

Oficina Cultural Maspalomas
Avenida de Tirajana
at Hotel Rey Carlos
Tel. 928 77 82 45
The cultural office has tickets for all major cultural events on the island and they will also arrange for transportation.

WHERE TO EAT
❶ Rias Bajas
€€€ – €€€€
Avenida Tirajana / corner Avenida de Estados de Unidos
Next to the Yumbo Centrum
Tel. 928 76 40 33
This fish restaurant is also popular among the local people and one of the best in town. Fish and seafood is cooked Galician-style. Table decoration is formal but there is no terrace. The owner has another fish restaurant with the same name in Meloneras (Shopping Centre Varadero).

❷ Mundo €€ – €€€
Avenida de Tirajana
Tel. 928 93 78 50
Closed Sat. and Sun.
Small bistro-style restaurant. The modern fusion cuisine covers everything from oriental falafel to Indian curries to Thai fishburgers.

❸ Rimini €€€
Avenida de Gran Canaria 28
(next to Eugenia Victoria Hotel)
Tel. 928 76 41 87
Nice little restaurant. Dine in a winter garden and enjoy classic Italian cooking like risotto, ossobuco alla Milanese and tiramisu.

❹ *La Casa Vieja* €€ – €€€
Carretera de Fataga
El Lomo 139
Tel. 928 76 90 10
www.grillrestaurantelacasavieja.com
A huge restaurant opened in southern
Gran Canaria in 1978 and is one of the
old favourites. It is located at the northern edge of San Fernando on the GC-
60 to Fataga. Grill dishes and classic Canarian cooking is on the menu, like goat
and marinated rabbit.

WHERE TO STAY
❶ *Riu Palace Maspalomas* €€€
Plaza de Fuerteventura 1   **Insider Tip**
Tel. 928 76 95 00; www.riu.com
Riu Palace offers the best view of the
dunes in Maspalomas. The rooms have
luxurious bathrooms. The garden is a
good place to relax. Both tennis courts
have floodlights and a gym and a beautiful sauna area are also part of the com-
forts of this house.

❷ *Vital Suites* €€€
Avenida Gran Canaria 80
Tel 928 73 02 33; ww.vitalsuites.com
Located in the quiet western part of Playa del Inglés, the 56 generous apartments, a thalasso spa designed like a
Roman bath and a wonderful view of
the Maspalomas golf course give this
facility top marks.

❸ *Aparthotel Barbacan* €€€
Avenida de Tirajana 27
Tel. 928 77 20 30; www.barbacan.es
The five-storey apartment building has
an inner courtyard with flourishing
plants and a pool. Some people will not
like the location. Even though all rooms
face the courtyard, the house is right in
the middle of bustling Playa del Inglés,

where the traffic noise has reached big-
city level. The apartments are well equip-
ped and have one or two bedrooms. The
food in the restaurants is excellent, and
the generous and varied breakfast buffet
deserves a special mention.

❹ *Casas Pepe* €
Avenida de Bonn 1
Tel 928 76 28 18
www.casas-pepe.com
The 53 roomy apartments are spread
over three two-storey buildings, located
at the upper end of the beach promenade and it is not far to the dunes either. Simply furnished but very popular
due to its location near the beach.

**❺ *Seaside Sandy Beach*
€€€**
Calle Los Menceyes 1
Tel. 928 72 40 00
www.seaside-hotels.com
A good place not only for parents. Playground, children's activities and professional childminding are available, so that
the whole family is satisfied. The 256
rooms are furnished suitably and have
balconies and marble bathrooms. But
the location in the cramped urban centre is not for everyone.

❻ *Hostal San Fernando* €
Calle La Palma 16
Tel. 928 76 39 51
www.hostalsf.comze.com
Don't expect much comfort or a good
view in the cheapest accommodation on
the Costa Canaria. This bed & breakfast
is on the northern edge of town and has
60 clean rooms without ensuite bathrooms. Especially popular among
young adults.

On a nice day no one is ever alone on the Playa del Inglés

about 6km/3.5mi away. The park has an area of about 11ha/27 acres and depicts the everyday life of the early Canarian settlers. Simple stone round houses, the residence of the guanarteme (king), barns and workshops, burial grounds – in short, a complete Guanche village has been built here in replica. Life-size figures depict everyday scenes, such as men and women working in the fields, priestesses performing rituals and even a public execution. There is also a small archaeological museum with original finds. The park has a spectacular location with an excellent view of the breathtaking mountains and Barranco de Fataga from several vantage points.

❶ daily 9am – 6pm, admission €10

✶✶ Pozo de las Nieves

─✳─ C 3

Höhe: 1,949m/3,094ft above sea level

Gran Canaria's highest mountain, Pozo de las Nieves (»snow well«) or Pico de las Nieves (»snow peak«), is in the centre of the island. Snow lies on the mountain for only a few days a year – and then only for a short time.

The peak of Pozo de las Nieves, where there are radar and TV antennae, is easy to reach on three roads that start at Cruz de Tejeda near Ayacata or in Telde. Coming from Ayacata drive past **Presa de los Hornos**, the highest reservoir on the island at 1,550m/5,085ft.

After the mountain restaurant La Cumbre near the picnic area Llanos de la Pez turn right onto the road to Telde; after 2km/1.2mi comes the turnoff to the right (GC 134) to Pozo del las Nieves. The peak is a military zone but just below it the Mirador Los Pechos offers a wide view all the way to the coast.

Mirador Los Pechos

A few steps below the observation point a »snow well« (Pozo de las Nieves) from 1699 was reconstructed. The island residents used to fill the shaft, which is 10m/33ft deep and 5 – 7m/16 – 23ft wide, with compressed snow in the winter. The ice remained until summer and was then transported to Las Palmas, where it was used for cooling during hospital operations, for example. There used to be three snow wells around the peak.

Snow well

From Mirador Los Pechos the narrow road leads around the military zone and ends after 600m/1,980ft at Mirador Pico de las Nieves, which offers a spectakular panorama of the Roque Nublo and Roque Bentaiga.

Mirador Pico de las Nieves

Pozo de las Nieves

WHERE TO EAT
Grill La Cumbre €€
Llanos de la Pez 2
Carretera GC-600 km 8
Tel. 928 17 00 69

The excursion restaurant is located at an elevation of 1,700m/5,610ft, the only one on the ascent to Pozo de las Nieves. Specialties are meat dishes with lamb, rabbit and baby goat. An open fireplace warms guests on cool days.

✳ Puerto de las Nieves

✦ B 2

Elevation: Sea level
Population: 660

The approach to Puerto de las Nieves on the road along the west coast commands a grand panorama of the town at the foot of the cliffs. The religious landmark of the »snowy port« is a chapel dedicated to the »Virgin of the Snow«. The rock needle Deo de Dios, which stood off the coast, was broken off by a tropical storm a few years ago.

Puerto de las Nieves was once a major port. Agricultural products from the region were loaded here; ships running between Las Palmas (Gran Canaria) and Santa Cruz (Tenerife) mostly called at Puerto de las Nieves as well. Then the port slumbered for decades. Today it is a port of call for **passenger and car ferries** that connect Puerto de las Nieves (Agaete) with Santa Cruz de Tenerife several times a day (duration approx. 1 hour).

North-west ferry port

There is a new yacht harbour, and colourful fishing boats bob in the water. Puerto de las Nieves has developed into a small tourist attraction in just a few years. There are apartment complexes around the centre of town. A pretty **promenade** runs from the port along the small beach and is an inviting place to stroll. Foreign tourists still only come for a short stopover. At weekends, when local people come to the many excellent fish restaurants, it can be difficult to just find parking in Puerto de las Nieves.

WHAT TO SEE IN PUERTO DE LAS NIEVES

The Ermita de la Virgen de las Nieves is located on the main road in a walled compound. The brilliant white chapel is worth a visit, especially for the triptych attributed to the Flemish painter Joos van Cleve (d. 1541). It was brought to Gran Canaria in the 16th century. The centre panel depicts the Virgin with child sitting under a canopy. During the **Bajada de la Rama** (4 – 7 August) the altar painting is carried from the chapel to the parish church of Agaete in a procession joined by most of the local population. The beautiful Mudejar ceiling of the chapel is also worth seeing. The model ships displayed along the walls are offerings from sailors for the Virgen de las Nieves, the Virgin of the Snow.

Ermita de la Virgen de las Nieves

At the Bajada de la Rama in front of Ermita de la Virgen de las Nieves

Puerto de las Nieves

INFORMATION
Oficina de Información Turístico
Calle Nuestra Señora de las Nieves 1
Tel. 928 55 43 82

WHERE TO EAT
Las Nasas € €
Calle Nuestra Señora de las Nieves 7
Tel. 928 89 86 50
The sky blue furnishings makes you
think of Greece, but the cooking is typically Canarian. Fish is served most often
under the high domed ceiling; there is a
small terrace in the back overlooking the
harbour.

El Dedo de Dios €€
Calle Muelle Vieja s/n above the beach
Tel. 928 89 89 00
The large fern hanging from the ceiling
catches the eye. This typical Canarian es-
tablishment has a huge picture window
that overlooks the beach. Specialty:
seafood of all kinds. .

WHERE TO STAY
Puerto de las Nieves €€
Avenida Alcalde José de Armas
Tel. 928 88 62 56
www.hotelpuertodelasnieves.es
A comfortable four-star hotel, one of
the few with a high standard in the almost tourist-free north-west Gran Canaria. It is located at the edge of town and
has 30 rooms furnished in a modern style. Spa with indoor pool, sauna, massa-
ges and various other therapies.

Roca Negra €€€
Avenida Alfredo Kraus 42
Urb. El Tumán; Tel. 928 89 80 09
www.hotelrocanegragrancanaria.com
This comfort hotel is located a little outside of town on a mountain ridge above
the sea. In the three-storey building
most of the rooms with modern furnishings have a view of Pico del Teide on
Tenerife. A paved path leads to a sea
water swimming pool in five minutes.

Dedo de Dios   A few hundred metres south of Puerto de las Nieves, Dedo de Dios
(»finger of God«), the town's landmark, juts out of the sea close to the
coast. The upper part of this 30m/100ft-high, unusually shaped monolith broke off during a violent storm on November 25, 2005.

** **Puerto de Mogán**

✧ D 2

Elevation: Sea level
Population: 1000

**Puerto de Mogán is the western outpost of the southern tou-
rist centre of Gran Canaria. The small town is located at the
mouth of Barranco de Mogán (▶Mogán), one of the most fertile valleys on the island.**

The Puerto de Mogán yacht harbor,
which has seen fast-paced development in tourism

Puerto de Mogán

SHOPPING
Mercado
Most of the day guests come on Friday, for the market is held between 8am and 2pm around the port.

BOAT TOURS
The »Yellow Submarine« starts from the port every 40 minutes to explore the undersea world (which is not very impressive in this area!). Boat trips along the natural coast west of Puerto de Mogán, on the other hand, are very pleasant. Choose between sailing or deep-sea fishing (experienced personnel help beginners). If that is too much trouble, take one of the local ships into the neighbouring towns of Puerto Rico or Arguineguín.

WHERE TO EAT
Patio Canario €€€
Urb. Puerto de Mogán s/n
Yacht harbour
Tel. 928 56 54 56
Located right next to Hotel Puerto de Mogán, during the day the rustic wooden tables are set up on the terrace and the guests have a nice view from there. Usually all of the places are taken up by day guests. Casuela de Pescados y Mariscos, a hearty fish casserole, is the house specialty.

Café de Mogán €€ – €€€   **Insider Tip**
Urb. Puerto de Mogán s/n
Tel. 928 56 55 58
The café is nice not only because of its location on the harbour basin; the ice cream menu and the large selection of cakes (apple streusel, Sacher torte), waffles and crêpes leave nothing to be

desired. The dinner menu offers good international cooking.

Tu Casa €€ – €€€
Calle La Zanja 2; tel. 928 56 50 78
This house is from pre-tourist times; now Spanish-Mediterranean cooking is served. Guests are seated outside on the terrace during the daytime and in the evening in neat little rooms under rustic wooden ceilings and with old black and white photographs on the walls.

La Caracola €€€€
Urb. Puerto de Mogán s/n
Tel. 928 56 54 86
www.seemuschel.com
Open from 7pm; closed from May to late August
The »Seashell« is one of Gran Canaria's gourmet establishments and has prices to match! As the name indicates, the restaurant is known for its fish; shark and swordfish are served in many tasty variations. With only 20 seats, reservations are an absolute must.

WHERE TO STAY
Hotel Cordial Mogán Playa €€€ – €€€€
Avenida Los Marrero 2
Tel. 928 72 41 00
www.cordialcanarias.com
The large hotel with almost 500 rooms and suites may not be located right on the beach, but from its location up the barranco the four-star resort is only a few minutes' walk away from it. The lobby with its giant dome and 15m/50ft high fan palms is overwhelming. The buildings follow this design and are

grouped around the subtropical swimming pool arrangement.

Taurito Princess €€€

Urbanización Taurito; tel. 928 56 51 80
www.princess-hotels.com
This all-inclusive resort has aged a bit and no longer quite lives up to its four stars. All 400 rooms have an ocean view. The huge seawater pool in the middle of lush green grounds is a special attraction (non-guests may use it for an admission charge).

Hotel Puerto de Mogán €€ – €€€

Urb. Puerto de Mogán s/n
Tel. 928 56 50 66
www.hotelpuertodemogan.com
DAlso known as Club de Mar, the two-storey house is attractive for its Mogán-style architecture and situation right on the yacht harbour. The bright rooms all have a view of the sea or the port. Steps from the swimming pool lead directly into the sea. The hotel also has several apartments, some with two bedrooms as well as a diving station.

Pensión Lumy €

Calle Las Manchas 5
Tel. 928 56 53 18
www.pensionlumy.es
A simple backpacker's hostel with ten basic but clean rooms.

While Puerto de Mogán was a well-kept secret in the 1980s time has not stood still. The town has expanded since then. The riverbanks are taken up by streetblocks and building continues to expand into the barranco. The large holiday resort complexes Cordial Mogán Playa and Cordial Mogán Valle alone have room for more than 1,400 guests.

Continued expansion

A shopping centre and sports fields were put up; there is also a new bus terminal with good connections to Maspalomas and Las Palmas. The main attraction is the complex along the yacht harbour, which was partly built into the sea. For a long time it was a model tourist resort and the Venice-like appearance is still very stylish. Two-storey white cottages with colourful door and window frames line the traffic-free lanes. Abundant floral decoration, pretty squares and many cafés and restaurants make it an inviting place to relax and shop. Gran Canaria is proud of its »Little Venice« since the whole community has shown that efforts are being made to get away from the negative aspects of mass tourism. The many day guests are spoiled for choice as far as gastronomy is concerned. Restaurants crowd around the small »village square« next to the harbour. Fridays, market day, the restaurants are especially full. West of the plaza the fishing harbour is only a few steps away. There is a dry dock where old boats are repaired.

**Little Venice

Many visitors leave without having explored the old part of Puerto de Mogán. By all means take the time to do so: whitewashed houses and cobbled streets bring the past to life.

Playa de Mogán
Puerto de Mogán is less of a beach resort than a venue for excursions, which does not mean that there is no beach. The 300m/1,000ft-long Playa de Mogán next to the holiday resortwas originally made of dark sand but later covered with light sand. A wave break ensures safe swimming for children. But the beach should not be compared to the ones on the Costa Canaria.

Lomo Quiebre
This part of Puerto de Mogán is located 1km/0.5mi into the barranco from the beach; it existed long before tourism came. The modest houses now house bed & breakfast accommodation for the backpacking crowd.

AROUND PUERTO DE MOGÁN

Playa del Taurito
4km/2.5mi to the east, Playa del Taurito (or Playa del Diablo) is also surrounded by tourist resorts. There is a large pool area with palm trees, flowers and water slides in the centre (admission charge for non-residents).

Playa de Veneguera
Playa de Veneguera is a small beach with dark sand and stones west of Puerto de Mogán. Access is only on foot on a traffic-free road. By car drive via Mogán and Casas de Veneguera (25km/15mi one way, only with four-wheel drive vehicles). At Playa de Veneguera another development with 20,000 beds is planned, but environmentalists have succeeded in delaying construction.

**Playa de Güigüí
The region's and possibly the island's most beautiful beach, Playa de Güigüí, is located further west (▶MARCO POLO insight, p. 214) and only accessible from here on foot after a hike of several hours.

Puerto Rico

✦ D 2

Elevation: Sea level
Population: 3,500

Puerto Rico on the south-west coast of Gran Canaria is completely oriented to tourists. Those who come here are less interested in entertainment than in sports. Puerto Rico has two yacht harbours, and almost everything revolves around water sports here.

Puerto Rico, the »rich port«, was built in a sheltered bay that is bordered by 100m/330ft cliffs. The apartment buildings climb up the

Puerto Rico

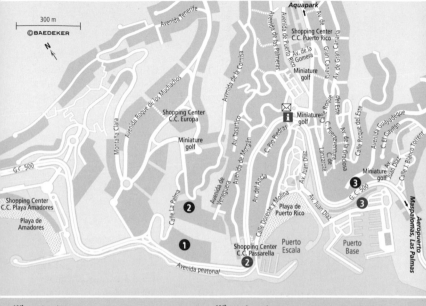

Where to stay
❶ Gloria Palace Amadores   ❸ Marina Bayview
❷ Hotel Puerto Azul

Where to eat
❶ Amadores B.C.   ❸ Don Quichote
❷ Puerto Rico B.C.

cliffs almost to the top. With about 30,000 beds Puerto Rico is the **second-largest tourist centre** on Gran Canaria. In the past decades it has become a favourite venue for Scandinavian and English guests. At first glance it might be difficult to imagine taking a vacation here, but a second look reveals many green oases that relieve the overall impression of concrete. There is one disadvantage: when the weather is good the small, artificial beach is full to overflowing. An alternative is a 30 minute walk away, Playa de los Amadores. But the wave break makes the beach idela for children, who can splash around here safely.

From Puerto Escala west of Playa de Puerto Rico ferries sail to Puerto de Mogán and Arguineguín. There are also sailing and surfing schools here. The terrace of the Beach Club Puerto Rico gives a view of the harbour and the hotel city that is built like honeycombs into the cliffs. **Puerto Base** on the eastern beach of the bay is the startiung

Puerto Escala and Puerto Base

Puerto Rico

INFORMATION
Oficina de Turismo
Avenida de Mogán s/n
Tel. 928 15 88 04

BOAT TOURS
Regular ship traffic (Lineas Salmon) connects Puerto Rico with Puerto de Mogán and Arguineguín. One way takes about 30 minutes. The ships run several times a day. From the harbour Puerto Base the catamaran Spirit of the Sea leaves several times a week to take passengers dolphin and whale watching.
Tel. 928 56 22 29
www.dolphinwhale.co.uk

NIGHTLIFE
Nightlife is limited in Puerto Rico and can't be compared to what the Playa del Inglés offers. Young people go to the bars and discos in the Centro Comercial. The restaurant La Bolera has live music and shows. Tel. 928 56 07
www.labolerapuertorico.com

WHERE TO EAT
❶ *Amadores Beach Club* €€€ – €€€€
Playa de los Amadores
Tel. 928 56 00 56
www.amadoresbeachclub.com
The elegant restaurant is located on the jetty on the northern end of the beach and has a beautiful view. Guests sit in comfortable armchairs in a relaxed atmosphere and enjoy the excellent cuisine and cocktails.

❷ *Puerto Rico Beach Club* €€
Puerto Escala
Tel. 928 72 56 94
Unlike the name suggests the restaurant is not on the beach but on the harbour jetty. Don't expect culinary revelations, but the terrace offers a wonderful view of the harbour and hotels.

❸ *Don Quichote* €€€
Edificio Porto Novo 19
Tel. 928 56 09 01
This restaurant right on the harbour serves fish, seafood, paella and flambé meat dishes. Porcelain plates on the walls commemorate Don Quichote, the »Knight of the Woeful Countenance«. Very popular, reservations recommended (closed Sun and Mon).

WHERE TO STAY
❶ *Gloria Palace Amadores* €€€
Calle La Palma 2
Tel. 928 12 85 10
www.gloriapalaceth.com
This four-star hotel dominates Playa de los Amadores. A lift brings guests to the promenade, from which the walk to Pu-

erto Rico takes 10 minutes and to Playa de los Amadores 15 minutes. The rooms are attractive; there is a miniclub and playground for children.

❷ Aparthotel Puerto Azul € – €€
Avenida de la Cornisa
Tel. 928 56 05 91
www.servatur.com
The hotel is not right on the beach, but a shuttle service brings guests to the beach in a few minutes. The rooms are very spacious and all have a roomy terrace with a view of the ocean. Some have a kitchenette for self-catering. A swim-

ming pool, two tennis courts, a playground and entertainment keep the guests occupied.

❸ Marina Bayview €€ – €€€
(formerly Ipanema Park)
Avenida de Guayadeque 3
Tel. 902 99 60 93
www.ipanemapark.net
www.marinabayview.com
The 114 apartments are modern and furnished functionally; above all there is a wonderful view over Puerto Rico bay. The descent to the beach is long and includes lots of steps. A bus runs to the town centre several times a day.

Playa de los Amadores near Puerto Rico is one of the most beautiful beaches on the island

To the Most Beautiful Beach on the Island

Many people think that Playa de Güigüí on the west coast is the loveliest beach on Gran Canaria. Since parts of this beautiful coastal landscape are a protected natural area, it will be saved from tourist development, at least in the near future. Playa de Güigüí is only accessible by boat or on foot, after a strenuous hike.

Those who opt for the **boat** can get a yacht or fishing boat to take them to the beach from ►Puerto de Mogán. The price is negotiable but will not be less then 75 euros. Remember that there is no jetty, so you will have to either swim ashore or take an inflatable dinghy.

A Strenuous Hike

The 12km/7mi tour starts at the hamlet **Tasartico**, which is only accessible by car. Allow at least five hours for the hike to the beach and back. There is a difference in elevation of 970m/3,200ft (round trip). The hiking trail is steep in parts, slippery and goes over gravel paths. There is no shade! Make sure you take enough water ...! It is only possible to get from E1 Puerto Bay to the larger Playa de Güigüí at low tide. The local newspapers list the times of the tides (bajamar = low tide, pleamar = high tide). Make sure that you allow enough time to get back to El Puerto during low tide. The way between the two bays is cut off at the onset of high tide. Until the tide turns again there is no way back ...!

Off We Go

The hike starts at the hamlet Tasartico in the barranco of the same name. A few houses are gathered around a small church. Follow the path that continues from the paved road into the barranco. Vegetables are grown in the valley, some in greenhouses. After about ten minutes go right after a green-

Walk to Playa de Güigüí

Playa de Güigüí
B.co de Güigüí Chico
Lomo de Güigüí
Barranco de Güigüí Grande
1 km
©BAEDEKER
Cebuche
Montaña de las Vacas
El Puerto
Llanos del Mar
Calzada de Aguas Sabinas
Mountain pass
Tasartico
Las Estaquillas
Montaña de Aguas Sabinas
Barranco de Tasartico
Los Canalizos

house and follow the path, which is easy to recognize, uphill. The dry vegetation on the slope includes tabaiba and euphorbia. After a few turns the path leads into the side barranco Cañada de Aguas Sabinas. After 15 minutes cross the floor of the barranco to the left. The path now runs uphill. It is long, steep and quite strenuous, in some places paved with stones and in others covered with loose gravel. The climb takes some time and finally arrives at a small marble cross and then the pass. This is the lowest part of the mountain ridge that divides Barranco de Tasartico and Barranco de Güigüí Grande. From here there is a wonderful view of wild mountain landscape with the blue, sparkling ocean in the background. The sound of surf can be heard from far off.

After a break, begin the descent. The old path is in better shape here and the far-off destination beckons already. The path winds in places and sometimes runs straight downhill. After about 45 minutes there is a fork in the trail: One branch leads straight ahead along the slope; follow the other path to the left into the barranco (a small farm can be seen further down).

In about ten minutes you will reach the valley floor. Follow the rocky rubble downhill – not the path, which soon turns off to the right. Walk under a pipeline that crosses the barranco. Soon after go left along a path into Barranco de Güigüí Grande and follow the valley. The rubble here is densely covered with Spanish cane; walk downhill on the right of the rubble

and pass along the lower border of a small farm. A partially sandy path leads down into **El Puerto Bay** via steps cut into the rock; Barranco de Güigüí Grande opens up into the sea here.

The Lure of the Beach

At low tide walk along the beach to the right into the sandy **Playa de Güigüí**; Barranco de Güigüí Chico runs into the sea here. Since this way is never completely dry, even during low tide, take your shoes off here to walk around the protruding rocks. Remember to return before the tide turns …! Follow the same route back, which now includes a strenuous hike uphill.

This text originally appeared in German in the Kompass hiking guide Gran Canaria. More information on www.kompass.at

Start: Tasartico
Length of hike: 12km /7 mi
Walking time: about 5 hours
Elevation difference: 970m/3,200ft
Gear: Good shoes and water

AROUND PUERTO RICO

*Peatonal Playa Amadores

In Puerto Escala a spectacular **promenade** begins at the Beach Club Puerto Rico, along which you can reach Playa de los Amadores in a good 20 minutes. The path is supported elaborately with walls and in parts it was blasted out of the cliff; it is one of the most popular hiking trails on the island, and it is used daily by hundreds of visitors to walk between Puerto Rico and Playa de los Amadores. Halfway along the path is a bar that was carved into the cliff by Hotel Gloria Palace Amadores, the lift that runs up the cliff here is only for hotel guests. The row of restaurants along almost the whole beach is unimaginative. The only exception is the Playa der Amadores Beach Club on the northwestern end. The attractively located minigolf course Las Caracolas is also nearby.

*Playa de los Amadores

The 400m/1300ft-long curved beach is considered to be the most beautiful on the island. It was only constructed a few years ago and is made of white sand. Jetties built into the sea protect the beach from surf and make it ideal for children. Above Playa de los Amadores a new exclusive holiday resort is being built into the cliffs.

Playa de Tauro

Playa de Tauro is located about 4km/2.5mi north-west of Puerto Rico (turn left after the campgrounds). The beach is about 400m/1300ftf long. The eastern part is the most attractive.

Playa de Cura

In the bay next to Tauro lies the Beach Hotel Riviera on a beach that is jam-packed during the high season.

Playa del Medio Almud

The next beach, Playa del Medio Almud, is accessible only on foot and is the preferred beach of the Canarians (a road turns off the coast road at km 78). While the beach is not very clean, the beach parties here are quite festive. However, the untouched setting will soon be gone: excavators are already on the march. The adjacent **Playa de Tritaña** has not yet been discovered by developers. A footpath begins at the coast road and runs 600m/2100ft to the narrow beach of fine-grained sand.

** Roque Nublo

C 3

Elevation: 1813 above sea level

Roque Nublo, the »rock in the clouds«, is at the centre of Gran Canaria only a few miles west of Pozo de las Nieves. It is the island's landmark because of its unusual shape.

Great views on Roque Nublo

Roque Nublo is a monolith that rises 80m/260ft over a mesa. The remarkable »needle rock« was once part of an even higher mesa and is all that remains after erosion. The rock was sacred to the Guanches.

Ascent

Roque Nublo is located in a romantically and very untouched landscape and only accessible on foot. The short **hike** (▶ MARCO POLO Insight , p. 218) starts at a parking lot on the road that connects Ayacata and Cueva Grande. There is a path from the parking lot to the rock, which is already visible. The »rock in the clouds« often lives up to its name. The best time to be sure to see it in sunlight is early in the morning.

Around Roque Nublo

When the weather is clear Roque Nublo looks like a raised finger from far off. The bizarre rock needle is one of Gran Canaria's landmarks and the destination for a very popular mountain hike. A well developed hiking trail leads to the foot of Roque Nublo. Many hikers leave it at that and go back the way they came after a visit to the rock. But walking around it is also very interesting.

The 1803m/5949ft high Roque Nublo (cloud rock) lives up to its name and is often covered by clouds. It is recommended to hike in the early morning before the rising passat winds often cover the mountains in a milky mist. The starting point the hiker's parking area **La Goleta**. From the holiday resorts on the southern coast drive on the GC 60 through Barranco Fataga and via San Bartolomé de Tirajana to Ayacata. Turn right there onto GC 600 and after 3km/2mi comes the hiker's parking area La Goleta. The drive from Maspalomas is a good 50km/30mi on narrow mountain roads, so it takes about an hour. The parking area has room for about 40 cars, on sunny days it is usually full by noon at the latest.

La Goleta is not accessible by **local bus**. People who want to take the bus should take bus line 18 from Faro Maspalomas towards San Mateo (about four to five times a day) to Ayacata bus stop. From there follow the street by the chapel to the right for a short distance and turn left at the traiul signed La Goleta; this is a shortcut and you will avoid the curving and in parts steeply ascending road. Allow an additional hour for walking from Ayacata to La Goleta parking area and back.

To the Cloud Rock

Two signed paths start opposite the parking area La Goleta (1580m/5214ft). Take the path on the left **marked PR GC-60** toward Roque Nublo; you will see Roque Nublo as you walk directly toward it. To the left of Roque Nublo are a smaller rock named Rana (frog) and the slender needle rock El Fraile (monk). There is a broad panoramic view of the southern coast; to the right are the terraced fields around the scattered village houses of La Culata.

After a quarter of an hour follow the left fork and at the fork five minutes later walk straight ahead. The path leads around a rock wall and then climbs to a rocky plateau, from there it leads straight to the foot of Roque Nublo (1,750m/5,775ft). It is possible to climb to the northern side of the rock across boulders for a view of Tejeda; above it you can see the Parador at Cruz de Tejeda, to the left is the mountain village Artenara.

Loop Trail

From Roque Nublo walk back to the last fork; those in a hurry can walk back to the parking area from here. For those who want to follow the worthwhile path around Roque Nublo, keep right and after 25m/80ft keep right again. The **panoramic trail**, which has a wonderful view, descends a bit and after 15 minutes comes a fork marked Hoyetas del Nublo (1,620m/5,346ft). The path to the left is marked El Aserrador, but follow the path to the right. After a good 15 minutes you will pass a fork marked La Culata; keep right to return to the starting point, La Goleta parking area .

Bus schedule
The tourist offices around Roque Nublo and Global Bus Company will have information on scheduled busses to Ayacata (www.globalsu.net).

Signs
The most important forks are signposted.

Walking time
The walk there and back will take about 2 hours.

Elevation difference
250m/825ft each ascending and descending

Equipment
Good hiking shoes and a warm jacket in the winter months.

Refreshments
There is a mobile refreshment stand at La Goleta parking area on days when the weather is good; it serves cold drinks and ice cream.
There is no other possibility on the hike itself, but Casa Melo in Ayacata is very popular.

Morning is the best time to hike around Roque Nublo

Volcanic Island World

The Canary Islands, which are located on the eastern edge of the more than 6,500m/21,000ft deep Canarian Basin, are an archipelago that owes its existence to a fixed hot spot under the African plate.

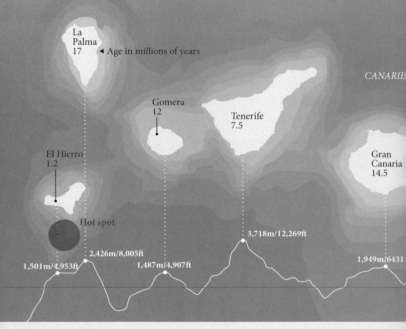

La
Palma
17   ◄ Age in millions of years

Gomera
12

Tenerife
7.5

CANARIE

El Hierro
1.2

Gran
Canaria
14.5

Hot spot

3,718m/12,269ft

2,426m/8,005ft

1,487m/4,907ft

1,949m/6431

1,501m/4,953ft

▶ **Plate tectonics and hot spots**
The African plate drifts to the north-east, but the hot spot remains fixed in the sa▮ place. For this reason the eastern islands Gran Canaria, Fuerteventura and Lanzar▮ lay right over the hot spot a long time ago while the western islands La Gomera, Tenerife and La Palma and Hierro only more recently and the volcano off the coas▮ of El Hierro only since fall of 2011.

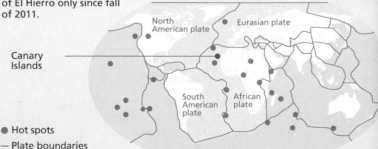

North
American plate

Eurasian plate

Canary
Islands

South
American plate

African
plate

● Hot spots
— Plate boundaries

...e 500km/300mi
...ng chain of
...ands runs from
...st to west. The
...rther west, the
...unger the island.
...is is considered
...be proof of the
...t spot theory.

E

Lanzarote
15.5

Formation of land
A submarine volcano has been active off the coast of Hierro since November 2011. Its crater has reached a height of 125m/410ft below sealevel.

Fuerte-
ventura
20.6

AFRICA

Island profile
Today the Canaries form a massive mountain range that is up to 4,000m/13,200ft high. But only 5% of it are above sealevel.

807m/2,663ft   671m/2,214ft
0m/0ft

©BAEDEKER   4,000m/13,200ft

...ot spot theory
...hot spot is a place where the outer crust of ...e earth's shell is thin and where hot magma ...es up and melts through the earth's crust, ...ated the volcanologist John T. Wilson in ...e 1960s.

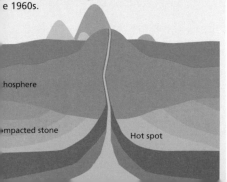

...hosphere

...mpacted stone

Hot spot

▶ **Volcanic eruptions on the Canaries**
In the last 500 years there were ten larger and numerous smaller eruptions. They not have an impact on the entire island world.

Tenerife	1492
	1604, 1605
	1704 – 1706, 1798
	1909
La Palma	1585
	1646, 1677
	1712
	1971, 1949
Lanzarote	1730 – 1736
	1824
El Hierro	2011, 2012

San Agustín

D 3

Elevation: Sea level
Population: 3500

San Agustín, a hotel town in southern Gran Canaria, borders ►Playa del Inglés, the island's largest tourist resort, to the west; to the east it extends in an almost unbroken line of construction to Playa de Àguila and Bahía Feliz. The somewhat worn holiday resort is preferred by guests who do not want the bustle of Playa del Inglés.

The core of tourist development on the southern coast in the 1960s was here, which can be seen in the sober architecture. While all of the hotels have been renovated several times since then there is still an old-fashioned atmosphere. Moroever no investments were made in public infrastructure; starting with loose paving to a lack of ramps for wheelchairs. San Agustín does not have a town centre. Hotels and other tourist facilities dominate the scene, but the many little lush and blooming gardens make it colourful. The GC 500 runs through the middle of San Agustín. Anyone who is staying north of it can get to the beach via pedestrian bridges.

The holiday resort owes its existence to the fine-grained sand beach, which is bordered by a promenade. The 600m/650yd-long beach is considered to be one of the best-kept on the island. On the east is Punta Morro Besudo, a rock promontory that protects the beach from the north-east winds. The waves in the cove are generally low and the gently shelved beach is safe for children as well.

Playa de las Burras

West of Playa de San Agustín the promenade leads to the »donkey beach« (**Playa de las Burras**) in the neighbouring bay. The fine, grey sand beach is used by guests from the surrounding hotels. Walking further brings you to the 4km/2.5mi-long superbeach at ►Playa del Inglés.

MARCO ◉ POLO TIP

!

Thalasso & wellness ^Insider ^Tip

Talasoterapia Canarias, the island's largest spa, is near the Gloria Palace Hotel. Here an area of 7,000 sq m/75,000 sq ft is devoted to rest and relaxation. There are several seawater pools, a sauna, various therapy and beauty treatments, a gym and a rest area. The pools are open daily 10am – 9pm, wellness and anti-stress packages over several days are also available.
Gloria Palace San Agustín
Thalasso & Spa
Calle Las Margaritas
Tel. 928 12 85 99
www.gloriapalaceth.com

AROUND SAN AGUSTÍN

The Playa de San Agustín is bordered on the east by small sandy coves. The 500m/550yd-long, but somewhat stony **Playa del Águila** is very pretty. It merges with **Playa de Tarajalillo**. The latter is part of the community Bahía Feliz (Happy Bay), a comfortable Moorish-style holiday village and at present the easternmost part of the Costa Canaria. Scandinavians and windsurfers stay in this quiet community. The well-known Club Mistral has a surfing station here.

Bahía Feliz

> **MARCO POLO TIP**
>
> ! *Gran Canaria from the air* **Insider Tip**
>
> For a bird's eye view, try a ride in a helicopter. They are available at Aerodrom El Berrial near San Agustín (from 15 minutes to 1 hour).
> Islas Helicopters
> Tel. 928 15 79 65
> www.islas-helicopters.com.

Just a few miles north-west of San Agustín a replica **Western town** has been built in Barranco de Aguila. Sioux City with its saloons, church, bank, jail and other buildings has been used as a setting for television shows. There are shows several times a day with lasso and duelling stunts, knife-throwing etc. – kid's favourites

Sioux City

❶ Tue Sun 10am – 5pm, admission €21

Drive 10km/6mi north-east from San Agustín to **Juan Grande** and then on to the fishing village of Castillo del Romeral. The name comes from a fortress that no longer exists; it was built to protect the nearby salt works. Fishing boats bob in the water along the jetty; there is a seawater pool instead of a beach.
The Cofradía de Pescadores (brotherhood of fishermen) next to the little harbour serves reasonable fish dishes; the selection depends on what was caught that day.

Castillo del Romeral

The average tourist is not likely to have heard of this small coastal settlement 16km/10mi north-east of San Agustín, but it is one of the sweetest-sounding names in the world in the ears of windsurfers as well as kitesurfers. This section of coast has hardly been developed and is o**ne of the best places in the islands for strong winds** thanks to continous blowing north-eastern passat winds which reach more than 30kph/18.6mph. A world cup race for surfing pros has been held here every summer for years.
The only facilities worth mentioning at Pozo Izquierdo are two surfing bars, a handful of the simplest guest houses as well as the public Centro Internacional de Windsurfing (CIW), where windsurfing and diving courses are offered mainly for local people; Pozowinds offers a wide range of courses for tourists (www.pozowinds.com). Nearby are the island's wind-power facilities and a salt works.

Pozo Izquierdo

San Agustín

INFORMATION
Oficina de Información Turística
El Portón
Calle Las Retamas 2
Tel. 928 76 92 62

NIGHTLIFE
Casino Tamarindos
Calle Las Retamas 3
Tel. 928 76 27 24
www.casinotamarindos.es
Roulette and blackjack daily between
9pm and 2am. There is also a hall of slot
machines.

Garbos Dinner Show
Carretera General del Sur
Bahía Feliz
Tel. 928 15 70 60
The dinner show with Swedish acrobats
and musicians is held four times a week
in the Nordotel in Bahía Feliz.
Admission incl. Three course menu:
46 €.

WHERE TO EAT
El Puente
€€
Calle las Dalias 3
Tel. 679 77 10 36
This restaurant is only open in the eve-
ning and has a fabulous view of the
coast. Closed Mon.

Balcón de San Agustín **Insider Tip**
€€ – €€€
Calle Los Jazmines 15
Tel. 928 77 89 67
The restaurant lives up to ist name: The
view from the promenade above the sea
goes as far as the lighthouse at Maspalomas; sunset is the time to be here. The

cooking is Canarian, service is quick and
friendly.

El Capítán
€€ – €€€
Calle Las Acacias 1
Tel. 928 76 02 25
www.elcapitangrancanaria.com
The restaurant benefits from its location
on Playa de San Agustín. During the
daytime sunbathers come by to eat pizza or pasta; on the large terrace sunsails
offer shade. In the evening many regu-
lars show up for fish and grill dishes;
one specialty is dentex (sama) in a salt
crust.

WHERE TO STAY
San Agustín Beach Club
€€€
Plaza de los Cocoteros 2
Tel. 928 77 16 40
www.luishoteles.com
Four-star beach hotel in a quiet location.
The 57 rooms face either the sea or the
garden; the small additional vharge for
the sea view is worth it.

Hotel IFA Beach
€€ – €€€
Calle Los Jazmines 25
Tel. 928 77 40 00
www.ifahotels.com
A typically functional five-storey 1970s
building, but the three-star hotel is well-
run, and there is direct access from the
hotel garden to the beach. Most of the
rooms have a sea view; the rooms on
the side are dark and face a parking lot.
The food is average; book the room with
breakfast only and eat dinner in a restaurant nearby.

San Bartolomé de Tirajana

 ✳ C 3

Elevation: 887m/2,910ft above sea level
Population: 54,000 (entire district)

The town is officially called San Bartolomé de Tirajana, but the residents still call it by its Guanche name Tunte as well. It is located on the edge of the Caldera de Tirajana, which borders the central mountains on the south. It is a good place to start exploring the mountains, even though it has no sights and hardly any tourist infrastructure.

San Bartolomé de Tirajana is the capital of the district of San Bartolomé de Tirajana, with 334.5 sq km/129 sq mi the largest municipio on Gran Canaria. Since the district includes the tourist centres Maspalomas, Playa del Inglés and San Agustín, the administration has expanded in the past decades. The population of the district has grown rapidly from only about 9,000 in 1950. Only about 3,500 people live in the town itself today, and it still has the character of an untouched mountain village. The mainstay of the local economy is fruit (almonds, plums, apricots and cherries), which is mainly used to make liquors and cordials. »Guindilla«, the sour cherry cordial made here, is a specialty.

WHAT TO SEE IN SAN BARTOLOMÉ

The church is dedicated to St James (»Santiago«), the Spanish patron saint. The Mudejar ceiling and the statues of Bartholomew and James from the atelier of Luján Pérez are worth seeing. The polygonal wooden sculpture »Santiago El Chico« (Santiago the Small), on the other hand, is unusual. It is about 70cm/28in tall and considered to be the oldest work of art in the sanctuary, going back to the 15th century. It depicts a soldier on horseback, swinging a sword, with a conquered Moor on the gorund at his feet.

Iglesia de Santiago

The Casa Consistorial opposite the church has been remodelled several times, most recently in 1966. The offices located off the inner courtyard make the building, which was begun in 1835, look more like a Canarian private home than an office building. The town hall can be viewed during office hours by walking past the police post. The town history is displayed and a fountain with two water-spouting frogs splashes on the patio. Most of the town hall's functions as

Ayuntamiento

San Bartolomé de Tirajana

WHERE TO EAT
La Cueva
€ – €€
Calle Tamaron 15
Tel. 928 12 73 00
This simple restaurant on the main street serves Canarian dishes, but also pizza and local wine.

La Hacienda del Molino
€€
Calle Los Naranjas 2
Tel. 928 12 73 44
Located opposite the church, there is a nicely restored inner courtyard and an old gofio mill with this restaurant. The cooking is typically Canarian.

Mirador de Tunte **€€**
Carretera de Fataga-San Bartolomé de Tirajana

Tel. 928 12 74 32
The best part of this large panoramic restaurant is the view from the terrace. It is a beautiful place when there aren't any bus groups taking it up.

WHERE TO STAY
Hotel Rural las Tirajanas
€€€
Calle Oficial Mayor Jose Rubio
Tel. 928 12 30 00
www.hotel-lastirajanas.com
The former Aldiana club hotel is now part of the Paradise Group, which also owns hotels on the Playa Taurito. Its four stars make it, along with the Parador, one of the best mountain hotels on the island, and it is used by hikers and hiking groups because of its good location. The rooms have beautiful views and are decorated in bright colours. The spa includes an indoor pool, a sauna and a jacuzzi; there are also tennis courts and an archery range.

La Hacienda del Molino **€**
Calle Los Naranjas 2
Tel. 928 12 73 44
www.lahaciendadelmolino.com
The small rural hotel at the northern edge of town is part of an ethnographic centre, which also includes an old gofio mill and a restaurant. The rooms are furnished simply and mostly used by hikers.

administrative centre for Playa del Inglés and Maspalomas have been turned over to that administrative offices that were built in Maspalomas in the 1980s.

The ethnographical museum shows how well-to-do rural Canarians lived in the early 20th century. A kitchen, living rooms, bedrooms and various utility rooms are grouped around the inner courtyard, all of them with a ceiling of solid teakwood. The rooms have been furnished with care and there is an old oven in the garden hut.

*Casa los Yánez

❶ Mon – Fri 9am – 2pm, free admission

Mountain village San Bartolomé de Tirajana in the mountainous island centre

AROUND SAN BARTOLOMÉ DE TIRAJANA

Caldera de Tirajana
To explore the Caldera de Tirajana, the semicircular valley bordered by mountains north of San Bartolomé de Tirajana, drive north on the GC 60 and turn off after 2km/1¼mi onto a side road to the east, which has beautiful views. Pass the settlements of Agualalente, La Culata and **Risco Blanco** (»white rock«). The latter gets its name from the brilliant white cliffs in the area. After driving through Taidia and continuing for a good 10km/6mi you will meet the GC 65, which connects Santa Lucía with San Bartolomé de Tirajana.

> **? How the caldera was formed**
>
> »Caldera« is the geological term for a crater that has been widened by collapsing walls or erosion, but there is no indication that Caldera de Tirajana has volcanic origins. The semicircle was probably formed by massive landslides.

MARCO POLO INSIGHT

From the GC 60 7km/4mi northwest of San Bartolomé de Tirajana a road turns off left to the **Embalse de Chira**, the Chira reservoir. Avoid it at weekends because of the many day-trippers. The first stop is the hamlet **Los Cercados**. From the sleepy community located on the northern shore the narrow road follows along the southern shore of the reservoir up to the **dam**. The paving ends here and the rest of the way south to Maspalomas on the unpaved and curvy road is only possible with a jeep.

Ayacata
Ayacata is located 10km/6mi north-west of San Bartolomé de Tirajana in a picturesque valley surrounded by high cliffs. Major tourist routes branch off here to Pozo de las Nieves and the reservoirs Cueva de las Niñas and Soria. Many holiday-makers use the chance to take a break in a restaurant here, of which Casa Melo is the most popular.

Hike from Cruz Grande to Pico de las Nieves
From San Bartolomé de Tirajana take the GC 60 towards Tejeda; after just 5km/3mi you will reach Cruz Grande at 1,250m/4,101ft elevation. The striking gorge is the starting point of a spectacular mountain hiking tour up to **Degollada de los Gatos** (»Cat Pass«) and on to Pico de las Nieves. 50m before the gorge the sign »PR-GC 40« marks the beginning of the trail. Soon a breathtaking path winds up the cliff in tight serpentines to the pass. At a dip in the trail after just two hours, follow the path to the right that is marked by little stone men to the Degollada de los Gatos only a few minutes away. To continue follow the ridge trail another 45 minutes toward the two radar domes on Pico de las Nieves up to Mirador Pico de las Nieves (altitude 1,940m/6,365ft). Allow five to six hours for the somewhat strenuous round trip. You can get to the starting point Cruz Grande from Maspalomas by bus.

Santa Brígida

✳ B 3/4

Elevation: 509m/1,650ft above sea level
Population: 19,000 (entire district)

Santa Brígida, a healthy 15km/9mi south-west of Las Palmas, is the capital's upper-class suburb. The elevation means it is always a bit cooler than Las Palmas, and the pretty scenery has made it the community of the rich and successful on the island.

The area around Santa Brígida and Tafira is Gran Canaria's main wine growing region. »Vino del Monte« is considered to be the island's best red wine. It is available in local bars and restaurants. The houses in Santa Brígida are scattered over hillsides, and some of the villas have large gardens. Tall eucalyptus trees give the village atmosphere.

The region around Santa Brígida has good wine

Santa Brígida

SHOPPING
Insider Tip

There is a flea market and art market in the Parque Municipal every Saturday morning, where bargains are still to be had.

WHERE TO EAT
Las Grutas de Artiles
€€

Carretara las Meleguinas s/n (GC 320) in Meleguinas
Tel. 928 64 03 73
This restaurant has existed for decades in Santa Brígida. It serves excellent Canarian food; the desserts are especially tempting. The restaurant is located in several caves, which gives it a unique atmosphere.

El Martell
€€€

El Madroñal
On the GC 15 to Vega de San Mateo
Tel. 928 64 12 83
Daily 12 noon – 5pm and
8pm - midnight
A typical Canarian restaurant with rustic furnishings. Wide selection of Canarian wines, including local red wine. It is full at weekends, so reservations are a must

WHERE TO STAY
Santa Brígida
€–€€

Calle Real de Coello 2
Monte Letiscal
Tel. 928 47 84 00
www.hecansa.com
The Santa Brígida has a long tradition: it opened its doors in 1898. Today it is associated with the Hecansa state school of hotel management. This means that the staff are very motivated and friendly, if not yet perfect! For the guests in the 41 double rooms, there are the obligatory swimming pool, gym and conference facilities.

Villa del Monte
Insider Tip
€€

Calle Castaño Bajo 9
Tel. 928 64 43 89
www.canary-bike.com
This finca with seven rooms is situated in a wonderful garden at an elevation of 800m/2,600ft. The rooms are all furnished individually, and along with breakfast, dinner is available in the evenings upon request. A pretty place not just for mountain bikers and hikers!

AROUND SANTA BRÍGIDA

La Atalaya The village of La Atalaya, about 5km/3mi south-east of Santa Brígida, is known for its **pottery**. However, hardly any of it is still made in the old style without using a potter's wheel. Since the village is a stop-off for many island bus tours, most of the potteries have gone over to mass production.
Some of the residents on the edge of town still live in caves, but most of the caves are no longer recognisable as such since they have conventional house façades. They are furnished with modern appliances and comfortable furniture.

Santa Lucía

─── ⋇ C 3

Elevation: 701m/2,800ft above sea level
Population: 66,000 (entire district)

Santa Lucía is only a few miles east of ▸ San Bartolomé de Tirajana, on the edge of the Caldera de Tirajana. The picturesque village is a popular stop on island tours. The mosque-like dome of the church in Santa Lucía can be seen from far off. White houses and palm trees are clustered around it.

WHAT TO SEE IN SANTA LUCÍA

The museum near Restaurant Hao, Museo Castillo de la Fortaleza, is the village's main attraction (about 50m/50yd from the main road; follow the signs). The »pseudo-castle« displays fossils and household articles of the Guanches. One room is furnished in typical 17th-century Canarian style. The special treasures of the carefully designed private collection include a Roman amphora from the 3rd century AD; it was found on the ocean floor near Lanzarote. A few old cannons are on display in the garden next to the museum and restaurant.

Museo Castillo de la Fortaleza

❶ daily 9am – 3pm, admission €2

AROUND SANTA LUCÍA

Fortaleza Grande or Ansite is a group of peaks south of Santa Lucía that were sacred to the Guanches. Coming from Santa Lucía, turn off the GC 65 to the right 2km/1¼mi outside town towards La Sorrueda. After driving through the hamlet set in a palm grove, a large open area appears after another 3km/2mi. A path runs from here about 100m/100yd to the cave entrance in Fortaleza Grande. Walk 20m/65ft through the cave to another entry. In April 1483 the early Canarians hid here during the Spanish conquest. Only their former

*Fortaleza Grande

Santa Lucía

WHERE TO EAT
Hao €€ – €€€   **Insider Tip**
Calle Los Alamos 3
Tel. 928 79 80 07
The proprietor of the museum also owns

the rustic garden restaurant Hao (bus tours welcome!). Try the delicious papas arrugadas with mojo sauce, but also marinated rabbit or baby goat from the grill.

guanarteme, Tenesor Semidan, who had already converted to Christianity, could convince the 1,600 men, women and children to give up and let Spanish forces take over Gran Canaria (▶ Gáldar). Ceremonies are held every year on 29 April on the assembly ground below the cave to commemorate this event.

Santa María de Guía

✦ B 3

Elevation: 186m/610ft above sea level
Population: 14,000 (entire district)

Santa María de Guía, Guía for short, is next to ▶ Gáldar in north-western Gran Canaria. When stopping here on the way to Cenobio de Valerón, be sure to taste the delightful »queso de flor« that is produced in Guía.

Guía was established in the late 15th century as a suburb of Gáldar. Recent Spanish immigrants settled here. Guía became an indepen-

Queso de Flor: Juice from artichoke blossoms gives it its special aroma

dent town in 1526. The streets of Santa María de Guía are full of life. The parish church (Iglesia de la Asunción) has neo-classical elements. Some of the statues inside – Nuestra Señora de las Mercedes is the most important – are by Luján Pérez (1756 – 1815), who was born in Guía and whose statues of saints can be found in all major churches in the archipelago.

In Calle San José the **Museo Néstor Álamo**, a small museum, is dedicated to the writer and composer of Canarian folk music Néstor Álamo (1906 – 1994). The typical Canarian house in the old town of Guía is also the artist's birthplace. Álamo played a major role in the restoration of Casa de Colón in ▶Las Palmas, Plaza Teresa Bolivar in ▶Teror and the construction of the León y Castillo in ▶Telde and Pérez Galdós museums in ▶Las Palmas.

> **!** *Don't miss it!* Insider Tip
>
> MARCO ⊕ POLO TIP
>
> Guía is known for its queso de flor. This cheese is made of sheep's milk and sap extracted from artichoke blossoms – hence the name. The sap gives the cheese an especially aromatic taste and also keeps it soft over a long period. The »floral cheese« is available in many shops in Guía (see below), but also in farmers' markets and the market halls of Las Palmas.
> Artesanía Canaria Casa Arturo
> Carretera General 17
> (near the supermarket Hiper Dino)

Tafira

— ✳ B 4

Elevation: 300 – 400m/1,000 – 1,300ft above sea level
Population: 3,000 (entire district)

Tafira, about 8km/5mi south-west of Las Palmas, just like ▶Santa Brígida, is a well-to-do suburb of the capital. It is divided into two parts, Tafira Baja and Tafira Alta. A visit to Tafira is worthwhile because of the Jardín Canario.

Tafira stretches for more than 3km/2mi along the four-lane road from Las Palmas to Vega de San Mateo. Many of the houses show that the owners are wealthy.

AROUND TAFIRA

Jardín Canario (Canarian Garden; officially Jardín Botánico Canario Viera y Clavijo) is located in the community of **La Calzada**, below Tafira Alta. The fabulous public gardens have two entrances. One is on the road from Las Palmas to Santa Brígida (GC 15), the other on

**Jardín Canario

Jardín Canario is a wonderful place

the Tamaraceite – Santa Brígida road (GC 308). The park extends into the Barranco de Guiniguada, along the valley floor and up the eastern slope. Many small paths and steps crisscross the somewhat confusing grounds. To avoid the steps use the lower entrance, but the other one is much more beautiful.

Jardín Canario was founded in 1952 by the Swedish botanist Eric R. Sventenius; it has been open to the public since 1959. Its name commemorates **José de Viera y Clavijo** (1731 – 1813), who wrote Lexicon of Canarian Natural History. The plants in the park are all natives of the Canary Isles or other Macaronesian Islands (endemic plants). The garden was planned to be like the native habitat of the plants and is a complete success: In the extensive grounds palm trees, laurel and dragon tree groves alternate with broad lawns and smaller plant beds.

Many of the plants that can be seen here are difficult to find in their natural habitat. The cultivation of these plants is intended to prevent their extinction. A large **collection of succulents** with rare varieties from Africa, Central and South America is attached to the park. In central and northern Europe they only grow in hothouses and then

Tafira

WHERE TO EAT
Restaurante Jardín Canario €€€€
Carretera de las Palmas
Tel. 928 35 52 45; daily 12.30pm – 5pm

The restaurant is located at the upper entrance to Jardín Canario. Along with its good Canarian and international cooking, it is known for its marvellous view of the park.

only as small plants; in Jardín Canario some have grown to a considerable size. The luxuriant vegetation and the generous water supply have attracted a wide variety of birds to the park. Canaries, goldfinches and Tenerife robins, to name a few, can be heard here.

❶ daily 9am – 6pm, free admission

✱ Tejeda

B/C 3

Elevation: 1,049m/3,400ft above sea level
Population: 2,200 (entire district)

Almost every tourist on Gran Canaria drives through the village of Tejeda in the centre of the island at least once. It has a picturesque location between the mountains and is a popular photo motif, but not very many tourists stop here; most of the tour buses stop at the highest point of the pass, the ▶ Cruz de Tejeda.

The picturesque location in the mountains at an elevation of more than 1,000m/3,300ft makes the mountain village a worthwhile excursion destination. The almond blossom season in late January / early February is the best time to visit. A large almond blossom festival is held then, the exact date depending on the blossoming time; tourist offices have information.

Insider Tip

WHAT TO SEE IN TEJEDA

The village is characterised by several nicely decorated Canarian rural-style houses. The parish church **Iglesia Nuestra Señora del Socorro** replaced a church that burned down in 1920. A wooden figure of Christ from the middle of the 17th century survived the fire. From the town square opposite the view of the impressive mountains is like the view from a balcony; all eyes are drawn to Roque Bentaiga.

Around Plaza Nuestra Señora del Socorro

Picturesque Tejeda illuminated at night

A few steps away is the **Parque Municipal** with its 4m/13ft high cacti. While the park is small, the benches between hibiscus hedges and climbing Bougainvillea are well-placed.

Museums The three village museums do not have any great art treasures, but they do give an impression of rural village culture. **Museo de la Historia y Tradiciones** is housed in a nicely restored Canarian rural house; on the ground floor the history of Gran Canaria is depicted in lively close-ups, beginning with the life of the original inhabitants until their subjugation and conversion to Christianity. On the upper floor agricultural topics are addressed, concentrating on almond cultivation in Tejeda. Unfortunately the information is only in Spanish.

A little way above the museum of history is the **Centro de Plantas Medicinales** (same hours), where healing plants from the region are shown. It is said that Tabaiba dulce, a spurge plant (Euphorbia balsa-

Tejeda

INFORMATION
Oficina de Turismo
Calle Leocadio Cabrera 2
Tel. 928 66 61 89; www.tejeda.es

WHERE TO EAT
Déjate Llevar € – €€
Calle Dr. Domingo Hernández Guerra 25
Tel. 928 66 62 81
www.letmetakeu.com
The opening of this trendy salad bar with wraps, quiche, milk shakes and freshly pressed papaya juice was a minor sensation in this somewhat traditional village, and it brought a fresh breeze. Sidewalk tables give a view of the mountains; there is a lounge area with Wi-Fi inside. A popular meeting place for gays.

WHERE TO STAY
Parador de Cruz de Tejeda €€€
Tel. 928 01 25 00
www.parador.es
The state-run four-star hotel is especially recommended in the summer half of the year; winters can get chilly in this mountain hotel at an elevation of 1560m/5150ft. Even though it is only a few steps to Cruz de Tejeda, the activity there is hardly noticeable. The sun terrace gives a magnificent view; Canarian-Spanish cooking, a fitness room and well-kept wellness spa round off the amenities. The small indoor pool, from which you can swim outdoors into the pine woods, is a nice touch.

Hotel Rural Fonda de La Tea €€
Calle Ezequiel Sánchez 22
Tel. 928 66 64 22
www.hotelfondadelatea.com
Opened on the main street in 2007, this small rural hotel has eleven rustically furnished rooms. The two top floors have an enchanting view of the moutains.

Casa Rural La Solana €
Tel. 928 39 01 69
www.ecoturismorural.com
This homey natural stone house has an especially charming location at 800m/2,600ft in La Solana. There is a living room with a fireplace and dinette, a well-equipped little kitchen and a furnished terrace.

mifera) common to the island, strengthens the gums and stimulates the flow of saliva, while the sap of cardón, also known as Canarian spurge (Euphorbia canariensis), which also grows wild in the moutains, is poisonous. At the end of a visit the guests are offered a cup of herb tea.

In the tourist information opposite the church a small exhibition introduces the works of the sculptor Abraham Cárdenes Guerra (1907 to1971).

Museo de Historia y Tradicionales, **Centro de Plantas Medicinales**:
Tue – Sun 10am – 3.30pm, admission €3

Exposición Abraham Cárdenes Guerra: daily 10.30am – 3.30pm, free admission

Hiking Tejeda is located in the middle of a popular hiking region; some of the old roads connecting the villages were repaired and signed recently. The three-hour Tejeda route via the neighbouring hamlet of La Culata and Cruz de Timagada is popular; the 350m/1150ft change in elevation in each direction is manageable. Hikes to Roque Nublo and Roque Bentaiga are also possible.

AROUND TEJEDA

Roque Bentaiga The 1,412m/4,633ft **Roque Bentaiga** towers over Tejeda. To get there drive 4km/2.5mi on GC 60 from Tejeda southwards and turn off to the right (signposted). After 500m/550yd keep left. Follow the trail on the right from the parking lot of the Centro Interpretación Roque Bentaiga (closed most of the time). It soon becomes rocky and leads up to the plateau below the basalt monolith. From there steps chiselled into the rock lead up to a Guanche religious site. The Roque de Bentaiga was sacred to them. They met here for sacrificial ceremonies (there are basins chiselled into the rock for libations) and festivals that lasted several days. They probably stayed in caves during these festivals; the entrances can still be seen on the slopes.

> **MARCO POLO TIP**
>
> ! *Sweet things* **Insider Tip**
>
> In Tejeda the Dulcería Nublo (Calle Dr. Hernández Guerra 15) is a popular stop for those with a »sweet tooth«. The little pastry shop sells local specialties made of almonds and marzipan. Try the piñones or pan de batatas made of sweet potatoes.

Cueva del Rey A particularly large cave (11m/36ft long, 7m/23ft wide and 2.50m/8ft high) west of Roque de Bentaiga and above the hamlet El Roque is called Cueva del Rey (King's cave). There are basins in the floor of the cave similar to those at the foot of Roque de Bentaiga. There are no signs to mark the cave – ask a local resident for help.

La Solana, El Chorillo A very winding and narrow lane leads from El Roque to the hamlets of La Solana and El Chorillo. The picturesque valley with terraced fields and small orchards is one of the most untouched parts of Gran Canaria.

Hike to El Carrizal El Chorillo and the neighbouring hamlet of El Carrizal are connected by a path. From the end of the road in El Chorillo climb the steps into the village and follow the old paved path up to a wooden cross. There is a wonderful panoramic view of Mesa de Acusa from the path. The last part of the way to El Carrizal is on a trail. After a refreshment at one of the two bars in El Carrizal follow the same trail back (round trip about 2 hours).

Telde

✦ **B/C 4**

Elevation: 116m/382ft above sea level
Population: 89,000 (entire district)

Telde, 15km/9mi south of Las Palmas, is the second-largest city on Gran Canaria. Various industries have settled around Telde. But there is still a certain amount of agriculture; citrus fruits are the primary crops.

The edge of town is characterised by large shopping centres, warehouses and factories. In the bustling centre the streets are usually jam-packed. Barrio San Francisco in the north and Barrio Los Llanos in the south of Telde are the oldest parts of town. The genteel citizens lived in San Francisco, while Los Llanos was the neighbourhood of the black slaves who worked on the sugar cane plantations. It is not surprising then that **San Francisco** with its narrow streets and attractive houses is considered to be a fine example of an old Canarian town.

Begin a tour of this quarter at Plaza de San Juan and its church, which is bordered by pretty old houses. Follow the lane up to Plaza de San Francisco, where time seems to have stood still. Until the Franciscans were expelled in 1836, the little church was their home.

History

Telde can look back on a long history. This area was the seat of the guanarteme who ruled the eastern part of the island in early Canarian times. The many pottery shards that have been found here and the reports of the Italian Leonardo Torriani indicate that the area was densely populated. The villages of Tara and Cendro were located here. Tara is known as the site where the most famous ancient Canarian work of art, the Idol of Tara (▶ ill. p 42), was found. After the Spanish conquest the cultivation of sugar cane and the sale of sugar were the main sources of income. Telde was also known for its slave market.

WHAT TO SEE IN TELDE

*Iglesia de San Juan Bautista

Iglesia de San Juan Bautista, in the northern part of Telde, is worth a visit. It was built from volcanic stone of different colours beginning in 1520. The 16th-century Gothic main façade survives. Changes were made in the 17th and 18th centuries; the nave was renovated in the 19th century. The two bell towers were added in the 20th century. Inside the church, which is dedicated to John the Baptist, the Flemish **retable** dates from around 1500. The artistic carving depicts six

The Flemish retable in Iglesia de San Bautista

scenes from the life of the Virgin. The main picture (top centre) shows the birth of Christ; other scenes show Mary and Joseph's wedding, the annunciation by the archangel Gabriel, Mary visiting Elizabeth, the circumcision of the baby Jesus and the adoration of the Magi. Above the altar there is a **statue of Christ** from Mexico. The life-size 16th-century figure weighs only 7kg/15lbs because it was made from the pith of corn plants. The niche to the left of the main altar is taken up by a sculpture by the sculptor Fernando Estévez; in the niche to the right is a Baroque statue by Luján Pérez.

Museo León There is a small museum in Telde dedicated to the brothers Fernando
y Castillo ▶ Famous People and Juan León y Castillo (Calle León y Castillo 43
– 45). Fernando was a government minister in Madrid who did much for his island home. The large port in Las Palmas was his idea. His brother Juan was born in this house in 1843 and carried out his

Telde

INFORMATION
Oficina de Información y Turismo
Calle León y Castillo 2
Tel. 928 013 312

WHERE TO EAT
Segundo €€
Calle León y Castillo 21
Tel. 928 69 93 65
This meeting place in the neighbour-
hood of San Juan with a usually lively

bar scene serves simple and affordable
Spanish-Canarian cooking. They also
serve small portions for smaller appeti-
tes.

Pastellería Opera €
Calle León y Castillo 4
Tel. 928 68 11 05
A pastry shop with a tiny café that ser-
ves various cakes, sandwiches and
freshly pressed juices.

brother's project. The typically Canarian house with a wooden balcony has furniture and memorabilia inside; pictures and plans of the
harbour are on display in the courtyard.
❶ Mon – Fri 8am – 8pm, Sat 10am – 8pm, Sun 10am – 1pm

AROUND TELDE

Montaña de las Cuatro Puertas (»mountain of the four gates«;   **Montaña de**
319m/1,060ft above sea level) is about 5km/3mi south of Telde on the   **las Cuatro**
road GC 100 to Ingenio. Four openings have been carved into the   **Puertas**
peak, which is accessible by car up to 200m/660ft. They lead to a
chamber that was used by the early Canarians as a religious site. The
area in front of the cave served as a tagoror, an assembly ground. On
the south slope of the mountain there are more Guanche residential
caves, some of which are natural while others were hewn out of the
rock. Steps can be seen that were carved into the floors of some of the
caves. The archaeological complex is open to the public.

✶✶ Teror

✦ B 3

Elevation: 543m/1,781ft above sea level
Population: 13,000 (entire district)

**Teror is considered to be the most typically Canarian town on
the island. In the centre, note the old houses with artistic wooden balconies and beautiful patios; some of them are decorated with coats of arms. The Sunday market is an attraction.**

The statue of the Virgen del Pino, the patron saint of Gran Canaria, is kept in the basilica. On 8 September every year the Fiesta de Virgen del Pino is the island's biggest festival, attended by Canarians from far and wide.

WHAT TO SEE IN TEROR

Calle Real

Teror's most beautiful street runs from the main thoroughfare directly to Plaza Pio XII at the basilica. Proud townhouses, some of which are decorated with portals, wooden balconies and Art nouveau elements in the gables line the street. The houses numbered 2, 6 and 8 are especially beautiful.

**Basílica de Nuestra Señora del Pino

The most important building in Teror is the Basílica de Nuestra Señora del Pino. It was built on the site where the Virgin Mary is supposed to have appeared to some shepherds. According to legend the »miracle« took place on 8 September 1481. The shepherds saw the mother of God in the branches of a giant pine tree, which was knocked over in a storm in 1684. Juan Frías, the first bishop of the Canaries, must have found the vision very convenient, since it gave the

Altar picture in the Basílica de Nuestra Señora del Pino

Teror

INFORMATION
Oficina de Información Turistica
on Plaza Pio II diagonally opposite the
basilica
Tel. 928 61 38 98

SHOPPING
Sunday market
There is a market every Sunday morning
around the basilica. It sells delicious and
very fresh groceries; checking out the
rummage and the craft items is also fun.

WHERE TO EAT
El Secuestro €€€
Avenida Cabildo Insular
Tel. 928 63 02 31
Grilled meat, rustic setting. The restaurant is only open Thu – Sun; it is crowded at the weekends!

Mirador El Balcón de Zamora €€
On the GC 21
1km/0.5mi before Valleseco
Tel. 928 61 80 42
At weekends it is hard to get a table at
this popular panorama restaurant. The
menu includes classics of Canarian cuisine like rabbit or hearty potaje (stew).

El Rincón de Magüi €€
Calle de la Diputación 6
Tel. 928 63 04 54

closed Mon.
Family restaurant located at the end of
a lane off the church plaza; the walls are
decorated with ceramic plates and posters from Seville. On Sundays Sancocho
canaria (fish stew) is served; or choose
from filled croquettes, meatballs and
other meat dishes, or try gofio.

La Villa € – €€
Plaza Nuestra Señora del Pino 7
Tel. 928 63 26 33; closed Mon.
In a pretty Art nouveau house that is
always full during the Sunday market.
There is a bar in front and a few rustic
wooden tables in the back, tasty tapas
and soups are served.

WHERE TO STAY
Casa Rural Doña Margarita €€
Calle Padre Cueto 4
Tel. 609 62 90 76
www.margaritacasarural.com
This representative townhouse from the
late 18th century is located next to the
town hall and only a few steps from the
basilica. Three apartments with two bedrooms each and room for four people at
the most can be rented. The rooms are
a little old-fashioned but stylishly furnished; the kitchens have all the necessities. Minimum rental time: one week.

Christianisation of the island a significant impetus. A chapel was
built on the site on his orders and replaced in 1692 by a larger church.
This one was almost completely destroyed in an explosion in 1718;
only the tower survived. It is integrated into the present basilica,
which in turn was built between 1760 and 1767.
The 1m/3ft-high statue of the **Virgen del Pino** survived the explosion of 1718 undamaged. The 15th-century statue stands in a silver

Procession in honour of the Virgin Mary

palanquin that was made in the 18th century in La Laguna (Tenerife). The two halves of the virgin's face have different expressions. One half appears to be suffering, while the other half is smiling softly. Those who want to see this can climb the stairs in the back of the church to see the figure up close. The Virgen del Pino was named the patron of the island by the pope only in 1914. Until then the Virgen de la Candelaria, the patron of Tenerife, was also the protector of Gran Canaria. In 1929 the Virgen del Pino received military honours: King Alfonso XIII declared her to be Capitan General. During the feast day, along with sacred and folk music, military marches take place and soldiers salute the statue. Another valuable relic in the basilica is a cross that was carved from the legendary pine tree; it is kept under glass.

❶ Mon – Fri 3 – 5pm, Sun 11am – 2pm and 3.30 – 5.45pm

Casa Museo de los Patrones de la Virgen Diagonally opposite Casa Museo de los Patrones de la Virgen (Plaza Nuestra Señora del Pino 3) there is a well-preserved example of Canarian architecture. The house was built around 1600 and was the summer residence of the Manrique de Lara family, the patrons of the Virgen del Pino. Today it houses a museum. The many exhibits (paintings, weapons, dishes, etc.) and the pretty patio give an attractive impression of life on the Canaries in the past centuries.

❶ Mon – Thu 11am – 6pm, Sun 10.30am – 2pm

The museum also exhibits some works of the German painter Georg Hedrich (1927 – 2010). He came in 1957 to work as a teacher for art history and drawing at the German school in Las Palmas and lived in Teror for almost half a century.

Georg Hedrich studio

❶ Tue – Thu 11am – 4pm, Sun 10am – 2pm, admission €3

The little plaza next to the church is named after Teresa de Bolívar, the wife of the leader of the Latin American freedom movement, **Simón de Bolívar** (1783 – 1830). There is a bust of the Venezuelan freedom fighter on the square. Teresa's great-grandfather is said to have been born in Casa de los Patrones.

Plaza Teresa de Bolívar

There is no sign ponting the way to the former **bishop's palace** on Plaza Pio XII, but the 50m/165ft long building with windows framed with ochre-coloured stones right behind the basilica can't be missed. It is now used as a house of culture and can be entered through the 1867 stone portal. Two halls off the inner courtyard are used occasionally for exhibitions. The **Casa Consistorial** (town hall) to the right of the entrance to the bishop's palace is flanked by two square towers with the Teror coat of arms between them.

Palacio Episcopal and town hall

With its avant garde architecture the culture forum just a few steps below the basilica looks like a foreign body in the historic old town. It has an auditorium that was opened in 2006 with room for 600 guests and is used as a stage for theatre and concerts as well as the annual trumpet festival in July (www.terortrumpetfestival.com).

Auditorio de Teror

AROUND TEROR

On the road to Arucas after 1.5km/1mi comes the large entrance gate to public estate (parking is usually limited on Sundays). The estate, which has an area of 207ha/500ac has belonged to the island government since 1981; it is now open for day-trippers, hikers and Nordic walkers.

Finca Osorio

From the gate a comfortable path leads after ten minutes to a picnic area with several massive oaks trees, some with a diameter up to 3m/10ft. To the right is the former manor house from the 19th century, which is now used for school camps. To the left of the building is a garden with bamboo, sago palms, various succulent plants and a fountain; there are grottos in the slope above the garden. Various excursions through the grounds are possible starting from the manor house; reforestation projects have been started are in order to reintroduce the laurel forests that were once common here.

❶ daily 9am – 5pm, free admission

Valleseco   The road from Teror to the village of Valleseco 8km/5mi to the west is very winding. The name »dry valley« is confusing since the area is very fertile. Potatoes, fruits and vegetables are grown. The village is located at an altitude of 950m/3,000ft above sea level and dominated by the white, Moorish-style parish church.

Balcón de   The observation point half a mile before Valleseco has the best view
Zamora   of Teror and the over-populated northern mountains. At exactly the right place there is a large tourist restaurant that is completely overrun at weekends.

Vega de San Mateo

✳ B 3

Elevation: 836m/2,743ft above sea level
Population: 7,700 (entire district)

Vega de San Mateo is a typical mountain village, located a good 20km/12mi south-west of Las Palmas. Most people just call it San Mateo. The country market on weekends is the big attraction.

Mercado de   Since the farmer's market opened its gates in 1983 it has developed
Agrícola   into into one of the best-known island markets. Apart from a broad selection of vegetables, fruits and cheese specialties, potted plants and cut flowers are also sold. The products all come from the immediate area, since the good water supply makes agriculture possible here. There is a price list at the entrance showing the average prices for all of the products.

❶ Sat 8am – 8pm and Sun 8am – 2.30pm

WHAT TO SEE IN VEGA DE SAN MATEO

Iglesia San   The historic old city plaza can be reached from the unattractive
Mateo and   through street via the cobblestoned Calle Rambla de la Constitución;
Ayunta-   the parish church and town hall are located on the place. Parroquia
miento   de San Mateo has a statue of St. Matthew, the patron saint of farmers and cattlemen, that goes back to the year 1652. From the church several narrow lanes invite exploring the small old town. Above the church behind a small pavilion is the Casa Consistoral, which was

Vega de San Mateo

INFORMATION
Oficina de Información Turística
Calle Dr. Ramírez Cabrera 11
Tel. 928 66 13 50

WHERE TO EAT
El Mercado € – €€
Avenida de Mercado s/n
Tel. 928 66 16 21
Visitors to the market can get typical Canarian food in this restaurant right next to the market hall, like gofio, chick pea soup and meat skewers. But the house wine takes getting used to.

Cafeteria Mallow €
Avenida de Tinamar 41
Tel. 928 66 21 55
Simple bar on the main thoroughfare, which functions as the local pub. Guests chat over tapas or churros, deep-fried pastry that can be dunked into hot chocolate.

built in 1943 in the neo-Canarian style. The observation point **Balcón de La Caldereta** behind the town hall offers a wide panoramic view of the surrounding mountains.

The San Mateo gofio mill is located in the unpretentious house at Calle del Agua no. 9. The roasted grain is ground freshly several times a week in the mill right behind the sales counter. Gofio in various degrees of quality can be bought during the usual business hours.

Molino de Gofio

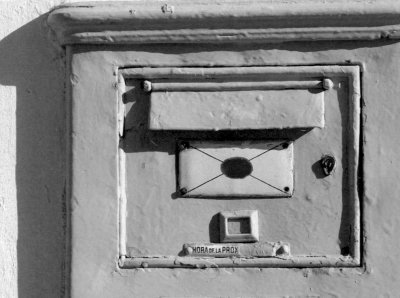

CORREOS

PRACTICAL
INFORMATION

What's the best way to get to Gran Canaria? How do you find information about the island before you go? What is island hopping between the Canary Islands like?

Arrival · Before the Journey

GETTING THERE

By plane There are **low budget and scheduled flights** to Gando Airport on Gran Canaria from all major European airports. Regular scheduled flights are worth considering as an alternative, such as Air Europa (www.aireuropa.com) from London. There are also connecting flights several times a day from Madrid or Barcelona with Iberia (www.iberia.com).

> **Island hopping** _Insider Tip_
>
> For first-time visitors to the Canaries, a tour including two or three islands is an attractive option. Many travel agencies offer holidays covering several Canary Islands. There is a large selection of air and ferry connections between the islands for those who want to organise the trip themselves (▸p.272).

Once a week (departure Tuesday evening) ferries run by the Spanish shipping line Acciona Trasmediterránea travel the route Cádiz – Santa Cruz de Tenerife – Las Palmas de Gran Canaria. The trip from Cádiz to Gran Canaria takes about two days. Passage can be booked with the shipping line.

IMMIGRATION AND CUSTOMS REGULATIONS

Travel documents As the Canary Islands are part of Spain, citizens of EU countries which are party to the Schengen agreement can enter without border checks.

However, travellers from the UK and Ireland need a valid identification card or passport. Children under 16 years of age must carry a children's passport or be entered in the parent's passport. For a stay of up to 90 days, citizens of Australia, Canada, New Zealand and the USA do not require a visa.

Car documents Always carry your driving licence, the motor vehicle registration and the international green insurance card. Motor vehicles must have the oval sticker showing nationality, unless they have a Euro licence-plate.

Pets Those who wish to bring pets (dogs, cats) require a pet pass. Among other things, it contains an official veterinary statement of health (no more than 30 days old), a rabies vaccination certificate that is at least 30 days and no more than eleven months old, and a passport photo. In addition, the animal must have a microchip.

AIRPORT
Aeropuerto de
Gran Canaria
22km/13mi south of Las Palmas
Tel. 902 40 47 04
Tel. 913 21 10 00
Taxi: about €30 to Las Palmas or
Maspalomas Bus: Line 60 of
Global bus lines runs every 35 minutes
between 6am and 7pm, between 8pm
and 1.30am only once an hour to
Parque San Telmo in Las Palmas.

FERRY
Acciona Trasmediterránea
Plaza Mr. Jolly s/n
Las Palmas de Gran Canaria
Tel. 902 45 46 45
(in Spain)

Main office in UK
Travel Gateway
Sutton Courtenay Oxfordshire,
OX14 4FH, UK
Tel. 0844 576 00 06
www.aferry.com

Customs regulations

The Canary Islands have a **special status** within the European Union member states: They are not treated as part of the common economic area within which the movement of goods for private purposes is largely duty-free. This means: The maximum quantities (for example 800 cigarettes, 10 litres of spirits and 90 litres of wine per person) applicable for journeys between other parts of the EU do not apply. Instead, it is possible to take in and out the quantities of duty-free goods that apply for travel between EU states and non-EU: for persons over the age of 15 500g of coffee and 100g of tea, 50g of perfume and 0.25 litres of eau de toilette, and for persons over the age of 17 1 litre of spirits over 22% or 2 litres of spirits under 22% or 2 litres of sparkling wine and 2 litres of wine, as well as 200 cigarettes or 50 cigars or 250g of tobacco. Goods with a maximum value of 430 euros may be imported.

HEALTH INSURANCE

National health insurance

Citizens of EU countries are entitled to treatment on Gran Canaria under the local regulations in case of illness on production of their **European health insurance card**. Those who do not have one should bring an alternative health certificate. Even with this card, in most cases some of the costs for medical care and prescribed medication must be paid by the patient. Upon presentation of receipts, the health insurance at home covers the costs – but not for all treatments.

Private travel insurance

Since some of the costs for medical treatment and medication typically have to be met by the patient, and the costs for return transportation may not be covered by regular health insurances, additional travel insurance is recommended.

Electricity

Gran Canaria uses 220 volt electricity; an adapter is generally necessary for visitors from the UK and Ireland. These are available at local shops and called »adaptador« or »ladrón« in Spanish.

Emergency

EMERGENCY NUMBERS
Fire department, police, doctor
Tel. 112

Multilingual police
Tel. 112

Etiquette and Customs

Clothing   In Spain it's important to cut a good figure. For this reason certain customs and rituals are part of everyday life for Spaniards and should be respected by foreign visitors, like choice of clothing. No matter if man or woman, Spaniards always look neat as a pin when they leave the house, even on humid summer days. A man wears long pants, on very hot days maybe knee-length Bermuda shorts, a short-sleeved shirt or a fashionable t-shirt. Short shorts, sleeveless t-shirts and worn out Birkenstocks are not really appropriate. For that matter beachwear is not worn in the city. People tend to be covered up. Women also dress fashionably in the city. They may show a lot of skin but they do it very fashionably and according to the latest styles. This applies especially to young people, who are very fashion-conscious and always follow the latest trends, including body piercing and daring tattoos when they are in fashion. Body hair of any kind, in the armpits or on the legs is absolutely taboo for women. Shorts and sleeveless clothing is considered inappropriate for both sexes in churches and monasteries. It is advisable to have at least one dressier outfit along for going out in the evening, whether to one of the many cultural events or to enjoy the nightlife.

> **?**
> **MARCO ⊕ POLO INSIGHT**
>
> *Strictly no smoking in Spain*
>
> Since January 2011 smoking has not been allowed in tapas bars, restaurants, cafés, discos, casinos as well as public buildings like railway stations and airports. Hotels are allowed to reserve 30% of their rooms for smokers, but many hotels in Spain do not allow smoking at all.

People embrace when greeting each other, whether man and woman or two women, even if they do not know each other well, and peck each other on both cheeks, but without too much bodily contact. Men greet each other by shaking hands firmly or thumping each other on the shoulder. Instead of using the more formal »buenos días« (»good day!« in the morning) or »buenas tardes (»good day!« in the afternoon or »good evening!«), the more casual »hola« (»hello!«) is being used in the meantime.

Greeting

Invitations are given quickly and happily, but the guest is rarely invited home. Instead, they are invited to bars or restaurants. But people do not linger and move on quickly.

The bar as living room

Spaniards do not like to go out alone, rather in small or large groups. If someone brings a friend to a nightly gathering, that person is quickly accepted and integrated into the group. This applies to foreigners as well. But do not expect a deeper friendship if the Spaniard casually says »call me sometime« when he leaves. He doesn't expect to hear from you on the very next day.

Excursions

Along with the island tour, the most popular excursions go to the central mountains, to Agaete, Tejeda or to Palmitos Park as well as on shopping tours to Palmas or on Sundays to some of the markets in smaller towns. Those who would like to make arrangements for a bus tour themselves needs a bit of time and patience, but all of the larger towns are accessible by public transportation (►Transport).

By bus

Gran Canaria is best explored with a rental car (►Tours). Organized jeep safaris are a enjoyable way to explore the island, as they go to untouched areas that are not accessible to normal cars.

By car

The range of boating excursions covers everything from short trips to day trips and to cruises lasting several days. Especially worth mentioning are shark fishing trips or a sail on the windjammer »San Miguel« (from Puerto Rico). The »Yellow Submarine« leaves from Puerto de Mogán for a fascinating trip to the world under the sea. There is regular boat passage between Puerto Rico and Puerto de Mogán and Arguineguín. A ride on a high-speed boat is also suitable for a day trip between Agaete (Gran Canaria) and Santa Cruz de Tenerife. The ships of the Fred Olsen company (www.fredolsen.es) run six times a day, and the trip takes only one hour. A side trip to Fuerteventura is also possible, but the trip from Las Palmas to Morro Jable (Jandía peninsula) takes about 2.5 hours (www.navieraarmas.

By boat

com). One-day boat trips to the other islands are not worthwhile because of the distances.

By airplane   Since each of the Canary Islands has a character of its own, day trips to a different island are eventful and thanks to the low airfares an affordable holiday pleasure. There is also a good connection to Marrakesh in Morocco; the flight takes two hours from Gran Canaria (www.bintercanarias.com). If you would like to see Gran Canaria from the air should go to Islas Helicopters (▶MARCO POLO tip, p. 223).

Health

Medical help   Gran Canaria has adequate medical facilities. Most doctors speak at least one foreign language. In an emergency contact one of the health centres listed below, where many English-speaking doctors work.

Medical insurance   Citizens of the EU are entitled to receive treatment in Spain according to the local regulations (▶Arrival • Before the Journey).

Pharmacies   Pharmacies (»farmacias«) are recognisable by the red or green Maltese cross. Opening hours are Mon – Fri 9am – 1pm and 4pm – 8pm and Sat 9am – 1pm. At other times there is a pharmacy with emergency hours. The address is posted in each pharmacy and called »Farmacia de Guardia«.

EMERGENCY
Tel. 112

HOSPITALS AND
MEDICAL CENTRES
*Hospital Universitária de
Gran Canaria Dr. Negrín*
Calle Barranco de la Ballena
Las Palmas
Tel. 928 45 00 00

Clínica Roca
Calle Buganvilla 1
San Agustín
Tel. 928 76 90 04
www.hospiten.com

Clínica San Roque
Calle Mar de Siberia 1
Urb. Meloneras
Tel. 928 06 36 00
www.clinicasanroque.com

Other clinics can be found in Playa Taurito, Playa del Cura and Puerto Rico

ENGLISH-SPEAKING DOCTORS
British Medical Clinic
Avenide Roca Bosch s/n
Bungalows Martinica 19
Costa Rica
Tel. 928 56 00 16
www.britishmedicalclinic.com

Information

SPANISH TOURIST OFFICES
In Canada
Spanish Tourist Office
Bloor Street West 2-Suite 3402
Toronto, Ontario M4W 3E2
Tel. +1 416 9613131
Fax +1 416 9611992
www.tourspain.toronto.on.ca

In Ireland
Spanish Tourist Office PO Box 10015,
Dublin 1
Tel. 0818 22 02 90
dublin@tourspain.es

In the UK
Spanish Tourist Office
PO Box 4009
London W1A 6NB
Tel. 020 7486 8077
www.spain.info

In the United States
Spanish Tourist Office
Fifth Avenue 666 - 35th floor
N.Y. 10103 New York
Tel +1 212 2658822
Fax +1 212 2658864
www.okspain.org

Spanish Tourist Office
Wilshire Blvd. 8383 - Suite 960
Beverly Hills California 90211
Tel. +1 323 658 71 95
Fax 658 10 61
losangeles@tourspain.es

On Gran Canaria
Patronato de Turismo
Calle Triana 93

Tel. 9 28 21 96 00
www.grancanaria.com

Centro Insular de Turismo
Avenida España, Yumbo Centrum
Playa del Inglés
Tel. 9 28 77 15 50
Hours: Mon – Fri 9am – 9pm, Sat until
1pm
The addresses of the tourist information
centres are listed under each location in
»Sights from A to Z«.

CONSULATES
Republic of Ireland
León y Castillo 195
Las Palmas de Gran Canaria
Tel. 928 29 77 28

United Kingdom
Calle Luis Morote 6
Las Palmas de Gran Canaria
Tel. 928 26 25 08
lapal-consular@fco.gov.uk

USA
Calle Martinez de Escobar 3
Las Palmas de Gran Canaria
Tel. 928 27 12 59
canarias@bitmailer.net

INTERNET
www.spain.info
Internet address of the Spanish Tourist
Office; information on the Canary Islands.

www.grancanaria.com
Official website of the Gran Canaria
tourist association, much useful information in various languages.

www.abcanarias.com
General information on all of the Canary Islands. Also check for hotels and holiday flats.

www.turismodecanarias.com
Website of the Canarian local government with diverse information, calendar of events and the possibility to make reservations.

www.grancanariacultura.com
Cultural gateway to the Canary Islands with information on events and museums. Only in Spanish.

Language

The staff of larger hotels and restaurants generally speak English. Only in smaller towns in the interior might there be problems in communicating.

Vowels The vowels a, e, i, o, u, are short and open in Spanish. There are no long vowels.

Consonants **c** before a, o, u like »k«
c before e, i voiceless lisped »s«, stronger than the English »th« (e. g., gracias)
ch like in English
g before a, o, u like »g«
g before e, i like German »ch« in Bach
gue, gui / que, qui u is always silent, like »g«, »k«
h is always silent
j always like German »ch« in Bach
ll like »ly« or »y« (e. g., Mallorca)
ñ like »ny« in canyon
z voiceless lisped »s«, stronger than the English »th«

Spanish phrases

At a glance
Yes./No.	Sí./No.
Maybe.	Quizás./Tal vez.
OK!	¡De acuerdo!/¡Está bien!
Please./Thank you.	Por favor./Gracias.
Thank you very much.	Muchas gracias.
You're welcome.	No hay de qué./De nada.
Excuse me!	¡Perdón!

Coaches are among the most popular ways to travel on the Canaries

Pardon?	¿Cómo dice/dices?
I don't understand you.	No le/la/te entiendo.
I only speak a little …	Hablo sólo un poco de …
Could you help me?	¿Puede usted ayudarme, por favor?
I would like …	Quiero …/Quisiera …
I (don't) like that.	(No) me gusta.
Do you have …?	¿Tiene usted …?
How much does this cost?	¿Cuánto cuesta?
What time is it?	¿Qué hora es?

Getting acquainted

Good morning	¡Buenos días!
Good day!	¡Buenos días!/¡Buenas tardes!
Good evening!	¡Buenas tardes!/¡Buenas noches!
Hello!	¡Hola! ¿Qué tal?
My name is …	Me llamo …
What is your name, please?	¿Cómo se llama usted, por favor?
How are you?	¿Qué tal está usted?/¿Qué tal?
Fine, thanks. And you?	Bien, gracias. ¿Y usted/tú?
Good bye!	¡Hasta la vista!/¡Adiós!
See you!	¡Adiós!/¡Hasta luego!
See you soon!	¡Hasta pronto!
See you tomorrow!	¡Hasta mañana!

Travelling

left/right	a la izquierda/a la derecha
straight ahead	todo seguido/derecho
close/far	cerca/lejos
How far is it?	¿A qué distancia está?
I would like to rent … .	Quisiera alquilar …
… a car	… un coche.
… a boat	… una barca/un bote/un barco.
Excuse me, where is …?	Perdón, ¿dónde está …
… the railway station	… la estación (de trenes)?
… the bus terminal	… la estación de autobuses/ la terminal?
… the airport	… el aeropuerto?

Breakdown

My car broke down.	Tengo una avería.
Would you please send me a towtruck?	¿Pueden ustedes enviarme un cochegrúa, por favor?
Is there a garage here?	¿Hay algún taller por aquí cerca?
Where is the next petrol station?	¿Dónde está la estación de servicio/a gasolinera más cercana, por favor?
I would like … litres of …	Quisiera … litros de …
… normal petrol.	… gasolina normal.
… super./ …diesel.	… súper./ … diesel.
… unleaded./ …leaded.	… sin plomo./ … con plomo.
Fill it up, please.	Lleno, por favor.

Accident

Help!	¡Ayuda!, ¡Socorro!
Careful!	¡Atención!
Careful!	¡Cuidado!
Please call … quickly	Llame enseguida …
… an ambulance.	… una ambulancia.
… the police.	… a la policía.
… the fire department.	… a los bomberos.
Do you have any bandages?	¿Tiene usted botiquín de urgencia?
It was my (your) fault.	Ha sido por mi (su) culpa.
Please tell me your name and your address.	¿Puede usted darme su nombre y dirección?

Going out

Where is there …	¿Dónde hay por aquí cerca …
… a good restaurant?	… un buen restaurante?
… a reasonable restaurant?	… un restaurante no demasiado caro?
Please make a reservation for us for this evening	¿Puede reservarnos para esta noche
for a table for 4 people.	una mesa para cuatro personas?
Cheers!	¡Salud!
The bill, please!	¡La cuenta, por favor!
Did it taste good?	¿Le/Les ha gustado la comida?
The food was excellent.	La comida estaba écelente.

Shopping

Where can I find … a market?	Por favor, ¿dónde hay … un mercado?
… a pharmacy	…. una farmacia
… a shopping centre	… un centro comercial

Accommodation

Could you please recommend … ?	Perdón, señor/señora/señorita. . . . . .
	¿Podría usted recomendarme …
… a hotel	… un hotel?
… a guesthouse	… una pensión?
I have reserved a room.	He reservado una habitación.
Do you still have …	¿Tienen ustedes …?
… a single room?	… una habitación individual?
… a double room?	… una habitación doble?
… with shower/bath?	… con ducha/baño?
… for one night?	… para una noche?
… for one week?	… para una semana?
How much does the room cost	¿Cuánto cuesta la habitación
… with breakfast?	… con desayuno?
… with half board?	… media pensión?

Doctor and pharmacy

Can you recommend a good doctor?	¿Puede usted indicarme un buen médico?
I have …	Tengo …
… diarrhea.	… diarrea.

... a fever.	... fiebre.
... a headache.	... dolor de cabeza.
... a toothache.	... dolor de muelas.
... a sore throat.	... dolor de garganta.

Bank

Where is ...	Por favor, ¿dónde hay por aquí...?
... a bank?	... un banco?
... a currency exchange?	... una oficina/casa de cambio?
I would like to change	Quisiera cambiar ...
British pounds into euros.	libras británicas

Numbers

0	cero	19	diecinueve
1	un, uno, una	20	veinte
2	dos	21	veintiuno(a)
3	tres	22	veintidós
4	cuatro	30	treinta
5	cinco	40	cuarenta
6	seis	50	cincuenta
7	siete	60	sesenta
8	ocho	70	setenta
9	nueve	80	ochenta
10	diez	90	noventa
11	once	100	cien, ciento
12	doce	200	doscientos, -as
13	trece	1000	mil
14	catorce	2000	dos mil
15	quince	10000	diez mil
16	dieciséis		
17	diecisiete	1/2	medio
18	dieciocho	1/4	un cuatro

Post

How much does ... cost?	¿Cuánto cuesta ...
... a letter ...	... una carta ...
... a postcard ...	... una postal ...
to Great Britain/USA?	para Inglaterra/los Estados Unidos?

a stamp	sellos
a telephone card	tarjetas para el teléfono

Restaurante/Restaurant
desayuno	breakfast
almuerzo	lunch
cena	dinner
camarero	waiter
cubierto	setting
cuchara	spoon
cucharita	teaspoon
cuchillo	knife
lista de comida	menu
plato	plate
tenedor	fork
vaso / taza	glass/cup

Tapas
albóndigas	meatballs
boquerones en vinagre	small herring in a vinegar marinade
caracoles	snails
chipirones	small squid
chorizo	paprika sausage
jamón serrano	dried ham
morcilla	blood sausage
pulpo	squid
tortilla	potato omelette

Entremeses/Starters
aceitunas	olives
anchoas	anchovies
ensalada	salad
jamón	ham
mantequilla	butter
pan	bread
panecillo	bread roll
sardinas	sardines

Sopas/Soups

caldo	meat broth
gazpacho	cold vegetable soup
puchero canario	hearty soup
sopa de pescado	fish soup
sopa de verduras	vegetable soup

Platos de huevos/Egg dishes

huevo	egg
duro / pasado por agua	hard-boiled / soft-boiled
huevos a la flamenca	eggs with beans
huevos fritos	fried eggs
huevos revueltos	scrambled eggs
tortilla	omelette

Pescado/Fish

ahumado	smoked
a la plancha	grilled on a hot griddle
asado	fried
cocido	boiled
frito	baked
anguila	eel
atún	tuna
bacalao	cod
besugo	bream
lenguado	sole
merluza	hake
salmón	salmon
trucha	trout
almeja	river mussel
bogavante	lobster
calamar	squid
camarón	shrimp
cangrejo	crab
gamba	prawn
langosta	rock lobster
ostras	oysters

Carne/Meat

buey	beef

carnero	mutton
cerdo	pork
chuleta	chops
cochinillo, lechón	roast suckling pig
conejo	rabbit
cordero	lamb
ternera	veal
vaca	beef
asado	roast
bistec	beefsteak
carne ahumada	smoked meat
carne estofada	pot roast
carne salada	corned beef
fiambre	cold cuts
jamón	ham
lomo	loin or back
salchichón	hard sausage
tocino	bacon
pato	duck
pollo	chicken

Verduras/Vegetables

aceitunas	olives
cebollas	onions
col de Bruselas	brussels sprouts
coliflor	cauliflower
espárragos	asparagus
espinacas	spinach
garbanzos	chickpeas
guisantes	peas
habas, judías	beans
lechuga	lettuce
patatas	potatoes
patatas fritas	french fries
pepinos	cucumber
tomates	tomato
zanahorias	carrots

Condimentos/Condiments

vinagre / aceite	vinegar / oil

ajo	garlic
azafrán	saffron
mostaza	mustard
sal/salado / pimienta	salt/salted / pepper

Postres/Sweets

bollo	sweet bread
dulces	sweets
flan	cream caramel
helado	ice cream
mermelada / miel	jam / honey
pastel	cake
queso	cheese
tarta	tart

Frutas/Fruit

cerezas	cherries
chumbos	prickly pears
dátiles	dates
fresas	strawberries
higos	figs
mandarinas	mandarin oranges
manzana / pera	apple / pear
melocotón	peach
melones	honeydew melon
membrillo	quince
naranjas	oranges
nueces	nuts
piña	pineapple
plátano	banana
sandías	watermelon
uvas	grape

Local Foods

bocadillo	filled roll
chorizo	red paprika sausage
churros	fried dough
migas	croutons

Beverages

agua mineral con/sin gas	mineral water carbonated/non-carb.
aguardiente	cordial
amontillado	medium sherry
anís	anis cordial
Brandy	brandy
cerveza	beer
café con leche	coffee with milk
café solo	espresso
café cortado	with a little milk
fino	dry sherry
leche	milk
limonada	lemonade
la Manzanilla	camomile tea
oloroso	sweet sherry
té	tea
vino blanco/tinto	wine white/red
rosado	rosé
seco/dulce	dry/sweet
zumo	fruit juice

Literature

A good deal of literature about many aspects of life on the Canary Islands is available in souvenir shops and bookshops on the islands themselves, but hard to get in other countries.

Jose Luis Concepcion: *The Guanches: Survivors and their Descendants.* Short account of the original inhabitants of the Canary Isles. The same author has written a book about the traditions of the Islands entitled Costumbres, Tradiciones Canarias (available locally in English).

History, culture

Florence du Cane: *The Canary Isles.* A. & C. Black, 1911. An entertaining view of the islands 100 years ago. Only available second-hand.

Felipe Fernández-Armesto: *The Canary Islands after the Conquest: The Making of a Colonial Society in the Early Sixteenth Century.* Clarendon Press, 1981. A scholarly work for those with a detailed interest in the subject.

José Luis Gago: *Arquitecturas Contemporáneas Las Palmas de Gran Canaria 1960 – 2000.* Excellent black-and-white photographs of interesting modern architecture in the island's capital.

José M. Castellano Gil: *History of the Canary Islands.* Centro de la Cultura Popular Canaria, 1993. A useful general survey.

Cooking **Jose Luis Concepcion:** *Typical Canary Cooking: The Best Traditional Dishes, Sweets and Liquors.* 1994.

Flora Lilia: *The Best of Canarian Sauces: Mojos, Adobos, Salmorejos, Escabeches.* Centro de la Cultura Popular Canaria, 2000.

Nature **Miguel Angel Cabrera Perez:** *Native Flora of the Canary Islands.* Editorial Everest, 2000.

Tony Clarke: *A Field Guide to the Birds of the Atlantic Islands: Canary Islands, Madeira, Azores, Cape Verde.* Helm Field Guides, 2006.

M.G. Sanchez and M.J.M. Valbuena: *National Parks in the Canary Islands.* Editorial Everest, 2001.

Noel Rochford: *Landscapes of Gran Canaria.* Sunflower Books, 2009.

Hiking The hiking map published by the National Geographical Institute (Instituto Geográfico Nacional/IGN) on Gran Canaria is very detailed with 20 pages at 1:25 000. It's useful both for walkers and mountain bikers.

Media

Newspapers Foreign newspapers and magazines are available on the island the day after publication. A good range of English-language papers can be found in the tourist centres.
The »**Island Gazette**« is published in English.

Television Five Spanish-speaking TV channels can be picked up on Gran Canaria as well as satellite channels, depending on the location, including English-speaking broadcasts.

Money

Euro The euro is the official currency in Spain. Spanish coins depict Juan Carlos I (1 €, 2 €), Miguel de Cervantes (50, 20 and 10 cents) and the cathedral of Santiago de Compostela (5, 2 and 1 cent).

Banks are open Mon – Fri 9am – 2pm, Sat 9am – 1pm. In the months   **Banks**
of June to September most banks are closed on Saturdays. **ATMs**
(bancomato) are available in all larg-
er towns and have operating instruc-
tions in several languages. Money
can be withdrawn using debit and
credit cards with a PIN.

Banks, larger hotels, restaurants, car
rentals as well as shops accept most
international **credit cards** like Visa,
Eurocard, American Express. Check
to see if your bank cards are valid
overseas.

What does it cost?

Petrol (Canaries) €1.15
Simple meal:
Tapas starting at €1.60
Cup of coffee:
€1.50 (café solo)

Prices in restaurants ▶ p. 8
Prices in hotels ▶ p. 8

MARCO ⊕ POLO INSIGHT

CONTACT INFORMATION FOR CREDIT CARDS

In the event of lost bank or credit cards
you can contact the following numbers
in UK and USA (phone numbers when
dialling from Gran Canaria, have the
bank sort code, account number and
card number as well as the expiry date
ready):

Eurocard/MasterCard
Tel. 001 636 7227 111

Visa
Tel. 001 / 410 581 336

American Express UK
Tel. 0044 273 696 933

American Express USA
Tel. 001 800 528 4800

Diners Club UK
Tel. 0044 1252 513 500

Diners Club USA
Tel. 001 303 799 9000

The following numbers of UK banks (dialling from Gran Canaria) can be used to
report and cancel lost or stolen bank
and credit cards issued by those banks:

HSBC
Tel. 0044 1442 422 929

Barclaycard
Tel. 0044 1604 230 230

NatWest
Tel. 0044 1423 70 0545

Lloyds TSB
Tel. 0044 1702 278 270

Post · Telecommunications

Postcards and letters are automatically sent by airmail and generally   **Letters**
take five days to central Europe. Postage for postcards (postales) and
letters (cartas) up to 20 grams within Europe costs €0.70. Large post-

cards cost €1.35. Stamps (sellos) can be bought where you buy the postcards or at the post office. The mailboxes are yellow.

Post offices Post offices are open Mon – Fri 9am – 2pm, Sat 9am – 1pm.

Telephone Phone calls to other countries can be made from public telephone booths using coins or a telephone card (tarjeta telefónica). Telephone cards can be bought in tobacco shops, kiosks and at some supermarkets.
Mobile telephones automatically connect to the local systems. A locally bought prepaid card can be cheaper. In Spanish mobile phones are called »móvil«.

Telephone numbers Spanish telephone numbers have nine digits. They begin with the area code (for Gran Canaria, Fuerteventura and Lanzarote: 928), which must be dialled when making local calls as well. Tenerife, La Gomera, La Palma and El Hierro have the area code 922.

COUNTRY CODES
To Spain
Tel. 0034

From Spain
To Australia: 0061
To the Republic of Ireland: 00353

To UK: 0044
To USA and Canada: 001

When calling these countries from Spain, leave off the zero before the local area code.

Security

Theft is common in the large tourist centres along the south coast. Be careful also in the port area Santa Catalina in Las Palmas, especially in the evening.

Time

The Canary Islands are in the **Western European Time zone** (WET), two hours ahead of Greenwich Mean Time. As European summer time is used from April to October, the time difference to other parts of Europe is constant all year round. Since the archipelago is so close to the equator the number of daylight hours does not vary as much between summer and winter on the Canaries as in northern Europe: The longest summer day has about 14 hours of daylight, the shortest winter day about 11 hours.

Toilets

Toilets are usually called »servicios«, »lavabos« or »aseos«. The ladies' is called »Señoras«; men's is called »Caballeros«, or simply the letters »S« and »C«.

Transport

The Canarians **drive on the right**, just like on the Spanish mainland and the rest of continental Europe.

Driving

Speed limits: Within towns the speed limit is 50km/h (30mph); outside towns it is 90km/h (55mph), on motorways 100km/h (60mph).
Right of way goes to the car approaching from the right (exceptions are marked). In **roundabouts** the car within the roundabout has the right of way. On some main roads in order to **turn left** it is necessary to exit right into a small roundabout and then cross the main road. Foreigners often do not understand this rule, thereby causing serious accidents. **When passing** be sure to blink left first and then right, and to leave the blinker on until passing is complete. Honking is required when passing and before entering a curve (flashing lights in the dark). **Passing is not allowed** 100m/300ft before the crest of a hill as well as on roads with less than 200m/600ft visibility.
Seatbelts are required in the front and back seats when driving. The limit for alcohol is **0.5 permille**.
Towing by private vehicles is not allowed.
In the case of a **breakdown** or an **accident** one warning triangle has to be set up in front of and one behind the car; but cars from other countries only need one triangle When leaving the car outside of town a **reflecting vest** must be worn.
Telephoning with a cell phone and without a hands-free system while driving is prohibited.

The best way to explore the island is with a rental car. There are rental agencies (alquiler de coches) in all tourist centres. It is practical to rent the car at home and collect it from the airport when you arrive. Car hire is cheap on the Canary Isles in comparison to most European countries. A car in the lowest category costs between €20 and €30 per day at international rental agencies, depending on the length of the rental. Rental contracts are generally made with unlimited mileage. Comprehensive insurance is recommended and costs about 3 € extra per day (damage to tyres when driving on unpaved roads is not covered). Smaller companies are generally cheaper. A **credit card** is absolutely necessary.

Car rental

AUTOMOBILE CLUB / TOWING SERVICE
Real Automóvil Club de de España (RACE)
Calle Luis Doreste Silva 3
Las Palmas
Tel. 928 23 07 88
www.race.es
Towing service: Tel. 902 30 05 05
If you are driving a rental car, it is best to contact the agency.

CAR RENTALS
Avis
Tel. 902 18 08 54
www.avis.com

Europcar
Tel. 922 37 28 56
www.europcar.com

Hertz
Tel. 901 10 07 77
www.hertz.com

BUS
Global
Las Palmas: Estación San Telmo
Avenida de Rafael Cabrera s/n
Tel. 928 36 83 35
Tel. 928 25 26 30
(bus schedule information)
www.globalsu.net

Useful routes
Line 30: Las Palmas – Maspalomas
(7am – 8pm every 20 min.)

Line 1: Las Palmas–Puerto Mogán
Line 60: Airport – Las Palmas

AIR TRAFFIC
Airport information
Aeropuerto de Gran Canaria
Tel. 902 40 47 04, 913 21 10 0

Binter Canarias
Central reservations
Tel. 902 39 13 92
www.bintercanarias.com

SHIPPING COMPANIES
Líneas Fred. Olsen
Puerto de las Nieves harbour
Tel. 928 55 42 62
Central reservations:
Tel. 902 10 01 07,
www.fredolsen.es

Naviera Armas
Calle Doctor Juan Dominguez Pérez 2
Las Palmas
Tel. 902 45 65 00
www.navieraarmas.com

Acciona Trasmediterránea
Plaza Mr. Jolly s/n Las Palmas
Tel. 902 45 46 45
www.trasmediterranea.com

TAXI
Las Palmas: Tel. 928 46 22 12
Maspalomas: Tel. 928 76 67 67
Playa del Inglés: Tel. 928 14 26 34 Puerto
Rico: Tel. 928 56 18 76

Taxis Taxi drivers are required to use the meter at all times. Trips at night, on Sundays and holidays as well as extra large luggage cost extra.

Bus transportation All towns are served by good bus lines. Global runs about 300 buses on about 120 routes and serves more than 2,400 bus stops on the island (www.globalsu.net). Bus stops marked with a »P« (parada) have

Canary Islands • Travel routes

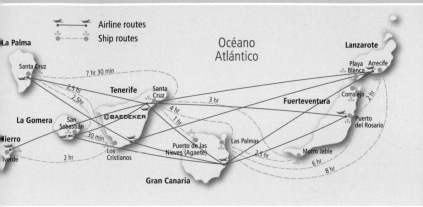

schedules posted (horarios); tickets can be bought from the driver. Schedules can also be picked up in the Global offices and at tourist centres.

In Las Palmas there is a close network of yellow city busses (Guaguas Municipales, www.guaguas.com). The most important junctions are Avenida Rafael Cabrera near Parque San Telmo, Teatro Pérez Galdós and the bus terminal Parque de Santa Catalina.

Ferries　Inter-island ferry service in the Canary Islands is dominated by the three large shipping companies Acciona Trasmediterránea (www.trasmediterranea.es), Fred. Olsen (www.fredolsen.es) and Naviera Armas (www.navieraarmas.com). All six neighbouring islands are served but only Tenerife and Fuerteventura directly.

Acciona Trasmediterránea ferries run from Las Palmas to **Santa Cruz de Tenerife**; the trip takes about 4 hours. From Agaete (Puerto de las Nieves) Lineas Fred. Olsen car and passenger ferries run four to six times a day to Santa Cruz de Tenerife (duration: 1 hour). From Las Palmas there is a free bus to Agaete (departure: Parque de Santa Catalina, 60 minutes before the ferry leaves); from Agaete buses depart for Las Palmas 15 minutes after the ferry arrives.

Naviera Armas runs a car ferry from Las Palmas daily to Morro Jable harbour (**Fuerteventura**), duration about 2.5 hours. Acciona Trasmediterránea runs the route Las Palmas–Puerto del Rosario (Fuerteventura) once a week, duration 6 hours.

Acciona Trasmediterránea runs once a week from Las Palmas to Arrecife on **Lanzarote**, duration with stop on Fuerteventura 8 hours.

From Gran Canaria to the western part of the archipelago (**La**

Gomera, La Palma, El Hierro) by ferry, change in Santa Cruz de Tenerife.

From **Puerto Rico** in southern Gran Canaria boats run several times a day to the nearby tourist centres Arguineguín and Puerto de Mogán (passengers only).

Air transport   All flights from and to Gran Canaria depart and arrive at Aeropuerto de Gando. It is located about 22km/13mi south of Las Palmas. Binter Canarias flies from Aeropuerto de Gando several times a day to Fuerteventura, Lanzarote, Tenerife (north and south airport), La Palma and La Gomera, to El Hierro several times a week. Flying times are between 25 and 50 minutes. **Early reservations** are recommended, especially before holidays; this applies above all to the smaller islands.

When to Go

The Canaries are often called the »islands of eternal spring«. This cliché comes from a climate that is much the same all year round (▶ p. 30). Temperatures vary no more than 6°C/10°F between the cold and warm months, so swimming outdoors is possible all year round. This makes the islands a popular destination in the **winter** for sun-starved Europeans. As far as the vegetation goes, March is an especially suitable time, when everything is in full bloom. While in the absolute high seasons Christmas and Easter require reservations far in advance, in the summer months many hotels are not full, even though the climate is then still very pleasant on Gran Canaria: There are few hot and humid days.

Index

List of Maps and Illustrations

Photo Credits

dpa/ Picture Alliance p. 26, 27, 53, 60,
   63, 64, C4 (left above, left below)
DuMont Bildarchiv/ Lubenow p. 3 (left
   above), 3 (left centre), 3 (right above),
   3 right below), 5 (above), 8, 9, 35
   (above), 37, 66, 82, 84, 87 (above), 74,
   76, 92, 93, 95, 96, 98, 101, 113, 117,
   132, 161, 180, 183, 193, 199, 207, 213,
   227, 236, 244, U3, U2
DuMont Bildarchiv/ Widmann p. 6, 21
   (right above, right below, left below),
   50, 78, 79, 107, 129, C4 (right below)
DuMont Bildarchiv/ Zaglitsch p. 2,
   3 (right centre), 4 (above, below), 5
   (below), 7, 8, 34, 42, 45, 56, 105, 126,
   139, 140, 144, 148, 152, 164, 173, 178,
   201, 217, 234, 242
Fan & Mross/ Friedel p. 1
fotolia / dulsita p. 86 (centre)
fotolia/ Carlos Pérez Gómez p. 87
   (below)
getty-images/ Nico Tondini p. 86
   (below)

Rolf Goetz p. 3 (left below), 30, 35
   (below), 72, 85, 90, 219, 248, 263, U8
Gran Canaria Natural p. 71
Huber/ Fantuz Olimpio p. 24
Huber/ R. Schmid p. 86 (above)
laif/ Andreas Hub p. 68
laif/ Dreysse p. 192
laif/ Piepenburg p. 175
laif/ Tophoven p. 10, 18
laif/ Zanettini p. 27, 156, 158, 191, 205,
   232
Look/ B. Müller p. 20
Look/ Friedel p. 100
Look/ J. Richter p. 12, 21 (left above),
   22, 33, 103, 108, C7
mauritius images p. 89
White Star/ M. Gumm p. 40, 87 (centre),
   110, 131, 200, 229, 240

Cover photo: Tips Images/F1online

Publisher's Information

1st Edition 2015
Worldwide Distribution: Marco Polo
Travel Publishing Ltd
Pinewood, Chineham Business Park
Crockford Lane, Chineham
Basingstoke, Hampshire RG24 8AL,
United Kingdom.

Photos, illlustrations, maps:
107 photos illustrations, 21 maps and
infographics, one large island map
Text:
Birgit Borowski, Achim Bourmer, Tobias
Büscher, Hans Jürgen Fründt, Rolf Goetz
Editing:
Baedeker editorial team (John Sykes,
Rainer Eisenschmid)
Translation: Barbara Schmidt-Runkel
Cartography:
Christoph Gallus, Hohberg;
MAIRDUMONT Ostfildern (island map)
3D illustrations:
jangled nerves, Stuttgart
Infographics:
Golden Section Graphics GmbH, Berlin
Design:
independent Medien-Design, Munich

Editor-in-chief:
Rainer Eisenschmid, Mairdumont
Ostfildern

© MAIRDUMONT GmbH & Co KG

All rights reserved. No part of this book
may be reproduced, stored in a retrieval
system or transmitted in any form or
by any means (electronic, mechanical,
photocopying, recording or otherwise)
without prior written permission from
the publisher.

Printed in China

Despite all of our authors' thorough research, errors can creep in. The publish-
ers do not accept any liability for this.
Whether you want to praise, alert us to
errors or give us a personal tip Please
contact us by email or post:

MARCO POLO Travel Publishing Ltd
Pinewood, Chineham Business Park
Crockford Lane, Chineham
Basingstoke, Hampshire RG24 8AL
United Kingdom
Email: sales@marcopolouk.com

FSC
www.fsc.org
MIX
Paper from
responsible sources
FSC® C011918

MARCO POLO

HANDBOOKS

www.marco-polo.com

Gran Canaria Curiosities

Enormous price differences, a house where Columbus stayed, whipping the ocean – Gran Canaria offers a few curiosities.

►Columbus

According to the city fathers of Las Palmas Columbus stopped in the Canarian capital city three times on his trips to the New World. He is supposed to have stayed in the Casa de Colón, which was named after him, and prayed in the Ermita San Antonio Abad. But not one of his stays can be documented for certain.

►Long journey

The first tourists to arrive from northern Europe by airplane had a long trip. They flew for a total of 16 hours with a landing in Madrid.

►Budgies

Budgies (canaries) became world famous because of their singing. But their »voices« were trained, for the wild budgies who live on the Canary Islands don't sing nearly as well. Moreover their feathers are not Canary yellow but mouse grey.

►High-rise hotels

In 1960 Gran Canaria had about 2,500 beds to offer guests, today it has more than 160,000.

►Making it rain

During the Bajada de la Rama in Puerto de las Nieves the ocean is whipped with pine branches and palm fronds. According to one legend the procession is supposed to cause rain.

►Price differences

A double room in Hostal San Fernando in Playa del Ingés costs €25. A suite in the Grand Hotel Residencia in Maspalomas, on the other hand, will cost you €1334 – a night!

►Sand from the Sahara?

It is often said that the dunes at Maspalomas were caused by sand blown across from the Sahara. But the sand comes from the sea, so to speak a local product.